D1327510

Praise for
I Would Die 4 U:
Why Prince Became an Icon

"I'm a Prince scholar and this is the ultimate Prince book." —QUESTLOVE

"Touré is one of my favorite writers and Prince is on the Mount Rushmore of modern music and this is the best book about Prince I've ever read." —Q-TIP

"It took the singular talent and journalistic skills of Touré to capture the wild genius and larger than life influence of Prince." —JANN WENNER, founder of *Rolling Stone*

"For those who understand how singular an artist Prince is, this book—every bit obsessive and revelatory as its subject—will be a great pleasure. For everyone else, it's mandatory. It unfolds like a good mystery, as cryptic clues are deciphered one after another." —JOE LEVY, Editor, *Billboard*

NOTHING
COMPARES 2 U

NOTHING COMPARES 2 U

AN ORAL HISTORY OF PRINCE

TOURÉ

PERMUTED
PRESS

A PERMUTED PRESS BOOK

Nothing Compares 2 U:
An Oral History of Prince
© 2021 by Touré
All Rights Reserved

ISBN: 978-1-64293-918-7
ISBN (eBook): 978-1-64293-919-4

Cover art by Tiffani Shea
Cover image by David Gahr/Premium Archive via Getty Images
Interior design and composition, Greg Johnson, Textbook Perfect

PERMUTED
PRESS

Permuted Press, LLC
New York • Nashville
permutedpress.com

Published in the United States of America
1 2 3 4 5 6 7 8 9 10

*Dedicated to Prince
and the amazing people of Princeworld
who have made me feel welcome
inside the Purple kingdom
over the past twenty years.
It's an honor to share your stories.*

"Ultimately, spiritual evolution is the axis on which inspiration and creativity spin...there r so many songs that I've written and recorded, sometimes it is hard 4 ME 2 believe it comes from one source! All of my musicality comes from GOD...the blessing/curse ensued when I kept sneaking back in2 the talent line dressed as another person...I got away with it several times be4 they caught me!!"

—PRINCE (from a 1994 email to me)

Contents

Foreword

by Susannah Melvoin

Life is filled with moments that change everything. I had no idea that this would be that moment.

One weekend in LA, Lisa and Wendy picked up Prince at LAX and brought him back to our little house. A minute or two into his visit, sitting around the kitchen table, Wendy and Lisa asked if they could play him the audition demo I had just finished recording. This demo got me my first big singing gig working for Quincy Jones. Back then, we had a small boombox that never left the kitchen table, and that's what they used to play the cassette. While I hid in my bedroom for what seemed like nine hours, they listened to the song. When it ended, the only thing I could hear were the small wooden chairs squeaking. I could barely keep it together. Then I heard a little clapping and Prince saying, "Aww." I walked out of my tiny room, scared of what he'd say or not say. He had a sweet smile on his face, looked right at me, and said, "You want to come sing with our family? You know you want to— come on." I stood staring at Wendy, Lisa, and Prince. I was so grateful to Wendy and Lisa for being supportive of my dream, and I was so happy to be asked to sing with my family and Prince.

Of course I said yes! But what was really happening is that he could see that the three of us were a family, and our union helped us to be great—because good family members make good band members. In a band, you need to learn the art of listening; to know when to back up the solo player; to hear when the vocals need blending; and to lay out, and let the music say what the music is going to say. Like in a family, sometimes it's better to listen than to speak. We learned that at home. Prince saw that we were a family and he wanted to be a part of it. He wasn't pulling me into his family; he was pulling himself into ours.

From that moment on, I spent years with Prince as partners, experiencing meaningful love, making plans for our family together, and creating incredible music. It changed my entire life. Over time, I intimately experienced the depth of Prince's desire to unite with family. It was a longing from early on. Prince would often tell me about his childhood when he'd pick me up and we'd drive around Minneapolis. Prince would tell me stories of his father, and it led me to think he wanted to be back in his father's life. Prince would find the family tribe he'd been longing for after he was thrown out of his father's home. He would find that tribe in the home of Bernadette Anderson—mother of his best friend Andre Cymone and her five older children. It was the perfect union of family and music, twenty-four hours a day. This was the beginning of a long history of making families with the folks he shared life and music with. There would be other families beyond the Melvoin/Coleman families that Prince would connect to throughout my years with him. Those families were the Rivkin Family, the Leeds brothers, and the Escovedo family. I know there are more. These are families who could communicate through music, and music was Prince's mother tongue.

Prince was known for his ability to do everything himself, but I believe he wanted a tribe to supplant his musical and emotional needs. Prince would always use the collective "we" when referring to any creative plans, goals, or ideas he had. He longed for his tribe to go all the way with him. I found that he was at his best when he had his chosen family with him. Family is what you make it, and Prince was all about family. He chose his family based on a harmony of purpose. I shared his purpose. To him, that purpose was to make music together, to love music, and stay connected physically even when it was excruciatingly difficult to do so. If I wasn't able to fly to where he was fast enough, he would question my love and devotion to him. When he needed me, or anyone, all ties that bind you to him were woven into the fabric of your ability to get to him quickly.

But I loved him. Deeply.

When Touré asked me to write the foreword to this book, I was overwhelmed with memories of our time as a family. What Touré has done here is to bring together a rich historical blend of Prince's chosen familial voices, to create a choir. When these voices meld together you can find resonance and harmony that only that family can understand. The music and relationships that make up the seasons of Prince's history, we all shared together. Since our time by his side, we've all grown in different directions, but nonetheless remained the roots of his family. It's beautiful and quite telling that Prince would choose a family that was black, white, Puerto Rican, Trinidadian, Mexican, straight, gay, Jewish, Christian, Jehovah's Witnesses, single, married, music makers, and life livers. It was always his idea to have his chosen family be diverse yet united in his purpose to make amazing music and make a life together with exceptional human beings. The bigger the family, the wider the scope of musical history that make up Prince's soul purpose. Who wouldn't want that?

Love and kindness,

—Susannah

Introduction

This oral history of Prince, one of the most complex celebrities of his time, draws on over twenty years of research and countless conversations with Prince and people who were close to him—musicians, lovers, engineers, managers, photographers, bodyguards—all sorts of Princeworld insiders who knew him well. I'll take you through Prince's difficult youth, his epic rise, his music, and the long, slow, tragic descent of a man who'd eschewed drugs early in his life but was dragged down by them later.

Close friends say Prince was doing opioids in his late twenties. At least one band member confronted Prince about abusing drugs, and he believes Prince went to rehab in his mid-thirties. The pain of constantly performing and never sleeping led to grinding, chronic pain in his hips, his hands, and his knees. He could barely keep up with the pain. As he got older and the pain increased, he sometimes showed up on stage without heels and debated whether he should get hip replacement surgery. Meanwhile, he was seeking stronger and stronger opioids. Why not just stay home if he was in pain? Because performing was at the core of his identity. It wasn't something he did, it was who he was, it was all he was. He needed it. Besides, in his last years, being home often meant being alone. By middle age, he was twice divorced and living in a small apartment inside Paisley Park. The drugs not only dulled his physical pain, they quieted the noise inside him, letting him escape from having to think about himself and deal with the deeper issues of who he was.

This is someone whose desire to be a superstar was launched because of pain. What pain? As a crazy man once wrote, look at this tangle of thorns.[1]

1

Nothing Compares 2 U

The Greatest Musician Ever

WENDY MELVOIN (Guitar, the Revolution 1983–1986): His gift was big, big, big, big, big, big. He knew he had a duty to be the best because his gift was so big. On any instrument, he was mind-blowing.

ALAN LEEDS (Tour manager 1983–1989, then president of Paisley Park Records 1989–1993): I was completely stunned by his innate musicality, just like everybody else who ever saw him.

WENDY MELVOIN: He was a great piano player.

BROWNMARK (Bass, the Revolution 1981–1986): He's an awesome drummer.

WENDY MELVOIN: He could play the hell out of his synth. He knew exactly how to bend and use his pitch wheel to elicit that thing where you'd feel a note just barely hit the beat.

BROWNMARK: He was an incredible bass player.

ALAN LEEDS: Everything he touched was brilliant. Not just good, but brilliant to the point where if all he did was play bass, he would have been a first-class bass player. Same with drums and keyboards. You just sit there and scratch your head and say, "How in the world could one musician become so proficient on so many instruments?" Each one of those instruments is a separate skillset. People like Chick Corea and Herbie Hancock will tell you it takes years and years and years of practice to master one instrument. The idea that you could become an elite level guitarist takes years and years and years of practice. But Prince never met an instrument he couldn't master quickly. This is not your average rock 'n' roll star.

WENDY MELVOIN: I don't think there was a better guitar player. There was a certain way he became his instrument. When you watched Prince play, there were blurred lines between the guy and the instrument. It was unbelievable. I've played with amazing players who I'm in awe of, but, with Prince, it wasn't an extension of him, it was him. He mastered that instrument with astonishing agility and ability. He mastered the neck. He mastered his tone. He knew exactly how to dance and choke the neck when there was distortion. He actually knew how to carve his distortion. He was able to control the tone, his foot pedals, everything was incredibly well-timed. He was able to control rhythm. He mastered his internal clock. His internal clock was beastly. His timing was unbelievable. He knew how to push and pull a rhythm that I am still amazed by. If you were slightly out of time, he sniffed it, and he would look at you and wave his hand to slow you down or speed you up. He was always right. And his feel was incredible. It was like part of the way his hands touched the guitar. He could think twenty steps ahead. It was incredible. His guitar playing was interstellar. And he got better over time.

BROWNMARK: He was one of the great guitar players in the world. The broad spectrum of genres this guy could reach is amazing. I'd sit there and watch him rip through some jazz like it was nothing. That's why Miles Davis liked him. If we wanted to do rock or country or blues, it really didn't matter. He just had this way where he could just find it no matter what. He always said, "If I can hear it in my head, then I can play it."

MORRIS HAYES (Keyboards, New Power Generation 1993–2012): In every position in the band, he could come over to your instrument and beat you so you had to really get it right. You had to crush it or else you were gonna have a headache because his antenna would go up. He'd walk over to your instrument, tell you to move out of the way, and then he'd show you how it actually goes. He did that to everybody. He'd take your bass away from you, he'd take your guitar away from you, he'd take your drums and be like, "Move out of the way," play the part, and then he'd say, "Now, you do it."

ME: He played everything except for horns, but if he absolutely, positively had to...

JILL JONES (Singer, Prince's girlfriend 1982–1990): When he was recording "My G-spot," he wanted a sax on it and Eric Leeds was not around, so Prince asked someone to get him a sax. He sat there all day and all night playing those riffs by himself. I was upstairs watching a movie or whatever while he was downstairs like, "Berp, beep, berp, berp." You could hear him making mistakes. I was dying, just cracking up, but he was teaching himself everything he was hearing in his head and after a while, he got it down and it sounded alright. He'd gotten the notes, but then he needed the feeling like a real sax player could deliver. He kept going after it all night long. He was so tenacious and so disciplined. I couldn't believe he sat there for like twelve hours playing this, "Berp, beep, berp, berp, berp."

SUSAN ROGERS (Prince's engineer 1983–1987): Who plays that well on that many instruments? Because he was one of the world's great bass players, and he's that good on guitar, and he's that good on piano, and on organ. Oh, and we're not done yet—let's put up a vocal mic. How many men have that chest voice and that falsetto and can give you that soul preacher vocal without ruining his voice? He never developed vocal nodes. He never destroyed his voice, and yet he could scream like any punk or rock artist, and he could shout like any gospel preacher. He could croon like Al Green. Who's got that range?

WENDY MELVOIN: He was a masterful singer. He could sing live better than most. He knew exactly how his voice sounded live and how to work it—never needed inner ear monitors, always relied on the monitors on the floor or the house sound.

SUSANNAH MELVOIN (Fiancée, lead singer of The Family 1984–1985): What makes him an amazing singer is he's completely not self-conscious. He's the opposite of self-conscious. He's totally in the unconscious mind. He's completely willing to bare himself, and to get a good vocal out you must let yourself be exposed. You must open yourself up and hear the shitty notes and hear the good notes and not compete with someone outside of you, but just be the best you that you can be and allow yourself to be your most vulnerable. He said, "The uglier you look when you sing, the better it's going to sound coming out of your mouth." Prince was willing to go 100 percent, never doubted himself, never doubted the vocal, never doubted his playing, never doubted any of it.

CHUCK ZWICKY (Prince's engineer 1987–1989): The most beautiful thing I ever found with Prince's vocals is when he does his background vocals. You listen to any one of those tracks on its own and it's a totally different personality singing. Together it conveys the sense of a group singing. Usually, if the lead singer sings the background parts, everybody's speaking in the exact same way but with Prince you felt like there's six people around you and some can sing better than others and they all have their own separate personalities.

MORRIS DAY (Childhood friend, drummer in Grand Central 1974–1975, front man for The Time 1981–1983, 1989–1990): As far as doing backgrounds, I know firsthand because I was in the studio with this dude on the other side of the glass producing, and it was a job. He would have me singing, and layering notes, and doing things differently each time until you just can't take any more. So, I know for himself, he took the time and layered his own vocals and put so many layers and different textures, and things on it that it was just crazy. He would just sit there at the board with the mic and do that all night, just working on structuring background vocals and arranging them.

ME: Many musicians say Prince's drum programming truly changed the game.

SUSAN ROGERS: His use of the drum machine had a lasting impression on the culture. He truly innovated the way electronic rhythm works.

QUESTLOVE (Friend of Prince, drummer in The Roots): To my ears, Prince is bar none the best drum programmer of all time. I'll put Prince up against my favorite hip hop drum programmers. He is the master. He is the only cat who programmed drums to make you feel like a human played 'em. He was able to take the Linn LM-1 drum machine and humanize it. When I was a kid, I thought that was him playing drums because he was smart enough to program little things that only drummers would notice. Why is this part speeding up? Why is this part slowing down? He wanted the sonics of the LM-1, but he wanted it as if a real drummer played it so he would do it in real time and he would purposely speed shit up during the chorus and slow it down during the verse, and all that would make me think a real drummer's playing. He created a sound with drums that you never heard before.

WENDY MELVOIN: The guy could play the hell out of his LinnDrum.

MORRIS DAY: He would try and get a real feel, because if you just straight up program a drum track, if you don't do something to offset it, it's going to feel really mechanical. He would do things to offset the beat a little bit, like he'd let some mistakes in there to make it feel more real.

ERIC LEEDS (Saxophone, the Revolution and New Power Generation 1994–2003): Prince was a really good drummer and as someone who was able to think like a drummer, he brought that musicianship to bear on the machine. He integrated the drum machine into the music as an instrument and not just a machine.

ME: He was also great with a pen.[2]

WENDY MELVOIN: With lyrics, he was a master. Especially when he really slowed down and became more universal with his lyrics and storytelling. Look at the lyrics to "Raspberry Beret." Forget about it. What a great story. Incredible. "Sign O' The Times." "Dorothy Parker."

MORRIS HAYES: We were sitting around one day and I said, "Prince, out of all of the stuff you do, what do you think you're best at, man?" He kinda did that look, put his hand on the chin, and looked up in the sky, and he said, "I think I'm the best at writing lyrics. Cuz, you know, I hate bad lyrics. At the end of the day, Morris, I'm a poet."[3]

ME: A girlfriend said he loved Nikki Giovanni. And Joni Mitchell. But perhaps what he was truly best at was his attitude toward music.

MORRIS HAYES: I remember once he did something really crazy. He played two instruments at once. He was playing his guitar and a keyboard at the same time, and I said, "Man, I can't do anything like that! That's impossible!" Really quietly, he said, "Morris, if you want to stay here, I don't accept impossible. I don't accept 'No.' We figure out how to win. If you want to stay here, you'll figure out how to win. I don't care how you do it, hieroglyphics, whatever you've got to do to figure it out, but you will figure it out, or you'll be gone."

ME: His determination was extraordinary. It shapes his life, but also Prince was working with a different level of brain power than most humans—he knew how to play multiple things simultaneously back when he was a teenager.

BOBBY Z. (Drummer, the Revolution 1978–1990): I saw him do a run on the guitar with his left hand and a run on the keyboard with his right and at the same time he's singing. Three different sides of his brain all at once. From there, you knew he was incredible.

ME: His mind's relationship to music was special.

MICHAELA ANGELA Davis (Prince's stylist): I remember once, a bunch of us were hanging out and he's making jokes—he's funny as fuck—and we're all sitting together, and then he just got up and left. You're like, "What?" Later, he said, "I think in music, so when you have words going through your head, I hear music and there are times I have to go." He had to leave because there was some melody that he had to go put down right away.

MORRIS HAYES: He once said to me, "When I play a song, it's already done in my head. I see the music done in my head, like I hear all of the parts, and I see it done, so when I play, I'm just executing the music I see in my head. Everything I do, I see it done first. I see it completed and then I'm just following through what I've already seen in my mind."

JILL JONES: He told me "Music must be a journey. It should be an escape into another world. It should be like a peep show into your soul."

ME: He was that rare thing—a genius who was a grinder.

ALAN LEEDS: Prince was the musical version of Michael Jordan—amazingly gifted and the hardest worker on the team. He realized that the gift didn't just work on its own. You had to do the work. And the work ethic he had was remarkable because the gift seemed to come so easy to him, but then again, how many of us saw him in his bedroom night after night after night after night after night playing his guitar until his fingers bled? How many of us saw him skipping lunch every day at school to bang on a piano?

ME: Also, like Jordan, he was insanely competitive.

SUSANNAH MELVOIN: He was competitive at everything, from being the best dressed, to being the best musician, to having the most drive, to working the longest hours, to anything. He always had to be the best. He could not cope with a loss. He would have been the finest athlete in any sport, if he'd decided to go that route. He had that kind of drive.

ALAN LEEDS: He was so extremely insecure that everything was a competition. He had to continually prove and reprove his dominance, his superiority, his intellect, over, and over, and over again. Every day, he had to prove himself somehow. If you watch a movie with him, it was a race to see who figured out how it would end first. You play basketball with him, he has to win.

ME: I played basketball with him, one-on-one and two-on-two, and I could see his competitive fire. He was dying to win. Also, I could see that he was really good at basketball. One more very important point: he really enjoyed playing with me. But we'll get to that.

MORRIS HAYES: I played basketball with him and he killed me so many times. I'm six-foot-five, and I can count on one hand the number of times that I beat him. He was an incredible ball handler and a good shooter, and that's how he beat a big Neanderthal like me, but Prince would cheat to win. Prince hated to lose. I don't care what it was, anything he did, he wanted to be the best at it. He wanted to win.[4]

ME: His competitiveness also led to him wanting to show up other musicians.

LEROY BENNETT (Lighting and set designer 1980–1993): He did a horrible thing to Sting one time. Prince had hand signals that meant certain turnarounds and accents and all that stuff. The band knew them. I knew them. But Sting didn't. He was playing along with whatever song they were playing, Sting was playing the bass, and then all of a sudden, just to fuck with him, Prince started doing all these hand signals. Sting was lost. Finally, he just threw up his hands and gave up. Prince liked to prove that nobody was as good as he was. It was his territory. It was his house. "I'm the boss." I think that's what was going on in his head.

ALAN LEEDS: Once in Europe there was an aftershow, probably in London or Paris, and Bruce Springsteen happened to be in town. As Prince would occasionally do, if there were celebrities in the house, he'd bring them up to jam. It was probably one of those ten-minute versions of "Baby, I'm A Star" or something. Anyway, Springsteen came out and played the guitar. At the end of the show, we're in the dressing room after Springsteen's gone home. Prince is sitting there cackling. He said, "See, I told you he couldn't play guitar. I told you he couldn't hang with us." It was like, why do you have to do that? You've proven yourself. You're selling more records than Springsteen right now. It's like, "Come on, dude." It shouldn't be about that on this level. His competitiveness served him really well when he was young and carving out his career. But once he was established as a superstar, his insecurity worked against him. You reach a point where you're so successful that behaving that way is beneath you and even detrimental because you can get more out of collaborating then out of competing.

ME: Competitiveness, drive, a massive gift, and determination led to Prince becoming world class in almost every aspect of music—he had a burning obsession to be great and he was a sponge of a learner. From his early teens, he was completely focused on becoming a rock-star musician and he spent years thinking of nothing else, shutting out every other aspect of life.

ALAN LEEDS: You're talking about somebody who really didn't have a life. For his first thirty-plus years, he didn't care about anything but music. He really lived, breathed, and slept music, and when you take that dedication, that sacrifice of a life, and combine it with this spooky natural gift, then you have Prince. You also see why there's only one Prince.

ME: That sort of tight, narrow focus may be critical to reaching a difficult goal, but it left Prince with some major deficiencies. It's like he ran away and joined the circus, and it left him a king in the big top and lost in the real world.

PEPE WILLIE (Cousin and mentor): The only time that Prince is normal is when he's on stage playing his music. That's when he's Prince. He doesn't even know how to be when he's off stage.

ME: Prince's years of focusing on developing as a musician, combined with the pain of feeling abandoned by his parents and rejected by his peers, led to him retreating into his shell and never really learning the basics of successfully interacting with people. Relationships with other people are critical for our souls. They help us deal with the complexity of the human condition; they make it possible for us to deeply enjoy the highs of life and to survive the hard parts. They help make life worth living. Talking about our emotions helps us make sense of them and is critical to maintaining mental health. And yet Prince was largely unable or unwilling to talk about himself or his feelings and couldn't have a one-on-one relationship that wasn't totally focused on him and his music. He was more comfortable on stage in an arena relating to thousands than he was in a one-on-one conversation.

ALAN LEEDS: He wasn't at home in front of people he didn't know well, and his lack of trust went so far as to inhibit his comfort level with people. I worked for James Brown and they were similar in the sense that James was also rejected by his mother and didn't trust anybody. He had very much the same trust issues. It's, ironically, very similar.

ME: Interacting with Prince off stage could be difficult. He was an enigma, even to those who knew him best.

ALAN LEEDS: It was hard to determine who the real Prince was. Every time I thought I had it nailed, he would say or do something that would send me back to the woodshed to rethink it.

WENDY MELVOIN: He was a shape-shifter. Underneath the shape-shifting, he was a complicated, incredibly intelligent person who was very funny but could be really mean. That was part of his complicated relationship to himself. I think what was easy for him was music. That was the form of language that came easiest. Communicating verbally was not his strong point. It just wasn't. He got used to a certain type of communication in his adult years, but the stuff underneath, where you say my heart hurts, that was really hard for him. I think the psychology of all that stuff was elusive to him, and he didn't really like that kind of communication. He was deeply self-conscious and, in private moments, whether it was one-on-one, or in a room with twenty people, it was difficult for him to talk. I think he was a really self-conscious guy, but he knew how to use that part of himself to become the most important person in the room. It was painful to watch him sometimes because he was so uncomfortable in front of a few people. If one hundred thousand people were standing in front of him, there was a certain dissociative quality he could muster and become the perfect version of himself that he wanted to be. In smaller situations he was too exposed. But he wasn't just one thing. Depending on what was going on in his life, he was either a bad guy who had good moments or a good guy who had bad moments. You couldn't predict. That's what I mean by shape-shifter. He was really moody. He used to say to me, "I'm whatever you want me to be."

ME: Several people said Prince's personality swings were so wide that they experienced him as four different people.

WENDY MELVOIN: We used to have personality names for him. Steve was the guy we really liked. He was sweet, funny, quiet, engaged, playful, available, touchy feely, huggy—wore tube socks that came up over his knees. Then there was Fred Sanford. You did not want him to come into the room. He was impatient, annoyed, aggressive, and mean. Fred Sanford was going to kick someone's ass. There was Marilyn Monroe—seductive, quiet, and just full of sexual energy. But she was treacherous, though, because sexual energy can be really manipulative. And there was Shaft. He would go on stage with us. He was ready to kick some ass like a vigilante. He was the guy that was going to make everything okay, but with an iron fist.

SUSANNAH MELVOIN: He had an extraordinary ability to compartmentalize his inner world.

BROWNMARK: Some days when he came in, he was not a friend—it was about business, about getting down to the music. But he also had a really funny side to him where he would crack jokes and pull jokes on you. He was just funny, and he had this heart-wrenching laugh, this deep laugh that came from deep down within, and that's when you knew he was really in a good mood because he would laugh about stuff and roll around on the floor like a kid. And talk about Marilyn Monroe, that was something that ran through his veins. He was a pretty man, and he knew it. He'd be like, "Mark, ain't I beautiful?" He had that whole side to him. He'd say, "Mark, I'm just too pretty. I'm just too pretty." Of course, he's joking, but he's for real.

WENDY MELVOIN: Most of the time, it was Steve, but if he hadn't slept in days, you didn't know what you were going to get. He'd go on jags where you knew he hadn't been asleep for three days, and you'd be like, "Oh my god, look at his eyes, they're like pinwheels." He'd be mute, his eyes would be red, and he'd be eating Doritos[5] and Toblerone, and it would be like, "Oh my god, don't talk to him." But, most of the time, it was Steve, and he'd be yummy and funny and kind and generous of spirit and playful and silly. Lisa and I used to call him My Little Pony. We used to sing that to him all the time because he was our little pony. He loved it. He loved hearing it. But you never knew if he loved you or hated you. And if you thought you knew, he could turn on a coin in two seconds. I believe that that was part of his pathology. He struggled with being annoyed by everybody and everything. He was easily burdened. He didn't want to have to communicate, so listening to other people's stories was a burden to him. He was annoyed by everyone. There was a lot that came out of his mouth that was egregious, and you just looked at him like, "Pump the brakes. What's the problem?" It was a lot of sticking up for yourself around him, and that was tiresome after a while. As an adult, I think what drove him was religion, and a moral compass created by his own definitions through his study. But I think the thing that controlled him was his drug addiction. His use of pain pills was probably longer than maybe some of us might have thought because, when he started getting his aches and pains, I think he really relied on it. And he was little. I think it just got worse for him over time. I know plenty of people in my life who've died of drug addiction. You get to a point where you need it so badly that when you're off of it, your pain is actually worse and your neurons, your nerve endings, are on fire. So, even when he tried to stop on his own, his pain was too much. I think it's an existential pain as well.

Morris Hayes: I came up with the theory that there were five personalities—I called them the Five Princes. Number one was the one I saw when *Purple Rain* came out. He was bigger than life. He was this enigma, a real rock star. That's how Prince was. He was The Kid. Number two is when I actually got in the band, and I started going to rehearsal, and said like, "Oh my God, this dude is rough. He's mean." I just learned from an insider's perspective, like, he's got the whip and the chain and everything. It would be like so tough, not like anything I've ever dealt with. This dude was hard. You've got to get it all and you've got to get it now and if you weren't getting it, he would wait until you did. He'd have everybody else just waiting for you. If you weren't conscientious about what it is you were doing, you were gonna have a problem. If it's my day and I'm messing up, his whole focus goes right to me and he'd be like, "I'm gonna break you down. You're gonna either get this right or you're gonna get so run over that you feel like a flat tire by the end of the day." Number three was the funny man. We'd play basketball, we'd play the dozens, and we'd be talking about each other's moms, like "Yo momma's selling drum machines down at Guitar Center." We'd be joking with each other and goosing each other and all this kinda stuff, just fun Prince. We'd rent out a movie theater or we'd rent out a bowling alley. We'd play jokes on each other and just laugh and run down the hallways like a bunch of kids. Number four was the sad Prince. It's like he's hurt, like he's having a bad day, so you're gonna have a bad day. And number five was give-you-the-shirt-off-his-back Prince. I'm sure there's some others, but those are the ones that were the most present to me, and the thing is, once I figured all of that out, I started shutting my mouth when he came in. I would let him talk first so I could see who showed up today. It was like, *Okay, number three is here, so it's a fun day today.* But if number two shows up, it's like, *Okay, uh, you better be on your A game or you got a headache.* I'd tell the band, "Number two's here today. I already talked to him, so you better have your parts ready." That really helped me because when I didn't apply that theory, I'd be lost. I would be like, okay, the day before we had a ball, we were hanging out with girls, doing whatever, having fun and I'd come in the next day on the same vibe, like, "Bro, man, that was a good time," and it'd be like, "Cut." That is not the dude from yesterday. And you hear the brake skid marks from a mile away, 'cause I had to readjust and get serious and be like, *Okay, Morris, we gotta focus, and get centered back in the right lane very quickly.*

JILL JONES: His genius became a hindrance to him actually having to be able to reveal his inner feelings. People didn't demand he show his feelings. It's too bad that he wasn't able to do it verbally, but he chose to wear different masks. You had to really pull him out to get to something real.

ME: It seems like Prince wanted to prevent people from seeing his real self.

MORRIS DAY: Prince kept himself at arm's length from people because I don't think he communicated with people very well. So, he just kept that wall up. He wouldn't let a lot of the employees in. He kind of controlled them with his moodiness, with awkward silence, and things like that. Everybody at Paisley Park was always worried about what his mood was when he got to work, when he got to the studio, when he walked in the room. They were like "Is he smiling? Is he happy?" Everybody was all running around worried about what kind of mood this dude was in. Sometimes he would come in and it's gloom and doom and serious, so everybody's quiet and on edge. Sometimes he was like Richard Pryor, a total comedian who would have everyone laughing. He was moody but that let him control the situation. But he was just all about music and I don't think anything outside of that he could really relate to. Outside of music, I don't think he really dug interacting with people.

ME: It feels like there were a series of masks in his music as well as the persona behind his songs shifted from Hypersexual Man ("Dirty Mind," "Darling Nikki,") to Romantic Lover ("Raspberry Beret," "Adore") to Supercool Dude ("Controversy," "Girls & Boys") to Artiste

("All the Critics Love U In New York," "Do U Lie?") to Spiritual Worshipper ("God," "Eye Know"). He could also be feminine ("If I Was Your Girlfriend") or obtuse ("Dorothy Parker") or afraid of what was happening to the world ("America," "Sign O' The Times") or exuberantly self-confident ("Baby I'm A Star"). Is this the work of a very multifaceted person or the ultimate code-switcher who knows how to give the audience so many looks that they never know who he really is? The person Prince was in high school was so radically different than the person who showed up a few years later on stage that one of his classmates famously said, "When did he get the personality implant?" Was it actually a shield protecting him from having to show his real self? Maybe—because in high school they saw him as an awkward nerd—one friend said in high school he was like Pedro from *Napoleon Dynamite*.

SUSANNAH MELVOIN: People were like, "What's up with the kid with the really light skin and the pens in his pocket and the huge afro who doesn't talk to anybody?"

JEROME BENTON (Background singer and dancer in the Revolution 1984–1986, valet in The Time 1981–1983, 1990): He was a high yellow Negro with a pretty afro and not much to say.

ME: Years later, people who worked with him saw the same thing.

LEROY BENNETT: He could be nerdy. He was shy. He was awkward.

ME: Becoming a rock star was meant to fix everything.

ALAN LEEDS: He was suspicious and paranoid of people and life in general and cynical and clearly troubled by his personal demons. And the more we learned about his background—how his mother basically walked away from him, and his father struggled to raise him and threw in the towel, and the kinds of rejection he suffered as a youngster—we can maybe understand why he was so suspicious of the world, and why he would maybe not grow up to be a secure, well-rounded individual. This is a guy who grew up with issues. He had mother/father issues. He had Small Man Complex. He had light-skinned issues. He had a taller half-brother who was a basketball star. He could outhoop his brother[6] but he didn't get any love for it cuz he was the short, goofy guy. He was the shortest kid in school and he was an excellent basketball player, but nobody took him seriously. If you can believe it, Prince was the short, obnoxious, nerdy guy in school. He got beat up a lot. He got bullied. Nobody liked him. When Prince was a kid, everyone in Minneapolis was like, "Oh, that crazy nerd."

ME: You can start to see why he decided that becoming a rock star would be his escape, and how the lack of a real family was helpful.

ALAN LEEDS: The only thing that really, really mattered to him was music. He didn't have the distractions most people have—no one in the family was going to stop him from making music all the time. His relationship with his mother was distant. He was also not close to his brothers and sisters, most of whom were half-brothers and sisters. He didn't really feel like he had family. In his mind, becoming a celebrity was a way to get back at his background.

ME: It seemed like the perfect way to roar back at everyone and everything—and music was really the only thing he cared about—so he put everything into it.

ALAN LEEDS: He sat down as a youngster and designed himself to be a rock star. Not a musician, but a rock star. There was an acceptance and a power and a security that he envisioned could come from massive appeal. It would liberate him from the ostracism he'd felt at school and the rejection he'd felt at home. It was pretty apparent in talking with him as well as people in Minneapolis who grew up with him that this was something that he had his sights on from junior high school, if not before. For him, celebrity was like "Okay, here's how I can get back at the world. Here's how I can get the girls and be the number-one guy and get the attention and, above all, never have to feel vulnerable or afraid or have to say I'm sorry." He emerged from his childhood with a very high degree of emotional neediness, and this is the only conduit through which he could establish any self-esteem.

The idea of celebrity was his way of looking at society and finding his place and establishing that he was never going to be a joiner, he was never going to be one of the gang; he was going to make his own rules and create his own place in this atmosphere out here called the music business, and do it in such a way that he would get the kind of attention and respect that he was craving.

ME: Prince fulfilled his childhood dreams beyond his own imagination, but he remained unhappy in many ways.

ERIC LEEDS: This is a guy who, after all the success, still looks at himself as a victim. It kind of pisses me off because I don't think he has a right to look at himself as a victim.

A GIRLFRIEND: He was tormented. He was struggling with this duality of good and evil, and sometimes you'd get happy, fun Prince but more often you'd get complicated, heavy Prince, and, a lot of times, it was almost like he was performing around me when it was unnecessary. He communicates on subjects he's passionate about like music, but he doesn't talk just to talk. He doesn't want to communicate about what's going on inside himself.

ME: He was famous for having lots of girlfriends, but it seems like in most of his relationships he wasn't forging deep, honest connections.

JILL JONES: I said, "Prince and I are back together again," and my mom goes, "You know the only time a pimp ever sleeps with a woman is when he's trying to get her back in check." My mom always thought that when Prince was sleeping with women, it was actually to control them. And when he wasn't sleeping with you, you were working. She said, "He's the best pimp I've ever seen." She said he was like the Iceberg Slim of his day.

ME: He became a megastar but remained deeply insecure, as if his wounded inner child never healed.

LEROY BENNETT: As a musician, he was a warrior, but as a human being, he was fragile. I think inside of him there was a hurt little boy, a frightened little boy, a fragile boy. It was like there were two people constantly fighting inside of him, that warrior and that boy.

ME: He was at war inside because even though he lived like a king, there was something he needed that he could never buy or create, and the lack of it may have led to his death. He wanted a family and he was never able to have one that lasted.

MORRIS HAYES: Prince put music as his first love, his second love, and whatever-other-number-you-want-to-put-on-it love. I don't think he ever allowed room for anything else. It's going to be hard for any significant other to accept that down-the-line position, because if it comes to him going home to eat dinner versus going to the studio or rehearsing with the band, the music is going to come first.

PEPE WILLIE: He got his wish to be a rock star, but you gotta be careful what you wish for sometimes, because Prince does not have one real true friend. I still love this dude! I still feel that he's part of my family, but you know what we call him? We call him The Lonely Guy. Christmas time, Easter time, Thanksgiving, where ya supposed to be? With your family! Not him, he's flyin' in the air somewhere! All alone. He ain't with his family! He don't have a family. He's The Lonely Guy.

2

When Doves Cry

Prince's Crazy Teens (1958–1977)

MORRIS DAY: John had some rules that he laid out—"Be in by this time," and "Don't bring no girls over to my house." But Prince and I had these girlfriends...

ME: Prince was twelve years old and had been living with his father, John Nelson, for about six months. A few years earlier, his parents had divorced. His mother remarried and Prince chose to leave her house to go live with his father. But now he was bringing girls into his dad's house, breaking one of his cardinal rules, and heading for one of the key moments of his life, perhaps the inciting incident that would set in motion everything else that would happen. That said, during his brief time living with his father, he had already chosen his life's path.

JILL JONES: Prince told me that when he was living there with John, he decided that he wanted to be rich. He was going to be rich and famous, and he was going to go from being abandoned to having complete autonomy and independence from those people that had raised him. He felt like then he would be free from everybody because there were abandonment issues. That definitely existed.

ME: He felt abandoned by his mother, who would remain a source of pain and resentment throughout his life. Prince's father was a musician. He led the Prince Rogers Trio—Prince Rogers was his stage name.

ANDRÉ CYMONE (Childhood friend, bass and cofounder of Grand Central 1975–1981): He was an unbelievable musician. Beyond that, he was a really, really cool person. He gave us a heads-up as musicians on the different things you can run into, different complications and women and all those kinds of things, the trappings and the pitfalls of being an actual musician. He would give us cassettes and say, "Listen to this." He'd give us a cassette of him playing, give us lectures about growing up and what we needed to do and how we needed to handle ourselves as young men.

ALAN LEEDS: Prince idolized his dad. He was a musician, he dressed cool, he was known in the community, and he had a measure of success. He approached music with a very unique personal style that was somewhere between Thelonious Monk and Sun Ra.

ANDRÉ CYMONE: The apple did not fall far from the tree. If you heard John play, you completely understood where Prince got the genes. Prince had a nice piano in his bedroom, a little upright, so his dad obviously said, "My son's talented." It was an unbelievable setup.

MORRIS DAY: John helped Prince get started. At an early age, he would take Prince with him to the church and they would play duets and stuff. I think he realized that his son had a gift. John and Prince were very similar to me. I didn't notice John's comedic side as much as Prince's. John was very serious and kinda moody. He reminded me of Vincent Price, and he kind of looked like him. He had this real deep voice, kind of like Prince did. They were very similar, which is probably why they ended up clashing.

ALAN LEEDS: As Prince grew up, he saw other sides of his dad that were difficult to idolize. He wasn't an attentive father other than to talk about the piano. He wasn't successful as a musician. He apparently had no interest in commercial music, so he didn't make a lot of money with music. I think he was basically a frustrated jazz man, a jazz man at heart who was never part of the real jazz scene. Whether he could have competed successfully in New York in those days when all the great jazz giants were playing in the city all the time, who knows?

MORRIS DAY: John was an avant-garde jazz musician, and I don't know what kind of market there was for that. There's a possibility that he was a frustrated musician.

ALAN LEEDS: John was a weird guy. Looking between his eyes, you could get a sense that his life had had a lot of drama. He worked at Honeywell in the factory. His day job is what supported the family. The musician side of John, financially, was a hustle. Prince saw that, and the older he got, the less he idolized his dad, but I don't think he ever stopped wanting to idolize him.

ME: John was still chasing his dream of being a musician and that may have made it hard to be a committed parent. He also had five other children.

ALAN LEEDS: John was playing nightclubs and strip joints for a living as well as working a day job. He didn't have much time to learn how to be a full-time parent. I don't think he was up to the task.

JILL JONES: I think that John couldn't live with a lot of people. I just don't get the feeling that he wanted a lot of people around. It was too much noise.

ME: Then came the night when John came home and realized Prince had again broken his rule.

MORRIS DAY: Prince and I had these girlfriends who were close friends, and we would hang out with them. You know when you kinda say you're sleeping over at somebody's house, but you're at somebody else's? We'd tell our parents we were going one place and then go to Prince's. One day, he sneaks the girl in. John had already threatened him about bringing girls up in his house, but Prince sneaks the girl up to his room, pulls the mattress off the bed, and throws it on the floor so there ain't no noise or squeaking. But John found out about it. I was there with him when it happened. We came in and said hello to John and he didn't say nothing. He just looked at Prince and said, "Put your key on the table." John called him Skipper. He said, "Skipper, put your key on the table." That was it. He was kicked out. There was no negotiating. He knew that that meant he was out.

ME: Suddenly, Prince had nowhere to live.

JILL JONES: I know that he called John on the phone to try to get back in. His dad was just like, "No." His dad was very strict.[7]

ME: Prince bounced from one family to another, staying on people's couches. He once told a reporter, "I was constantly running from family to family. It was nice on one hand, because I always had a new family, but I didn't like being shuffled around. I was bitter for a while, but I adjusted."

SUSANNAH MELVOIN: He just didn't have a place to be. He found himself going all over the place, living all over town.

ME: He was at his dad's because he had escaped his mom. He felt like she had abandoned him by remarrying. He felt unloved by her, and he hated his stepfather. He would forever stay hurt and disappointed and angry with his mother. So, as a boy, he already had the two key pieces of emotional baggage that would propel him into the incredibly driven teenager who was dying to become a rock star. He needed to get back at his mom for abandoning him and he wanted to win his Dad's love after he'd shunned him. Friends say Prince felt like becoming a rock star would prove his mom was wrong—see, I do matter—and it would also capture the attention of his father. Succeeding in music where his dad had failed would surely make Dad proud of him and win his respect.

JILL JONES: Prince had this vibe of, "I'm gonna punish my mom forever." He would do stuff like fly his dad first class and fly his mom in coach. Some really strange things went on, and he made it very difficult for her to be really warm with anyone, but his father got off scot-free. I thought that was really patriarchal of him.

ME: Let's go back to the beginning. Mattie Shaw was a jazz singer who met John Nelson in a nightclub. Both of them had grown up in Louisiana and then moved to Minneapolis, both of them loved music, and both of them had children—Mattie had one (Frank Jackson) and John had four (Sharon, Norrine, Lorna, and John Nelson). John was seventeen years older than Mattie. They met in 1956. She sang with his band until they married in 1957. She called him Prince. Prince was born in 1958. Also in 1958, John and his prior wife had a son named Duane. In 1960, Mattie and John welcomed Prince's sister Tyka. Sounds like it was complicated.

SUSANNAH MELVOIN: When he was growing up, he thought his mother was the most beautiful woman in the world. He used to look up to her, and he would say that when she was very, very young, she looked like Elizabeth Taylor. She had great hair, a beautiful body, and carried herself in a specific way. He was enamored with that, and he would talk about that. He looked at her curves, the way she put her lipstick on, the way her eyebrows arched. She was kind but she had a great swag about her, like her demeanor was incredibly hot. He would show me pictures of his mom and he'd say, "Wasn't she beautiful?" I would say, "Oh yeah, you look like her." It's really odd—he put his makeup on like his mom did. That was the way he wanted people to look at him.

MORRIS DAY: She was a nice lady. He always told me that he got singing from her because he said, in the car, when he was a kid, she would sing, but she would never sing the lead note. She always sang harmony notes. He said that he picked up harmonies from the way she approached singing songs as she was doing her karaoke thing in the car. The times when I was around her, she just always seemed like a nice lady.

JEROME BENTON: Miss Mattie was sweet. Very sweet lady. Beautiful. Light skin, like them yellow yellow girls. Beautiful lady. Very respectful. Proud of her son. She didn't talk a whole lot, but she embraced us and was very endearing.

CHILDHOOD FRIEND: She was never a momma bear with him. She wasn't a great caretaker. She was a party girl. She wasn't like a mom to him. I think she paid more attention to Tyka. And his mom is a twin. [Her sister's name was Edna Mae.] He had a real problem with his aunt and his mother's relationship. This twinning, he did not like.

ME: They had a nice house.

MORRIS DAY: I actually lived on the same block as Prince when he was eight or nine years old. They had the nicest house on the north side. I didn't know who he was. I just saw these two little kids who played outside in the driveway. I used to see Prince and his sister Tyka, but I didn't find that out until years later.

ME: John and Mattie's relationship was rocky.

ANNA FANTASTIC (Prince's girlfriend 1988–1989): Prince said that his dad had told him that women are no good. Once, he and his father were at a gas station with Prince's mom and she had on a polka-dot dress. She got out of the car and was kind of just standing by the car and Prince's dad went into pay for something when this other real fancy car drove by. When Mr. Nelson looked, he thought she was flirting with the driver of the other car and he was like, that's when I knew women are no good. That was one of the stories Prince shared about his parents.

ME: In Mayte's memoir, *The Most Beautiful: My Life with Prince*, she says Prince told her about a time when he was seven and his mother had come home from a shopping trip. In her rush to get back, she had put her shirt on inside out. Prince's father saw that, thought that she'd been cheating on him, and went ballistic. Mayte said that as he told her about the violent scene that followed, she could see how deeply it still affected him. She said the movie *Purple Rain* is about "what it is for a child to witness the psychological warfare between his parents." In 1981, Prince told *Newsday* that his father, "felt hurt that he never got his break because of having the wife and kids and stuff...There were constant fights." In his brief memoir, the *Beautiful Ones*, Prince wrote: "The sound of Ur parents fighting is chilling when U're a child. If it happens 2 become physical, it can b soul-crushing. One night I remember hearing them arguing & it got physical. At some point my mother crashed in2 my bedroom and grabbed me. She was crying but managed a smile & said, 'Tell Ur father 2 b nice 2 me.'"

ALAN LEEDS: It was pretty clear that his childhood wasn't peaches and cream. From everything I've heard, there was drama in the house, meaning the father and mother had issues.

ME: John and Mattie separated when Prince was seven and divorced when he was nine. John left behind a piano that Prince spent hours playing on. His musical interest was clear from a young age. His mother said that when he was very young, if they went into a department store, Prince would always find his way to the keyboards. But then Mattie married a man named Hayward Baker. Prince hated him. This is when his relationship with his mother began to fall apart.

A CHILDHOOD FRIEND: After John and his mom broke up and John went on his own, he saw his mother get involved with this stepfather guy. She would get all dressed up and she'd drink and she'd party and they would party and they would have all this fun. Prince found it really disturbing. He was incredibly put off by that. Like, "You're my mom. You're not supposed to do this shit." He just became a kid who was bumming everybody out.

SUSANNAH MELVOIN: He started to really despise his mother when she got involved with his stepfather. Prince literally paid no attention to him. It was like he was the most insignificant human for him. He almost never spoke of him. But he spoke of his mother and how disappointed he was in her. If she ever came up in conversation, he would get incredibly disturbed by it. He'd be like, "Fuck her. I don't even want to fucking talk about my mother." He'd give you that look like, "Mother? Never." He never really talked about the things that he loved about her, except for how beautiful she was.

MORRIS HAYES: He talked about how difficult it was with his stepdad and everything. He just said, "I don't think he wanted me in the house. He would do anything to get me out of the house. You know, like, go pick the dandelions or whatever."

ANDRÉ CYMONE: Some stepfathers can be really, really cool. Some stepfathers not so much. It's hard for me to really speculate on where he was at, I just know he was making Prince do a lot of stuff. I don't want to call him Cinder-fella or anything like that but, you know.

OWEN HUSNEY (Prince's first manager 1976–1978): I do know that there was something very funky going on in Prince's home with his stepfather. I don't know exactly what, but I do know that it was bad enough that he felt he needed to get out of that house to save his life.

JILL JONES: I have a little bit of empathy for his mother because I get the feeling Prince might have been a bit of a terror.

ME: When Prince was an adult, he saw his stepfather from time to time.

BOBBY Z.: We saw him a lot at the airport. Hayward was a skycap, a baggage handler for Delta. Very outgoing, friendly, always happy to see us.

ME: In his memoir, Prince described moving out of his mother's house as one of the happiest days of his life.

ALAN LEEDS: He felt sharply that his mother had abandoned him and, if you can't trust your mother, you can't trust anybody. He grew up with that. That's the template for his life. "I couldn't trust her, so I'm gonna trust you?" He never completely trusted anybody, and the lack of trust was right on his sleeve. It was so transparent once you got to know him. The inability to trust begets the need for control. Prince is a control freak because anyone assuming any kind of control frightens the hell out of him. He obsesses over having total control and has that fear of anyone else having control. So much of what he does is driven by fear. Fear of someone else having control. Mom had had control and that had been a disaster and that would never happen again.

ME: After Prince moved on, Mattie had another son, Omarr, and she went on to get a master's degree in social work from the University of Minnesota. She spent two decades as a social worker in the Minneapolis school system and, by many accounts, was a beloved presence in the lives of many young people. In her obituary, many people spoke of how caring she was in her job. But when Prince was twelve and semi-homeless, he did not feel like he could or should go to her place. But he knew someone his age who loved music just as much as he did: André Anderson, who would grow up to become the recording artist known as André Cymone.

JILL JONES: I don't think André was seen as the good boy that you'd want your son or daughter to hang out with. André was edgy as all get out.

ANDRÉ CYMONE: I had to be twelve or thirteen when I met Prince. I was from the projects. My family came from a different side of reality, so when we moved into Prince's neighborhood in North Minneapolis, a kind of an upper-middle-class Black neighborhood, it was a different reality. It was a different mentality. My mom worked hard, and she was able to move her family out of those circumstances and move us into this really nice neighborhood, but the thing is, you don't move into a neighborhood like that and change overnight. I was still very, very rough around the edges. I was a handful as a kid. It didn't take long for people to realize that. I don't want to say I was a thug, but I was a very curious kid and I got into a lot of stuff and I was very creative in the things I got into. Anybody who hung around with me wound up having a lot of fun, but it was fun that was always a little bit on the edge. After meeting Prince and hanging out, I think I might have been thirteen when I pulled up in front of his house in a brand-new Cadillac, white on white, and I honked the horn. It wasn't mine. It was a whole thing that I had it but that's a whole other story. Anyway, I honk the horn, thinking he's going to run out and I'm going to take him for a little joy ride because cars like that you only have two days and then pretty much time's up, all bets are off. I honked, and I was like,

"You should come out." His mom came out and was like, "What are you doing in that car? Whose car is that?" I didn't expect that. I'm like, *Uh oh. I got to make up a real quick lie.* I said, "It's my uncle's car. He let me drive it." She said, "You ain't got no license and what uncle?" I'm like, "Uh, my Uncle Tommy," because my Uncle Tommy always had Cadillacs. I think he worked at a Cadillac dealership. I thought that was a good one but she knew my uncle. She was like, "He would never let you drive his car. Get away, leave!" I had to slink off. She forbid him to hang out with me, as did everybody else's parents after that.

ME: Prince needed a place to live and he dug André.

ANDRÉ CYMONE: He came and said, "Can I stay with you guys for a while?" I was like, "That's fine with me, but you've got to talk to my mom." So he talked to my mom and she said, "It's cool but I'm going to have to talk to your mom."

ME: André's mother, Bernadette Anderson, knew Prince's mother—they were both Seventh-day Adventists and the Minneapolis SDA community wasn't large. Also, André's father had played in the Prince Rogers Trio for a bit.

ANDRÉ CYMONE: She said it was cool. He stayed. A week turned into a month, a month turned into a year and, before you knew it, it was five or six years, something like that. I saw this man almost every morning and every night for six years, maybe more. He was just there, living at my mom's crib. He wore Converses. He was cool. He was like a brother. He was really cool, really talented. I mean, he was my best friend.

ME: It was a perfect fit. Prince needed a maternal presence and Bernadette had a huge heart. In the neighborhood, she was called "Queen Bernie."

BOBBY Z.: The house on Russell Ave [Bernadette's place] was a pivotal house in politics in Minneapolis. The city had a rough time after MLK, and Bernadette was a strong force in the community.

ANDRÉ CYMONE: Anybody who met my mom and came into contact with my mom, you'd want to move in. She'd make you feel like not only could you do anything, but you could be the best at it. That's how she was. My mom was our anchor and, in some ways, I think if I'm going to be really honest, there were times where I thought she actually, kind of, looked out for him in some ways like she was his biggest fan. I felt a little bit slighted, but then she pulled me aside and said, "You know what? He's going through what he's going through. We're all here together." She really made me understand and made me really comfortable with it. I think she made all of us really comfortable.

JILL JONES: Bernadette was amazing, lovely, loving, warm, nurturing. I can't say enough. She was so warm and such a charismatic person, too. She mothered Prince when he lived there. Not to take anything away from Mattie, but Bernadette raised him. I think it was just what he needed.

MORRIS DAY: Bernadette was a really cool lady. She was all about the kids. We hung out at her house, we ate up her food, and we took up her space, and she never complained about it.

JEROME BENTON: Oh my goodness, she was amazing. I never saw her mad. She was always ready to nurture. And that's what she did. She nurtured young men and women of the north side. She was a nicer version of my mom. She was a presence.

JILL JONES: Bernadette got things done. She was an independent woman who made things happen. He adored her. Her teachings stuck with Prince and he never forgot her. Never. That family, somehow, managed to find a way. I think she had a way with her children that they're all really high achievers to some degree.

OWEN HUSNEY: She made sure that people stayed on the path. She kept things running in that house. This was not a house where everybody was laying around and being silly. She kept things rolling. She kept things moving in that house. Nobody had any money over in North Minneapolis, that's not a wealthy neighborhood. Most people over North were living hand-to-mouth. I mean, it was a nice house that they lived in, but the neighborhood was very depressed. Bernadette instilled some discipline. She made sure that homework was done. She made sure that garbage was taken out. She made sure that they were taken care of. I cannot underestimate the influence of Bernadette on Prince. She always looked out for Prince. She loved Prince like a son. And Prince, I believed, developed an element of discipline that absolutely came down from Bernadette.

ALAN LEEDS: Bernadette was a surrogate mother to Prince, and he remained grateful and close to her for the rest of her years.

ANDRÉ CYMONE: She was his first big fan. We had this thing. We'd go back and forth writing songs—he'd write, I'd write, he would play me stuff and I'd go, "Oh yeah?" Then I'd go write more while he's upstairs playing then I'd play him stuff. We were constantly playing music for each other. And then we'd meet in the kitchen and play them and my mom would be in there and say, "Oh that's great! I like that, I like that!" It was just really loving and tender, the caring that she bestowed on him.

ME: Years later, Prince would reference her in a song called "The Sacrifice of Victor" as if she were a saint giving great advice about discipline and sacrifice.

MORRIS DAY: Bernadette was real encouraging, because we were at her house rehearsing in her basement, and she would always comment on the rehearsal. She'd say, "You guys sound good," and just be very positive about it, very embracing, and just a great spirit.

ME: Prince was just one of Bernadette's many responsibilities. When he came into her life, she was a divorcee and a single mother with six children—André was her youngest—and she was pursuing an advanced degree in social work. She was incredibly busy and thus she gave Prince a lot of freedom. Prince told some early interviewers that Bernadette "would let me do anything I wanted to."

JILL JONES: She put food on the table too, but ultimately they made decisions for themselves. Bernadette was not hovering over her kids, so Prince started to be able to make his own decisions.

BOBBY Z.: Bernadette had less pulse on us. If he got in trouble outside of the house then he was in trouble with her, but if he didn't, then he didn't. It was a don't ask, don't tell sort of thing. She was lenient.

ANDRÉ CYMONE: She was the voice of reason and the voice of wisdom but she also let us do our thing, just let us grow and gave us the freedom to do our thing. That was really invaluable.

ME: The freedom shaped Prince for better and worse—he spent no time confronting his pain or learning how to trust or even interact with other people, but, down in Bernadette's basement, he found all the time he needed to develop as a musician.

MORRIS DAY: If you want to know what Bernadette's basement looked like, just go look at *Purple Rain*. That's exactly what Bernadette's basement looked like. It almost mirrored what he put together for *Purple Rain*. It was a little dark, dusty basement with a bed and posters and all of that.

OWEN HUSNEY: It was a basement basement. We're not talkin' about a nice basement. I think they drew a line down the center of the floor and one area was Prince's and one area was André's and you would not cross areas. I think eventually they put a curtain down there to separate the beds so if they met somebody, they could hang out.

ANDRÉ CYMONE: We would go back and forth about what music we were going to listen to to go to bed. Is it going to be Seals and Crofts? Is it going to be the Natural Four? Is it going to be Parliament Funkadelic? Is it going to be Joni Mitchell?

PEPE WILLIE: Him and André used to have contests of who could write the most songs in an hour.

OWEN HUSNEY: These guys were tighter than brothers. I mean blood brothers. André was a big influence on Prince because they would jam at all hours and André could keep up with him. André's an excellent musician in his own right and was very formative in what later became known as the Minneapolis sound. André was instrumental in creating that. André needs to get his due. You just can't underestimate

André's impact on Prince's life. They were both dedicated musicians. Both of these kids had a drive. But Prince's drive was beyond. I remember Bernadette saying to me that quite frequently everybody would be sleeping, it would be three o'clock in the morning, and she could still hear Prince down in the basement playing the guitar.

ANDRÉ CYMONE: I would say this to Prince all the time. "There's somebody somewhere right now practicing while we're sitting here eating dinner. Somebody out there is practicing so we need to be practicing." I was always thinking if we want to make it, we've got to be better than everybody else, which means we've got to practice. He was the same way. It didn't take much swaying. But I was making some nice money hustling, so I was like, if I'm going to give that up, we've got to be serious. Prince didn't need much swaying.

ME: Prince and André were very serious, practiced all the time, and remained serious when they took little breaks.

ANDRÉ CYMONE: Any chance we got, we played basketball. He was phenomenal. There was a little hoop at the house next door that we'd use. We played whenever we'd take a break from practice and, obviously, at North Commons we played a lot. I remember because we used to play two-on-two with guys from the south. At the time, we were both kind of short, so people would say, "You want to run a game?" Actually, we'd have to ask because it wasn't like people were going to ask us. They didn't think we were going to run a good game. So I'd be like, "Hey you guys want to run a game?" They'd look at us like, "Come on." I'd say, "Okay how about we play for two dollars? For five dollars?" I'd get my hustle on. We would almost always win because Prince could drive and he could shoot. I was good from the outside, and I was just a warrior because, no matter what, I was getting back up. I was like, "I ain't done yet. We ain't done yet." We could play.

PEPE WILLIE: Me, him, and André was over south one time playing basketball, and we beat these white boys. They were so mad that we whupped them, and they're acting like they wanted to fight us for real.

So Prince, the littlest guy there, says to this guy, "You guys act like y'all want to fight or something." He got hard all of a sudden! I'm like, *Wow*. I didn't know he was gonna get real like that!

ANDRÉ CYMONE: One summer, my mom got us a summer job together where we were playing with these kids during their recess, which was weird because, at the time, we thought we were rock stars so we'd come in wearing our gear with our hair done. He had naturally curly hair. My hair was not naturally curly so I would have to press and curl it and go through a whole rigamarole. But we would hang out with these kids for an hour or so and play bombardment. Other people call it dodgeball, but we called it bombardment. We had nicknames—they called me "The Cannon" and they called Prince "The Whip." We kinda named ourselves, but the point is our job was just to play with the kids. For us, during bombardment, our targets was the kids' heads. It ended because one of the kids called me a jungle bunny.

ME: André had five older brothers and sisters and several of them had a major impact on Prince.

ANDRÉ CYMONE: He parachuted into a crossroads of dysfunction with all the different characters and personalities in my family. These are very dynamic people. Without them, I know I wouldn't be the person I am. I can't imagine that Prince would say much different. You can't be around my brother Sonny and not be influenced. You can't be around my brother Eddie and not be influenced. Eddie managed him for a while. You can't be around my sisters, especially my older sister, and not be influenced. You can't be around my mom and not be influenced. My brother just came from Vietnam, that whole thing. My other brother just got out of prison. My sister just came from Europe study-ing fashion. My mom had just gotten divorced and everybody was in this house together. You can't be around the characters that came into our house—boosters, people selling stuff, selling coats, selling stereo systems, selling albums. My mom would throw parties and they'd be down there gambling. You can't be in that environment and not be influenced. If you're a shy person, you can still be a shy person, but you start to look at the world from a different perspective because all those people that used to be strange, you can put them in context. Okay, he's a hustler. Okay, he's a pimp. Okay, he's a this or she's a that. You start to put people in context and you start to understand the world around you. My brother Eddie, if you said that you wanted to be in journalism, he would come the next day with a stack of books about journalism and how to get in, what to do, and all the nuts and bolts. That was his thing. So, for me and Prince, he would come and drop business and music books. He would sit there, read passages whether you'd want to hear it or not, like, "You need to understand this," You have to understand, my brother. I think one of the things that when you go to the clink, you come out and you learn, you educate yourself. You read and you get knowledgeable about different things so you never wind up in that situation again. He definitely exemplified that mentality. He also knew we were just getting into sexual experimentation, so he brought books on different aspects of how you can maximize tantra. Every book about sex, he brought to us. It's like, there it is, an education on sexuality. My brother Sonny was a pimp. He had the ride, he had the women, he had three bad women. They would come through sometimes, no clothes on. There was no sexual inhibitions going on in our house.

JILL JONES: Prince looked up to Sonny. He talked about him over the years to me. Everybody looked up to him, and he ventured into the world of being a pimp. He had a lot of women and the full-on pimp getup with the hats and the canes. He was that archetype and Prince grew up watching all of that. He was like a little goody two shoes at the beginning, and I think those guys reshaped that. André and his brothers were instrumental in making Prince not the little mama's boy. I believe all those characters were indelibly marked in his head.

MORRIS DAY: Sonny was the kind of guy who'd come over during rehearsal, and he could just hop on any instrument. He'd hop on the bass, the guitar, the drums, the keyboards, and he was a hell of a singer. He was in a rival band called Back to Black. He was all about the music, and he would teach you if you wanted to learn. Sonny came over to my house when I got my first drum set. Now mind you, I only had a kick drum, a snare, and one cymbal. No high hat, no chair. This dude got on my drum set and absolutely mashed it. He was playing "Cold Sweat," you know, James Brown, and I was never the same after that. He really took me to another level. Sonny was definitely influential for all of us, and especially Prince.

ME: Prince spent his youth pursuing excellence and mastery and building himself into a rock star, playing music to the exclusion of almost everything else that a normal childhood would include, using music to quiet his pain around his parents turning their backs on him. But, at the same time, his dad had not forgotten about him.

ANDRÉ CYMONE: His dad always gave him allowance. He was lucky as far as that was concerned.

ME: Sometimes Prince collected it from John at a strip club.

ANDRÉ CYMONE: It was a place called the Copper Squirrel. We'd have to go catch the bus to get there. I remember sitting there and looking around. It was interesting.

ME: Eventually, they were able to play there.

ANDRÉ CYMONE: We were backing another group, a four-guy singing group, and, when they took a break, we got to do a couple songs.

ME: Then Prince and André started Grand Central.

ANDRÉ CYMONE: We came together and said, "Let's start a band." He was guitar. I was originally the horn section, but later, through some shenanigans, I became the bass player. Actually, originally there were some other dudes because when you start a band, you start a band with whoever has equipment. When we did our first couple of talent shows, this guy named Jerome Dunham was playing guitar. It wasn't like we could just go out and get whatever we wanted. Jerome had a great guitar and a really cool outfit. At the start, Prince didn't play guitar, he played keyboards but sometimes he got his dad to let him use his guitar. Then there was this kid named Lem Perry because he had a bass and an amp. I think Michael Shaw might have been related to Prince, he was supposed to be one of the horns but he never came to any practices so I was the horn section because I played trumpet, saxophone, trombone, tuba. I played all that stuff. But I also played bass because my dad was a bass player. That was my main thing, but I didn't have a bass, and I couldn't get my mom to buy me a bass because we were broke. I actually got the first guitar that Prince and I shared because I was a hustler. I was able to hustle up this guitar. Then I finally got a bass and became the bass player.

ME: In time, the band grew into Prince on guitar, André on bass, Prince's cousin Charles Smith on drums, and André's sister Linda Anderson on keys.

ANDRÉ CYMONE: The sound was good and we started to build a little following. We were doing covers mostly. We did "Slippery When It's Wet" [the Commodores], "Can You Handle It" by Larry Graham, "Once You Get Started" [Rufus], which was one of Prince's main things. We did "Wildflower" [first done by Skylark, popularized by the O'Jays]. We'd always slip in a couple of originals, too. I always thought we were really good. I thought that we had a ways to go, but I was very, very hard on all of us. I was hard on my sister, I was hard on Charles, I was hard on him. I was just like, "We've got to be the best." I was a hustler. I was making nice little chunk off hustling. I was not interested in being broke. But I saw an opportunity in being in a band. I knew we could make some noise. I was in the streets, so I was always seeing what was going on on the ground level. I would see what was happening, and I said, "I could see us slipping in there. I could see how we can make this thing happen." I thought we were a really good band. We kicked everybody's ass.

ME: Then, Morris Day started trying to get in the band.

MORRIS DAY: I found myself in the middle of this really creative time. Back then in Minneapolis, there was a band on every block. I would hear a few guys play and go home and woodshed on my drums. That's pretty much all I did. If I wasn't chasing girls or something, I was playing my drums. So one night, I was supposed to meet a girl at this school dance in a cafeteria at North High, and I get there and this band is playing. They're my age, fourteen, fifteen years old, and they're playing Hendrix; Carlos Santana; Earth, Wind & Fire, real sophisticated stuff, and they're playing it like they're in their twenties. Prince is ripping guitar solos and André's playing all this Larry Graham-type bass. They were just ripping it up, and I was mesmerized. I forgot all about the girl. I was standing there pretty much in front of the band in awe the whole night. They take a break and I go up to André and I'm like, "You guys are amazing, man." We hit it off and started to get to know each other. I mentioned that I play drums but, you know, just mentioning it and actually finding out what somebody's capable of are two different things.

ANDRÉ CYMONE: Morris would come to our gigs and he would always say, "Hey man, I could play drums." I'm like, "Yeah, we've got a drummer," and he's like, "But I'm really good!" "Well our drummer is good, too." Then he would come to another gig and say, "You've got to hear me play." He was very persistent. Then when I graduated from ninth grade to tenth grade, I went from Lincoln High to North High and Morris saw me in the hallway and he came running up like, "André! Man, you've got to hear me play drums!" I'm like, "Dude, we've got a drummer." He's like, "Let's just go into the band room." So, we go in the band room and there's a drum set. He starts playing but the drums are set up on a riser and there's no carpet, so when he starts playing the drums are slipping and he's trying to pull them back as he's trying to play, but, eventually, the drums start falling off the risers. I was like, "I'm getting out of here," because they always blame the project Negro. He runs after me and he's like, "You've got to come over to my crib, you got to hear me play!" I'm like, "Dude, I don't go over to dudes' cribs." He's like, "No, no, you've got to come by," blah, blah, blah, blah. Eventually I'm like, "Alright. Cool."

MORRIS DAY: We started hanging out, skipping school together, smoking weed, all that stuff. Kids, I don't recommend it, but that's what I did. One day, we were skipping school, and I invited him to come over to my house. I wanted him to know that I played the drums.

ANDRÉ CYMONE: We walk over to his house and he introduces me to his mother and his mother is gorgeous. I completely fall in love. I mean, completely in love. She's like Pam Grier fine. Eventually, she became our manager. We go upstairs and Morris has his drums set up. He has this amplifier and put on "What Is Hip" by Tower of Power and played it lick for lick. I was like "Damn."

MORRIS DAY: I then came back with some "Soul Vaccination," playing Dave Garibaldi note for note. When I stopped André's sitting there looking at me with his mouth open. He's like, "Man, I didn't know you could play like that." Next thing I know, he said they were having problems with their drummer who was Prince's cousin. He was chasing girls and not coming to rehearsal. To these guys, it was all about rehearsing and professionalism. He said, "You should bring your drums by and audition." I hopped at that opportunity because I had wanted to be in the band from the first time I heard them. I took my drums over, set them up, and never broke 'em down, man.

ANDRÉ CYMONE: I told Prince, "Man, this guy needs to be our new drummer." We wound up jamming with Morris and, sure enough, he was in. That's how Morris came in.

MORRIS DAY: Prince was real quiet at first, few words, just trying to vibe me. We talked about song arrangements and stuff like that. Musically, we hit it off right away. We would cover stuff from pop music to fusion to jazz, just all over the place. We went through some serious grooves and spent a lot of time doing it. If we weren't playing something structured, then we were jamming. It was deep, man. Our stuff was deep. When we jammed, Prince would get on the bass and I would be on drums, and we would just go at it for hours. Even in his early teens, his ability was very unusual. He was an awesome guitar player and keyboard player. But other than music, he was standoff-ish and keeping his distance and maintaining his little mystique. He's had that whole thing ever since he was a kid. Eventually, we got to be close, but it was a process. It took a few months before we started to really hang out and get to know each other and become friends. A year or two later, we're like the best of friends. He had a really good sense of humor and he was a cool cat to be around, but also difficult to be around at times, which never changed.

ME: Being one of Prince's best friends meant he would call you in the wee hours of the night. Morris had a four-track recorder and he lived around the corner from Prince and André. Prince would write songs and then swing by Morris's, wanting to use his recorder to lay them down. This could happen at midnight, or at 1 a.m., or 3 a.m., or whenever.

MORRIS DAY: He would stop by my house and knock on the front door. If it was late, I might try and duck him, act like I wasn't home, but he'd go from the front door to the window to banging on the back door. You'd think I stole something from him, but he just wanted to come in and record. That went on all the time. He's hollering for me, and it was all because he had a song in his head that he wanted to record, and he just wasn't giving up on the idea of that. I don't think Prince ever slept on an idea. Sometimes, things might pop in my mind, and I'll mari-nate on it. I might hum something into my little tape machine and, you know, let it marinate, but this dude, if he got an idea, he would act on it right away. The difference between Prince and me is like, I'm not really a workaholic. I can do my thing musically, but then I got to have my leisure time. This cat, he was just all about it.

JEROME BENTON: He was driven. Being with him I saw what drive was.

ANDRÉ CYMONE: He wanted to be a rock star. I always said I wanted to write the most amazing songs in the world. His goal was always to be a rock star.

JILL JONES: André told me a story where they were coming out of a 7-Eleven and Prince looked at André and said, "Don't get used to this because there'll be a time when we won't be able to do this." That was one of the beautiful things about Prince—he really believed in hard work and manifesting your dreams. What he did was he created the world around him, and if the people didn't fit the dream, they were gone.

MORRIS DAY: He was very serious and very positive. The whole band, Grand Central, all they talked about is not if, but when I make it. "When I make, it I'm going to do this, I'm going to do that." That changed my attitude as a musician. All we did was rehearse seven days a week. The only times we didn't was when one of the parents of whoever's house we were at told us it's not a good day. Other than that, it was all about the music. He had a drive at a young age that was incredible. By the time I got in the band, he already had a Mead notebook, a little spiral binder, and he already had a hundred songs written in this binder. To me, that was unheard of. I thought I was a serious-minded musician until I met Prince, but I wasn't even thinking in terms of writing songs. His drive and determination were unparalleled. He was on another level, always thinking ahead, always had his eyes on the prize as far as his career was concerned.

ME: He had everything a budding rock star needed—a specific, vivid dream, mountains of determination, painful inner wounds he was trying to heal, and a surreal work ethic. He was the kid who was waiting outside the school's music room when they unlocked the door in the morning and the one they had to kick out at the end of the day so they could lock up. Then he went home and practiced for hours, playing until his fingers bled. He definitely wasn't putting much energy into school.

SUSAN ROGERS: One day, I saw his report cards. His mother came to the house and she brought a cardboard box with some of his stuff from childhood. That's the only time I ever saw her. I saw her for a minute and then she left. The box was sitting there and Prince saw me looking at it and he said, "You can look in it if you want." I went over, and there were things from childhood including his report cards. I went through his report cards and I looked at the grades he got and I looked at the comments that his teachers wrote about him and they wrote about the same guy that I knew, the guy who was sitting there next to me. He's quiet, he's respectful, he's polite, he's obviously very bright, but he keeps himself apart from the other kids for the most part and he's a lovely boy. That's essentially what they're saying, he's obviously very bright and also incredibly shy.

SUSANNAH MELVOIN: He was actually like the geeky pen-in-his-pocket kid. He taught kids how to play piano. He was a piano teacher.

ALAN LEEDS: He was not a joiner. He was a loner. He was short. He was made fun of by kids who were tall, the typical kind of stuff that happens to a nerdy kid who sits in the corner and plays the guitar while everybody else is out playing football or whatever.

MORRIS HAYES: Prince told me that these two guys used to beat him up at school. They would take turns, like, "Is it my day to beat him up? You beat Prince up yesterday, right? So it's my day to beat him up today, right?" He told me that was happening and how he hated school. They all thought he was mentally challenged or something, like this kid's slow, but it turns out he had an IQ near Einstein. He couldn't thrive in a place like that because he was way beyond everyone. He just was so far ahead of folks. They just thought he was weird and they persecuted him and what he really liked was being on his own with his thoughts. Of course, one of the guys who beat him up ended up playing with him in the band.

ME: It sounds like a Hollywood movie—in a world where he was tossed aside by his parents and unseen by his community, he decided that the perfect way of showing them all that they were wrong, and that he did matter, was to become a rich celebrity. Because becoming a rich celebrity is the best revenge.

MORRIS DAY: I could see that Prince felt there was something to prove from not being able to stay at his mother's house, and not being able to stay at his dad's house and just kind of feeling forced out into the world. And maybe feeling like he had something to prove. I think that could have been a factor in his drive.

ALAN LEEDS: You also have a situation where his mother had left him with his dad early in his childhood. When you get that kind of situation, it only reads as rejection to a youngster. I think he was looking for acceptance. Maybe his seeking of celebrity was replacing his mother. He was more than just someone with massive talent and an amazing work ethic, he was also someone who had something to prove. He had someone he wanted to show up.

WENDY MELVOIN: I think underneath it all, what drove him was a need to break away from his family and be more successful and be better.

ME: Prince had determination, drive, insomnia, creativity, and heaps of talent, but he still had a lot to learn.

MORRIS DAY: We were playing clubs and playing shows at the VFW and the Nacirema [a legendary local club] and these little hole-in-the-wall clubs that adults frequented, and he basically stood in front of the mic, played the guitar, and sang. As far as performing, it wasn't about that. He wasn't much of an entertainer then.

PEPE WILLIE: Prince and them played "Sex Machine" and it was good, but then he stopped in the middle of the song. He told Linda, "Those are not the chords I want you to play." He puts down his guitar, goes over to Linda, and starts playing the keyboards. I'm like, "Okay, he plays keys, too." He goes back and straps on his guitar and they start jamming again. Then he stops. "André, let me hold your bass." André gives him the bass and he starts playing the funkiest stuff that you could imagine. I was like, "This guy plays bass, too?" Then he jumps on the drums. I said, "Man, this guy is talented." Then they started playing this song called "You Remind Me of Me" and at first I'm like, *Okay, alright*, and then, all of a sudden, it turned into a jam session. These guys are just jamming and I'm going, *Wait a minute*. I stopped them and I said, "The basic construction of your music is not right.

You have to have an intro, then you have to have a first verse, then you do the hook, then you do the second verse, then do the hook again, then you either do a third verse or a bridge and do the hook again and vamp out. The hook gotta appear in the song at least three times because that's what people are going to remember until they buy the record and they can understand what you're saying in the lyric form. But as far as what they're going to remember, that's the hook." And everyone was singing the wrong words, so I made everybody put down their instruments and write the lyrics on this blackboard so everybody knew what it was. Then I said, "Prince, you ever been in a recording studio before?" He said, "No." I said, "You want to play with me in the studio?" He goes, "Yeah!" I said, "Okay. You can play guitar for me," because I was playing acoustic guitar and Prince had an electric. I gave him a copy of the songs that we were going to do. He rehearsed for a couple weeks, but Prince didn't have a driver's license, so we had to go pick him up. So we get to the studio, we got five songs to do and we kick it off. We went into the first song. No mistakes. Everybody is grooving. Finish that. Then, before the second song, Prince goes, "Wait a second." He tunes his guitar a little bit, "Okay, let's go." Two, three, four, boom. Second song, perfect. Third song, perfect. Fourth song, fifth song perfect. And we're done. One take and it came out awesome. I mean awesome. But later that night Prince calls me up and he goes, "Pepe, there's something I have to fix." I said, "What do you mean something that you have to fix? It's great!" He says, "No, the second chorus, I didn't do the guitar part right." I'm like, "Well, I didn't hear it." He says, "Believe me, it's there." Now, for him to say to me that it was incorrect and I couldn't hear it, I just took it like, man, this guy is good. I called the studio the next morning and I said, "Let Prince in the recording studio, he's gotta fix a part." I went golfing.

ME: Seems like teenage Prince only got respect when he was playing music.

PEPE WILLIE: He wasn't hip at all. Prince was a square. Nobody really wanted to hang out with him because he wasn't, like, cool. He would just do square things, man. Like, we'd go outside, smoke a doobie and come back upstairs, and he goes, "Oohhhh, ooohhh, look at you! Your eyes are red! Look at you, look at you!" And we'd be going like, "Oh, man, come on." He was square. He didn't do any drugs, didn't drink, and, matter of fact, when we were rehearsing, he didn't even take breaks. Prince would always be up in the attic while me and Morris and André would be downstairs having some chocolate cake that his mom made or smoking a doobie on the stoop, in front of the house. He never took a break. When we came back, he still has his guitar, and he's playing the stuff. He'd come over and rehearse at my house for ten hours straight and leave and go right into more practice. You would think that he'd be trying to get something to eat, but no. Once, after he left my house, I went over his house, and I'm banging on the door and didn't get no answer. I knew he was home because his car was there. I go around the side of the house, and I hear this rhythmic banging sound. I peek through the basement window, and Prince is down in the basement playing drums after ten straight hours of practice. The one thing I liked about Prince: he had the desire to be successful. This man did not want to fail. The work ethic that Prince had is unbelievable. I tried it. One day I said, "You know what? I'm going to be like Prince, man. I'm going to work real hard and just keep it going. I like working hard. I like putting eight to ten hours in at the studio." But I couldn't do it again the next day. I was worn out. He did that every single day. He was just a worker all the time. He was all music, all the time. That was it.

ME: Interestingly, the wannabe rock star rejected one thing that was almost expected from rock stars: he was super sober.

PEPE WILLIE: Prince didn't want no drugs, period! He didn't want no drugs in his band at all. He don't want you smokin' weed around him, he don't want you doin' nothin. He wanted a completely straight band, and I can understand that. He didn't want anything to come in the way of his success.

MORRIS DAY: We would sit around as kids and smoke a little weed, drink a little wine, just me and some of the guys in the band. Prince was never into that. He would never partake. He would maybe sit around and kind of get high off of watching us, and wonder what that was all about, but he was never really interested in getting high or drinking with us. It wasn't his thing. He just wanted to get back to playing the guitar and rehearsal. He wasn't interested in any mind-altering drugs or drinks. He liked to be in control.

ME: Except this one time.

MORRIS DAY: Once he was like, "Can you get some mushrooms? I want to try and get high tonight." I don't know why he said mushrooms, because I never really smoked mushrooms any damn way, but I guess he heard that it was some kind of hallucinogen or something, so I went and got some mushrooms, and we both tried them. We went to a club and this dude starts freaking out. Next thing I know, he's sitting on the floor with his head in his hands, and he was tripping like his mind was playing games on him. He was like, "I'm not never doing this shit with you no more."

ME: Meanwhile, Grand Central was growing.

ANDRÉ CYMONE: Grand Central became a very known band. He was definitely respected, but we had a reputation as a group. One thing that exploded us was we went to do a battle of the bands at North High. At that time, it was just me, Prince, and Charles. I don't think my sister was playing. Prince had this guitar that me and Charles had bought for him. It was the first guitar he had that was not his dad's guitar, a little Silvertone. But we had these little cheesy amps and our drummer had drums that didn't have heads on both sides. They weren't going to let us play in the Battle of the Bands because we didn't have enough equipment. They were like, "You can't be in. We can't let you guys. You guys aren't ready yet." I'm the mouth so I was able to talk to the other bands and say, "Listen, we're young and we don't have amps and you guys have big amps, We won't hurt anything." They said, "Yeah. Okay.

Fine." So we went on and people started leaving as soon as we came on. But we started playing Billy Preston's "Out of Space" and people started coming back. Before you knew it, everybody was back. Before you knew it, we had them. We was doing our own thing. We kicked everybody's ass and two of the biggest bands in the city at the time were there, so this was like a big deal. There was all these bands that were really at the top of their game, and we won. We were like fifteen, but, if you've done your work and your due diligence, then success is where preparedness meets opportunity. Just be prepared when the opportunity comes. We exemplified that mentality, that mindset. I think we won seventy-five dollars and a recording session. When we went in as a band to record, Chris Moon came to me and said, "Hey, listen. I do jingle things if you want to make some money on the side. So, if you want, you can come and record some jingles." I said, "You need to talk to my manager." I was always leery about people coming and approaching us trying to get in. I thought that's what he was doing. When we get back to the crib, Prince said, "Yeah, dude came up to me." I said, "Are you going to do it?" He said, "Yeah." He saw that was an opportunity.

ME: Prince's friendship with Chris Moon, a local studio owner, led to him getting a set of keys to the studio, which meant Prince basically living at the studio, sleeping on the floor, and spending all his time studying it. You can imagine young Prince being in the studio in the middle of the night, pressing every button, exploring every possibility, teaching himself how to use that massive tool.

MORRIS DAY: The period in Prince's life when he came across Chris Moon changed him because for him, having access to a real studio was more important to him than food or sleep. Eating and sleeping was on the backburner. Being in the studio around the clock meant everything to him.

ME: Prince was close to getting a record deal and achieving the first part of his dream, but there was still a lot of work to do and a lot to be nervous about.

Bobby Z.: There was a real chance it would all fizzle away.

Dez Dickerson (Guitar, the Revolution 1979–1983): Our first public performance was a disaster.

3

Onedayi'mgonnabesomebody

He Never Said If I Make It,
He Always Said When (1977–1979)

OWEN HUSNEY: My secretary buzzes into my office and says, "There's a guy here who says he's got one of the greatest artists around." I said, "Yeah? Tell him to wait." I'd heard this a million times. But Chris Moon sat in my reception area for like four days, so when my secretary buzzes to say, "He's still here," I said, "Alright, alright, I feel so bad, send him in! Send him in!" He comes in and he's professional, English accent, very proper, and he says, "I want you to hear this..."

ME: Moon played a demo of "Soft And Wet" that Prince had made.

OWEN HUSNEY: I listened to it, and I said, "Holy shit! This is great! Who is the band?" The band was unbelievably tight, the musicianship was really, really excellent. I noticed that the songs kinda rambled and went on and on, and there were some elements that needed to be changed, but it struck a chord with me because the musicianship was beyond what I had heard. Sometimes sloppy musicians like the Rolling Stones can be good, but this was like perfection. So I said to Chris, "Who is the band?" And he said, "It's one guy playing and writing everything. He's like sixteen or seventeen and he's playing everything." I immediately wanted to know, "Who

48

is he?" And, "Where the hell is he? Let's get him over here!" He said, "Well, he's with his sister Sharon in New York trying to get a deal." I said, "Well, let's get him back here in Minneapolis. Let's call him." We called him at his sister's house and I said, "Listen man, I get it. I get what you're doing. If anything, my role right now is to protect your creativity. You're very young and there's a lotta people trying to take advantage of you, and that ain't gonna happen. I will put this thing together like it's made for you and we'll get this done." I brought in other people to help him. I raised money, about $50,000 from a doctor and a lawyer, and we were able to get Prince a little place to live and some instruments and new clothes and stuff like that. He never took advantage of that. He was a very, very unique human being. When you met Prince, there was nothing untrustworthy about him. His focus, his drive, his intelligence, his sincerity was everything. He wasn't hung up with BS; he had the drive and the focus of a forty-year-old businessman.

ME: Husney introduced Prince to drummer Bobby Z. and they started jamming with André Cymone in Husney's office every night after everyone else went home.

OWEN HUSNEY: He knew how much he had to work to achieve what he wanted to do and he was more than willing to do it. There were letters that he wrote to me that were so brilliant and so spot-on while most kids his age were experimenting with drugs, running away from home, and being stupid. That was not him at all. He was very disciplined. He had that work ethic.

ME: When they went into the studio, Husney was blown away.

OWEN HUSNEY: He was doing the demo tape, and I hired a string section so he had real strings. I remember him being in the control room and sort of disgusted by these old men trying to play these parts he'd written, and he went in there and worked with them 'til they got their parts right. This eighteen-year-old kid was not gonna let anything get in the way of what he wanted to do, and he was going to accomplish it by just being very, very smart.

49

ANDRÉ CYMONE: Owen knew someone who worked for Warner Bros. He said, "Hey I've got this kid," brought him in, had him play some stuff, showed them he could play all the instruments, and they signed him. I want to say he got $300,000, $350,000, somewhere around there. I'm not completely sure. It was more money than any of us had ever dreamed of having.

OWEN HUSNEY: Prince wanted creative control and that was kinda tricky, but I knew I had to get it. A&M and I think Columbia offered us deals, but we could only get two-album deals. Warner Bros. gave Prince three albums. That was unheard of. Parenthetically to all of this, I don't think that I could get Prince signed today given the environment of this business. Labels now would not give him a chance to develop over several albums. They would've kicked him out after the first album.

MORRIS DAY: He got the deal and he comes back and he's showing us pictures of his check from Warner Bros. for $80,000 with his name on it, and we're like, "Wow, man that's really cool." I had never seen a check for eighty grand before. Prince bought a Fiat Spider, a little convertible, and we thought that was hot shit, man. It was like him having a Ferrari or something. He left the band maybe a month or two before he got the record deal and, personally, I was a little salty about it because it kind of messed up a good thing for us. I really liked our band and to see him leave was hard. Of course, everybody's like, "Why didn't Owen take all of us to Warner Bros.?" But at the end of the day, it was all good.

PEPE WILLIE: When he got signed to Warner Bros. I said, "Prince, this is what they're going to do." I knew everything. He got $85,000. That was his upfront money. Now what the whole deal was I don't know, but I know they gave him $85,000 as an advance and he had $80,000 in tour support. They didn't give that $80,000 to him, but that was available for him. And then his budget for the album was like $20,000. All I wanted to do was protect him and make sure that he got to where he was going and nobody screwed it up for him and he wasn't taken advantage of. I started his publishing company for him so he could have his copyrights. They wanted Maurice White from Earth, Wind & Fire to produce his first album. Prince was like, "No. No way." He said, "I listen to Earth, Wind & Fire, I picked their shit apart note by note by note by note, and I ain't going to be Earth, Wind & Fire." It was too simple for him. He said, "I'm not going to have Maurice produce me because I'm better than him." He didn't say that exactly but that's what he was insinuating when he said, "I picked his shit apart." He didn't want to sound like Earth, Wind & Fire. He wanted to do it all himself.

OWEN HUSNEY: They wanted Maurice White to produce him and Prince was extremely respectful of Earth, Wind & Fire and of Maurice White and Verdine White [Earth, Wind & Fire's bass player], he was in awe of their talents, but I think Prince knew that there was gonna be an ending for that sound and I think he felt that if he let somebody like that produce him he was gonna get locked into their sound and he didn't wanna do that 'cause he felt there might be a time when that sound was gonna end and he might be locked in.

ME: Prince also did not want to end up being slotted as a Black artist and aligning himself with the sound of Earth, Wind & Fire would lead to him being perceived as a Black artist. He wanted to be a pop artist. The difference was much more than semantic—the industry then tended to put Black artists in departments labeled Black music or urban music but those departments had smaller budgets and smaller staffs and less power than pop music departments. Prince knew that it was harder to become a megastar when you started in the smaller pond.

OWEN HUSNEY: Some people in the Black music department at Warner Bros. took serious offense, but he knew early on that he did not wanna get pigeonholed.

DEZ DICKERSON: He understood the industry, he understood the segregation of the industry, and he said, "I'm not going to be James Brown.

I have to position myself so they can't categorize my music that way. I have to have white people in the band and girls in the band. Sly Stone had the right idea. I'm gonna do what Sly did and they're gonna cross me over from Jump Street, otherwise I'll forever be just a Black artist."

ALAN LEEDS: It was not so much about wanting white approval, but simply wanting a bigger audience that could support a more successful career. It wasn't a racial thing as much as it was a thing of numbers. He saw what happened to Black artists and how difficult it was for them to get out of the musical ghetto and crossover to pop. He was smart. We're talking about a very, very bright individual, somebody whose brain is just as quick as a spaceship, and he constructed a vision and part of his vision was to not be typecast. He could see that the programmers of pop radio had quotas of how many Black artists they would play, and he was determined from day one to beat that system.

PEPE WILLIE: He said they had to allow him to do his own production, but he was so young they wanted proof that he was playing all these instruments. Warner made him audition on all these instruments to make sure he was the guy doing all of them.

OWEN HUSNEY: The label had a lunch for him because they didn't believe that Prince could play all the instruments. They actually booked studio time at Village Recorders and the president came down to see this kid play all the instruments. Then in the middle of this big luncheon for Prince in Los Angeles, Dean White comes in and sits down. That's Maurice White's brother, and they're pretty much at the height of their career at that point, and Dean White says he wants to produce Prince's album. Prince leans over to me and whispers, "No, he's not. Let's get outta here!" Prince knew that if somebody was gonna produce him, that was not gonna be good for him. He knew instinctively that it wasn't right for him. It wasn't anything about that person, they had tons of hit records, but Prince knew exactly how talented he was. He knew he was a motherfucker and nobody was gonna produce him. I had to go to Warner Bros. and march Prince into the Chairman's office and say, "Excuse me, mister chairman, this eighteen-year-old kid who's never made a full album in his lifetime, he's gonna produce himself." This was a lot—playing all the instruments was one thing, but producing an album was something else. The Chairman said, "How are we gonna do that?" I said, "I've got an idea. Fly Prince out to Los Angeles, tell him he's got free studio time, and let him go and make a song and see what happens." They agreed to do that. That's the magic of Warner Bros. at the time. That would never happen in this day and age, but back then, it did. Now, I did not really want him in the LA bullshit. He was still young and the town was rotating on cocaine and, not that he would've done cocaine, but who needs that? But they wanted to see how good he was, so Prince went into the studio and worked and he didn't know who was walkin' in on the control room, but there were all these top producers of the day coming in—Russ Titelman, Lenny Waronker, top, top producers, they're just waltzing around, and they were fuckin' blown away! At the end of the session, the president says to me, "The kid's got record sense." He meant he knew what making a record entailed, what it needed to sound like, how it needed to be structured.

ME: Once he got the deal, he was not open to people walking in on his sessions.

PEPE WILLIE: I remember Prince being in the studio in LA recording his album, and this is when Prince started really honing in on what he wanted. He did not want to fail. Some Warner Bros. executives walk into the studio. They want to see what he's doing. He stops. He stops the whole session. They're looking at him, and he goes, "When you guys finish touring, I'll get back to work." When they left, he went to work. He went triple overbudget on that first album [*For You*] and he only sold like seventy-five thousand.

ME: The label was nervous.

PEPE WILLIE: Warner Bros. people didn't think that he was quite ready for prime time. Remember those tights that people were wearing? The shiny type of tights? He was wearing that. And he had these boots.

I don't know if it was girly clothes per se, but this is what he wanted to wear and God bless him.

ME: A lot of people were not quite sure what to make of him.

PEPE WILLIE: We went to North Carolina on a plane and he goes to the bathroom. I'm sitting there waiting, like, *What's taking this guy so long? What's he doing?* Eventually, he comes out of the bathroom in curls. He was in the bathroom on the plane with a hot comb and curlers, curling his hair. He comes out with all these curls in his hair and the first thing I think is, *Is this dude gay?* He wasn't but I wasn't the only one to wonder. When I took him and André to New York to do sessions with Tony Sylvester from the Main Ingredient, there was a girl named Gigi who was Tony's girlfriend and she came up to me while we was in the studio and she goes, "You know your friend Prince? I think he wants to be me." I'm like, "What are you talking about? Did he say he likes what you're wearing?" She said, "No, the read I get from him is that he wants to be me. To be a woman." People were always asking me stuff like that, and I can see where they got that from because he did have a little feminine thing about himself. But people who knew him never said anything like that. He had a bunch of girlfriends then. He was starting to get more confident with women. They were coming to him because he was a known musician so it was easy for him. But he was still tricking them. He told me that he told this girl that he was a virgin. He told lots of girls that he was a virgin. He said they'd be like, "I'm gonna teach him how it's done!" He played that virgin role and the girls would be like, "Oh you haven't? Well come over here, sit down, let me show you." That's how he would get them. He did that with a lot of girls.

ME: This interestingly echoes the strategy he would take years later on his records—over and over he positions himself as less knowledge-able, less experienced, and less freaky than the women in his songs. Think of "Darling Nikki," "Sister," "Little Red Corvette," "Raspberry Beret"—over and over in his love songs, he's the one who's being taught, not the one who's dominating.

SUSAN ROGERS: He was so eager to empower women to seduce him. Prince loved the women who seduced him. He admired and respected the women who seduced him. And man was that good for us. It helped women; it helped how we saw ourselves. That subtle point was lost on many of his imitators. He was a highly evolved male in that regard.

ME: That said, he was always ready to drop a woman the second his career called.

PEPE WILLIE: I remember this girl that he was going with, her name was Kim. They were really tight. Kim was with him from the very beginning, before he got signed. She was there for him, she helped him out, she was a really good person for him. We got tight and we used to talk. Then Prince bought her a diamond ring, I think it was like $20,000 or $30,000. He was probably on his second album. But then she had an argument with Prince. And you know, girls they do what they do, she was like, "Well, you could take your ring..." She calls me up and she says, "Yeah, me and Prince had a fight and I threw that ring back." I said, "That's the dumbest thing that you could have ever done." She said, "No, he's going to call me, you watch." I said, "Kim, the minute that he thinks about calling you, his phone will ring and it'll either be his manager or Warner Bros. or some musician, and then he's forgotten about you already. Because his career is bigger than you are. That's what's going to happen. He might want to call you, he might pick up the phone, but then it'll be like, 'Oh, wait a minute, somebody is calling me—Hello, Owen, what's going on? I gotta be where? Okay.' And then he'll start gearing on that and not thinking about you no more." He never went back to her.

ME: Prince started putting together a band to back him. He hired his old friends André Cymone and Bobby Z. to play bass and drums then held auditions to find new people.

DEZ DICKERSON: I had heard something about him in the wind around Minneapolis. He'd stepped into that urban legend status of "Hey, have you heard about this kid? He's like the new Stevie Wonder." He played all these instruments. It wasn't until after the Warner Bros. deal that the word really started to circulate in musician circles. No one was getting signed out of Minneapolis, so that was a big deal. We met in the context of me auditioning for the band. He was maybe nineteen and I was twenty-two. At the audition, I felt like this guy is mature beyond his years. He didn't say much, but when he did speak there was a depth to the words coming out of his mouth that you didn't see with cats that age. And there was this look about him. During the audition, he didn't say a single word, but he had a look on his face and in his eyes you could tell this dude is thinking nonstop. After the audition he had me step out in the parking lot and we talked for about fifteen minutes. You could see it in his face that he was deep. He asked me some very mature, career-minded questions, trying to get a handle on where I was coming from.

ME: He quickly realized the depth of Prince.

DEZ DICKERSON: In every band that I had ever been in, I had always been that guy that was more driven than anybody else. Not just anybody else in the band that I was in, but anybody else that any of them had ever known. Then I encountered Prince and I said, "Wow. This guy is even more driven than I am." It's like there are people who love a good steak but, at some point, they push the plate away and savor the moment that they just enjoyed. But there are other people who immediately order another steak. There are some people who can't enjoy a day off. There are some people who can't rest a beat. That was the difference between us. For him, driven was just a continuous state of being. He could rehearse the band for eight hours and then the band would leave and he'd go on for another four or five hours on his own. That was his normal. Being driven was just his baseline. I came to realize, you know what, there's this thing about wanting to be the best and he has it way more than I do.

BOBBY Z.: André and Dez joined on the premise that they were never staying. They wanted to do their own solo work. André joined reluctantly like, "Okay, I'll help you," but they weren't supposed to stay.

ME: This is why Prince didn't name his band at first—it wasn't clear how long these guys were going to be around. Still, as he went to fill out the rest of the band, he had a vision of what it should look like.

PEPE WILLIE: It was known that he wanted a mix. He said, "I don't want an all-Black band." He wanted to be like Sly and the Family Stone.

ME: Sly and the Family Stone was an iconic, incredibly funky 1970s group led by Sly Stone that was diverse—it was made up of Black men, Black women, white men, and white women. Prince knew diversity was key.

DEZ DICKERSON: The one thing Prince talked to me about a number of times in the early going was that he wanted us to be the multicultural Rolling Stones. That's the way that he wanted it to come across. He wanted he and I to be the Black version of the Glimmer twins—to have that Keith and Mick thing, and have a rock 'n' roll vibe fronting this new kind of band. That's what he wanted. In fact, there were some folks that we auditioned that didn't get the nod because they didn't fit the branding template he had in mind. He wanted a multiracial, male-and-female band. He was a young cat who thought things through. Plus, the Twin Cities had always been a place where you had multiracial bands that did a wide variety of music. That had always been a part of the fabric of the town musically.

JILL JONES: There were tons more musicians who could have pulled that off just as well, but he handpicked everybody for crossover potential. Having white people in the band made it seem like it was just this diverse group of people. Then he could be anything. All of that was totally calculated.

ME: Prince ended up hiring Black men—André and Dez—as well as white men—Matt Fink on keyboards and Bobby Z. on drums—and a white woman in Gayle Chapman on keyboards. And Morris Day, well, at the right time he was at the wrong place.

MORRIS DAY: I had left Minneapolis shortly after Prince got his deal. My mom moved to Maryland, so I was there working odd jobs. I was working at a car rental counter, renting people cars and shit, and one day I'm at the counter and I hear this record come on, and the DJ's like, "Here's a new one by Prince!" It was "Soft And Wet." I was like, "Damn!" I'm telling random people coming up to the counter, "That's my friend! That's my buddy on the radio!" They were like, "Yeah, right, whatever," and looking at me like, "You're lying. And why you telling me this?" But I was done. I packed up, left Maryland and went back to Minneapolis thinking *I'm gonna get in the band!* So I get back and hook back up with Prince and he was glad to see me. We started hanging out right away and doing what we do. Then I'm like, "So, uh, you know, am I gonna get in the band?" He's like, "I already have a drummer." And that was that.

DEZ DICKERSON: Our first public performance was a disaster. It was a place called the Capri Theater in North Minneapolis, and it was initially set up as a public-slash-private showcase for the Warner Bros. execs to come in and see the progress of their prodigy.

BOBBY Z.: It was just stage fright at the Capri. The moment overwhelmed him.

DEZ DICKERSON: At that point in time, Prince had not done a lot of shows. He was transcendent at the musical side, but as far as performing live, that was a whole other thing. He was not yet comfortable, so it was challenging. In that show there were a lot of awkward moments. The few times he did address the audience and speak was with his eyes closed, standing at the microphone and barely speaking above a whisper. At that point, he was just more comfortable letting the music do the talking.

ME: His nervousness on stage was a repeated issue. In late 1979 Prince and the band had their first TV appearance on *American Bandstand* hosted by Dick Clark. They performed "Why You Wanna Treat Me So Bad?" from Prince's sophomore album, *Prince*, and that went well, but what people remember is Prince's interview with Clark where he answers in short, terse, monosyllables as if he was playing a joke on Clark. His awkwardness in interacting with people was on full display.

PEPE WILLIE: It was totally stage fright. Totally. When he came home, I said, "What in the fuck happened to you?" because, to me, he was like my little brother. I'm the only one to talk to him like that. Nobody else talked to him the way I talked to him. I said, "What the fuck happened to you, man? What the hell was that shit on Dick Clark?" He goes, "Pepe, man, when Dick Clark came and started talking to me, I got freaked out." But he says to me, "Pepe, that will never happen again." He didn't like that. He didn't like that feeling. After that, he started controlling his interviews. After that, he didn't want to do interviews. He didn't want to talk to anybody. I did a promotional thing for him out in Chicago, going to radio stations and telling the radio people "Yeah, I'm going to make sure that Prince gives you a call to say thank you for playing his record." That was one of the things that had to be done for him to become a successful artist. You gotta call the radio stations and thank these guys for playing your record. When I got back from Chicago, I told Prince, "Hey you gotta call the radio stations in Chicago and thank them guys for playing your record." He says, "No." I said, "What do you mean? You gotta do this so you can get more play and sell more records." He said, "Do you think the record's a hit?" I said, "Yeah, I think it's a hit." He said, "Then I don't need to call them." After that thing with Dick Clark, he didn't want to talk to people anymore, and for a long time, he didn't do no interviews.

ME: Prince made his sophomore album, *Prince*, all alone.

BOBBY Z.: He made the second record practically trapped in the valley. He was in LA. Nobody was around. He made the record by himself, living out there. He makes it through that and had a hit with "I Wanna Be Your Lover," which helped drive the train into the third album.

ME: Now he was laser focused on becoming a strong performer.

DEZ DICKERSON: One of the things that drove him was the fact that André Cymone and myself, we had that performing part down already. The fact that there were these cats on either side of him who were just tearing it up and he was trying to hold it together, he wasn't going to let that keep happening. So he did what he always did. He decided that he was going to flip that script and he was going to become the best in that area. That's who he always was—he may, at one point, be the student, but you can bet that once he latches on, he will become the master. If he doesn't know how to do something, once he focuses on it, it's not going to be that way for long. That's his greatest asset. Part of the myth and the legend is that he just kind of dropped from the sky fully formed, but the reality is that his greatest strength and his greatest asset is the ability to recognize both what he is and what he isn't and work harder than anybody else in developing those aspects that he knows he needs to develop. In the beginning, he was not a great performer by any stretch, but he changed that and he changed that at a history-making level. That's where that asset comes in. He had that boundless drive connected with teachability and that's a formidable combination. You get somebody who's that driven and has that ability to absorb and assimilate and then do? That's part of what makes him extraordinary. One of his chief strengths was his ability to observe, assimilate, and then reinterpret. And he was doing this with everyone he was around—every engineer he worked with, he was observing and assimilating their recording techniques. With every band member, he was observing and assimilating performing techniques and song-writing and anything that was happening inside the band. All of that shaped him.

OWEN HUSNEY: Prince had the ability to absorb what's in your mind so if you were really, really good at what you do, he'll absorb that like a sponge and soon he won't need you anymore. That happened several times when I was around him. He would work with an engineer for a month, a month and a half, an accomplished engineer with platinum records on his walls, and after a month Prince would come to me and say, "Owen, I know everything he's doing. I don't need him. Tell him go to home."

BROWNMARK: It's pretty amazing how Prince developed as time went on. He kept learning and kept absorbing from people. A lot of people think he was just born with all this, or he was walking down the street and all of the stuff just fell out of the sky into his brain. It wasn't like that at all. He absorbed everything. He absorbed my bass style. He sucked it up. He's like a sponge. Every lick, everything that I did, he absorbed it and he transformed it for himself. He just listens and makes it his own.

ME: Prince's ability to learn quickly seemed like magic even to people close to him.

MORRIS DAY: He went from being a great musician and an okay entertainer to a level where he was totally captivating in all facets and playing at a level that was hard for me to believe. That's something he morphed into in his own time. It had to be developed. It took time for him to really come into his own as a performer. I had the opportunity to watch him grow. I don't know how it happened that he turned into the entertainer that he became. I think he went down to the crossroads like Robert Johnson.

ME: Robert Johnson was a blues guitar player from the 1930s. According to legend, Johnson was an average guitar player who longed to be great. One night in rural Mississippi, he took his guitar to a crossroads and met with the Devil. In exchange for his soul, Satan granted Johnson his wish and made him great. Six months later, Johnson re-emerged as a master and went on to become one of the most important figures in blues history.[8] It's one of the great stories of music history, and while it's fun to think of someone becoming great through supernatural intervention, there were no fallen angels helping Prince.

BOBBY Z.: We were practicing every day in front of big ballet mirrors. Every one of those moves and winks and jumps and spins and smiles and everything, all of that was practiced for hours and hours. And we were taping the shows and watching them back. We did that over and over. Prince watched Jackie Wilson and James Brown and Rick James through that debacle of a tour. He watched Robert Plant, Janis

Joplin, Dolly Parton, Jim Morrison, and all these people. He watched film and he watched himself and he put in work and he evolved and he practiced every little thing until the metamorphosis happened. He developed the ability to take icons from all eras of space and time and spin them back out in new ways. Once the door was unlocked, it was a different guy. Ancient stuff would just flow out of him.

ME: He was extraordinary at learning, but that skill was aimed at certain aspects of his life. He was a genius at music and if we could map his brain, that area would be hyperdeveloped like a gorgeous modern urban landscape. His interpersonal intelligence was underdeveloped like an abandoned town. The Lonely Guy was a peerless musician, but he achieved that at the cost of learning how to deal with people in basic social situations. It created a useful mystique, but it also kept him from being able to make meaningful human connections. He was a person who could not or would not share who he really was or how he really felt, and if the conversation wasn't about music or some aspect of his career, he had zero interest. Even dating him could be strange.

4

Lady Cab Driver

Prince's Relationship with Jill and with Jesus (1980–1981)

JILL JONES: We always had a really weird relationship. Everything was quite random. I had my own line in my parents' house that he could call, but he deliberately called my parents' line in the middle of the night. I was only eighteen and still used to boys from high school coming over with flowers and coming at the right time. Not Prince. He'd show up at three and throw rocks at my window, and they were like, "Who's this rebel?" But I'm running out the door like, "Bye!" I had never met anyone who broke the rules the way he did. I'd say, "You can't call at this time because my parents are sleeping," but he didn't listen. Or, "You can't do X or Y," and he would just do it anyway. I sort of liked that. I was really attracted to the fact that time and rules didn't seem to matter to him. He'd be sitting outside in his black car with tinted windows. You open the door and it's Stravinsky on the stereo. I know my neighbors were like, "What the hell is going on out there?" But it felt like such a rebellion. He was so quirky. He was unlike anybody else I had ever dated, and I really felt like I was embarking on something that would change my life. I just felt like this is something that's going to become incredibly meaningful one day. I don't even know if he would call what we did dating. It was just sort of like we were hanging out, just two people coming together. Sometimes, we'd meet at the Dunkin' Donuts that used to be on Ventura in Laurel Canyon at like two in the morning. I was never great at roller skating, but I was completely comfortable roller skating with him. Dates with him, when he would take you to a restaurant, it was strange. We could sit there in a restaurant that overlooked everything and he would have a glass of wine, or a Coke, or something. If those were dates, I don't know. I think he was afraid of dates. I think that put it into a real conventional thing and I just don't think that was really his steelo. It kind of was weird. I always liked the spontaneous thing. Let's just hang out and see what we can get up to, those kinds of nights. But he was absolutely seductive and he knew that.

ME: Usually they'd end up at the studio.

JILL JONES: It was fantastic, but it was definitely all centered around music. He had a tremendous amount of energy and focus on his songs. He would live, breathe, eat, and sleep his music. And he only slept about four hours a night. I think that he was an alchemist, in a way. He had the brain type of an alchemist who always needed something to motivate them, always needed to keep being innovative. I've never met anyone who was that creative, but also incredibly focused on doing all of the work. Usually, you find people who slack off. Not him. It was just full-on dedication all the time. He gave it all he had every day. I don't think I've ever worked with a musician who had that much fever to get something done. I've worked with people who do their work then take breaks. They sometimes go and have a nice Mediterranean meal in the middle of the day. That wasn't Prince. It was a race to get to the next one. He wanted it done because he believed everything was a chain reaction. He could hear the music. He could hear the bassline. He could hear it as he played the piano. He could hear everything, and then, he'd make his move. "Get the bass. I heard it." Then he's fooling around on the keyboard, doing that part, and he's like, "I know what I'm gonna do. Get me the drums. Set them up; I know what I'm gonna do." It was like he was finding the puzzle pieces.

ME: Outside of the studio, their relationship felt weird, but he made her feel comfortable when they were in the studio together.

JILL JONES: Recording with him was great. We'd do anything—moaning, groaning, whatever we were gonna do, we'd go for it.

ME: Jill met Prince in 1980 on Rick James's Fire It Up Tour, where Prince was opening up for Rick while Jill was singing backup for Teena Marie, who was also on the opening bill.

JILL JONES: Prince was shy from the day of meeting him during the *Dirty Mind* era. He was so shy. You had to pull him out to get those little things about him. His brain worked in a different capacity and he could be so funny, really funny.

ME: Over the course of that tour, Rick began to see Prince's ability and power and appeal were rising and Prince was threatening to outshine Rick. He grew threatened by Prince's presence and he did things to hurt Prince's stage show like reducing the size of the stage he could perform on.

BOBBY Z.: It was a cold war.

JILL JONES: I said to him, "Where are you from?" He said, "Minneapolis." I was like, "Where's that? Up near the North Pole?" He goes, "Oh, you don't know your geography?" It just went back and forth like that. There was always some kind of ribbing going on. And we had this really weird game going on. One night, I was hanging out with André and some of the other members of the band, and André said, "Are you married?" I was like, "No, I'm not married. I'm eighteen." And he goes, "Prince told me you were married." I kind of knew right then that there was something between us. Over the course of the tour, we were staying at the same hotels and we started sharing cars to the venue to sound checks, and he and I became friends but in a really antagonistic way. It was very kidlike. We would pick on each other all the time.

ME: After the tour, when Prince went to LA, he would call Jill. So she could drive him on his dates.

JILL JONES: I was always driving him places. I think "Lady Cab Driver" happened because I was driving him everywhere. He'd bought this new BMW and he showed up at my house with it and then for some reason, I was always driving that car. I even overheated it going up the hill to my parents' place. I was driving him all over LA and Malibu showing him things. Even when we went back to Minneapolis, I was driving him because I think his license got suspended because the police were always on him when he started getting nice cars. He had a lot of speeding tickets. So, yeah, I was the real lady cab driver. We did "Lady Cab Driver" in LA at Sunset Sound. We did the moaning and groaning and the bed springs and it was the most fun ever because it was just like two little naughty kids coming up with all this. There wasn't anything he wouldn't try in the studio. It was great recording with him because there was such an amount of freedom and no restrictions. I wasn't fearful about recording anything with him because he was always so open for whatever. Didn't matter if it was moaning or groaning or whatever, we're gonna shoot for the moon. The wilder the better. You had to stay fearless when you're around Prince. He didn't like being around people who were fearful. We knew what we were doing and how edgy it was and how it was going to make some of his fans go "What?" I got punched in the stomach once by some woman on tour. She was like, "What were you doing with him?" He gave you the freedom in the studio to do whatever. He wasn't a stickler for your pitch if he thought you really felt it, if you really believed what you were singing because sometimes that could win. And that was great because he and I did a lot of screaming. I mean, he felt like if you really believe the lyrics, it's probably going to work.

ME: She became his girlfriend. Sort of.

JILL JONES: We definitely had a bond and had intimacy, but girlfriend wasn't a word that was gonna cut it. I feel like he thought I would always be around, always be there and always be completely important in his life, and I thought he would be the same for me, but it was complicated. It was very codependent. Every step each of us made to get away from the other led us back together, so it was difficult, but girlfriend and boyfriend, that's tricky. There was one time he said girlfriend, and I remember being in shock and horror that he said it, but his dad told me, "Prince really loves you a lot." It was a weird relationship.

ME: Prince had strange relationships with his bandmates, too.

GAYLE CHAPMAN (Keyboards, Prince's band 1979–1980): He was immature in a lot of respects. He was eighteen, nineteen years old and his dealing with band members—well, he wasn't exactly a band leader when I was there. He was still working on himself when he hired us, which is fine. We were all willing to work with him and let him do what he needed to do. But he was so lousy at dealing with personnel issues. He had the manager take me on a drive around LA to tell me I was fat and needed to lose weight. He took my hand and said, "Look at your nails. Get your nails done." It was clearly Prince talking, but what Prince didn't seem to understand is that fingernails were a big challenge for me. I couldn't grow my fingernails and play the keyboard because if they were too long, every time I pounded on those keys, the nails would break. They would break backwards. One time, when he was not pleased with what I had worn on stage, Prince came to my door. He was really upset with me and he told me that he would fire me if I didn't do something different. I said, "Okay, fine, I'll do something. No big deal. All you got to do is say something." Then he sent his girlfriend Mary down with a paper bag and she reiterated to me that I had to wear this or I was fired. I opened the contents of the bag and it was multicolored metallic underwear and a bra that were clearly the wrong size for me. I put my fist in the cups of the bra and I said, "Mary, this is a C-cup. I can't fit into this. Surely you understand. But I know what he wants. I'll go shopping. Tell him not to worry. I'll get him something that he wants." I have always had a great deal of respect for Prince and I loved my two years with him. I wouldn't trade it for the world. It was tons of fun. But the way he handled certain issues was hard and we're talking about things that, in my opinion, are really simple to talk about. So anyway, I went to a local lingerie shop and told the owner of the shop what I was doing and why I was there and he locked the doors and started racking up a bunch of stuff. I was there for like an hour and a half, drinking wine as I tried on stuff. That night, I didn't reveal what I was wearing until we walked up on stage. The guys hadn't seen it. I had on a robe and when I tossed off the robe, I revealed this new outfit and the band was not paying attention to the audience. They were paying attention to, holy shit, Gayle!

ME: One of his ironclad rules for himself and his bands was that they had to dress like stars no matter when or where they were. Prince cared deeply about how he and the band were seen when they were on stage and off. People who saw Prince in the morning said he had incredible custom-made pajamas that he could've worn on stage.

JEROME BENTON: The look and attitude of cool, we were required to have that at all times. Prince was like, "You've never seen me in blue jeans and you never will!"

MORRIS HAYES: He said, "Rock stars should always look like rock stars. I don't want you guys going out looking like you just got through shoveling the driveway or whatever. We gotta be like superheroes. We gotta make an impression. When people see us, it should be a spectacle, it should be bigger than life." He needed us to echo that ethos because, for him, it was like, this is my crew and this is how we get down. When we go out, we're a team. And I'd be like, "Prince, I don't wanna wear my sparkly red velvet pants down to Walgreens." He'd say, "Morris, we're in show business. We're rock stars. You should always look like a rock star. I'm never turning back into Clark Kent. I'm Superman all the time."[9]

ME: This was harder for some people than others.

GAYLE CHAPMAN: He felt like he had to threaten to fire me to get me to change what I was wearing instead of simply saying, "Can we look at some different clothes for you?" I would've said "Sure! What do you got in mind?" His biggest concern was making sure his band did exactly what he wanted. How we dressed when we were in public was a law—no matter where you were going. If you walk out of your hotel room, you were supposed to be in your rock 'n' roll garb. You never left your room not looking like you were ready for work. Full makeup, hair, spandex. Whatever. When I did that, I got so many stares. They thought I was a hooker.

ME: Ultimately, Gayle's impact on Prince was far greater than his impact on her.

GAYLE CHAPMAN: I told him he was blessed by God. Because he was. But so was I. It wasn't because of anything special in particular. That's what God does in my belief. He blesses everybody.

ME: Prince took it to mean that he alone had a special relationship with God.

DEZ DICKERSON: It didn't help that Gayle was telling him that he was blessed by God with some special dispensation. He ate all that up. It was very convenient information. I think it allowed him to indulge himself in certain ways.

ME: Prince believed he was the Chosen One. One friend told me that once, after a gig, Prince said, "Do you ever think that I was Jesus Christ? 'Cause maybe I just am. Maybe I am the second coming."

DEZ DICKERSON: Prince feels like he has a special talent and God gave it to him. He told me we were sent to help people see. That was a recurring theme in the inner conversation of the band that he initiated. He had this sense that he was enlightened and we as a band were messengers who were there to bring this enlightenment to people who needed it. It was a musical mission. That's why he put the Lord's Prayer in the middle of "Controversy." There's some redemptive purpose in exposing people to the Lord's Prayer in the middle of this other jam because we were the messengers of some higher level of understanding in the guise of punk-funk or whatever the hell we were doing. I think in his mind he was lending voice to the gospel message as he perceived it. In his own way, he's speaking for the messiah. He felt he had a sense of being called, of being a special messenger of some sort.

ERIC LEEDS: Once, we were playing an outdoor concert in Japan and it was threatening to rain. We were all concerned about having to play a gig in the rain and one of the guys on the crew just laughed and said, "Don't worry, it's not gonna rain. Prince will talk to his buddy upstairs and make sure it doesn't rain." There was always this feeling that he had the inside track. That he had like a special line to God. By the way, it drizzled, but not enough to disrupt anything.

ME: Was the guy who said, "Prince will talk to his buddy upstairs," being sarcastic or did he kinda believe that Prince had a special connection? Either way, he and everyone around that guy knew that Prince believed he had a special connection. Maybe that guy was buying into that, maybe he was mocking it, but what really matters is that Prince believed it. When he strapped on his guitar, when he stepped on stage, when he grabbed the mic, he believed that God was with him and he had the power to do anything he could dream. I mean, he was already living out his dreams, so his feelings about God were more of an attempt to understand his life.

SUSAN ROGERS: I think he felt especially blessed. I think he felt especially fortunate and his relationship with God was a really good coping mechanism. I mean, how do you make that journey from being a nobody in a family that's not well-known with no money and no great accomplishment, how do you start from that and leap over everyone you know into a brand-new world of wealth and fame? How does that make sense? What allows you to be so special and not Morris Day, or Jesse Johnson, or Sheila E., or André or any of the many, many other talented people you know? What do you attribute that to? I think in order to remain sane, you have to recognize that there has to be a causal factor outside of you.

ME: Friends said he felt like a vessel through which music poured at a rate beyond his ability to control.

A GIRLFRIEND: He has no control over his life. The music is channeled through him. When the music tells him to play, he does. When the music tells him to sleep, he does. He considers it a blessing and a curse.

ALAN LEEDS: I've always believed that he thinks he has an in with God. I have my own hunch as to where that comes from and that is this: the guy sits there and says, "How in the world did someone like me get the gift I have?" Where does that come from? Because the level of his gift is spooky. I've been around a lot of brilliantly creative people, from Miles to James Brown to D'Angelo, and I've never seen anyone who's a portal for music the way he was in those years. He's trying to sleep because he hasn't slept in two days and he can't because he's gotta write down lyrics and then it's like, "Can you find me a studio? I gotta get this out. Gotta get it out. Get it on tape. Once it's on tape, it's out and then I can sleep." It was crazy. I've never seen anything like it. And you can't say, "Well, Prince there's a studio in the next town and we've got a day off..." "Nah, I gotta get it out." And there's gotta be a time where he sits and says, "What is this about? Where does this come from? Why me?" There's a lot of good guitar players. There's a lot of good singers. There's a lot of great songwriters. He's all of that. For a lot of artists, it's what they do. For him, it's not what he does, it's who he is. You cannot divide Prince from the music. That's why he plays aftershows to the point of exhaustion. Because he has to play. To the point of obsession that's borderline sick. It's like, "Goddamn, don't your fingers get tired? Don't you wanna watch a ballgame?" It's crazy. Maybe he sat there and decided "God anointed me. Because He gave me so many gifts." The gift that allowed him to pick up any instrument and figure it out quickly to the point where he's not really playing the instrument: it's just music coming through him through the instrument; it's just part of that funnel from whatever this source is. You can't separate his work from his spirituality.

ME: For Prince, being spiritual was not in conflict with his sexuality—the two were deeply intertwined.

ALAN LEEDS: The guy had a very provincial, evangelical attitude toward the world. He really believed all the sin is real and God is gonna punish us and blow this world up. He really believes that. But this shit is fun, so I'm gonna roll with it, and I'm gonna make dirty songs along the way.

DEZ DICKERSON: He wanted to be the poster child for hedonism, but he also had this deep-seated sense that spiritual consequences are a real thing. He wrestled with that. But, of course, he was conflicted: he was wrestling with three personas. He had a very calculated marketing mind. That's where the idea of embodying pure sex comes from. He's also dying to be the baddest musician there ever was. And he holds religious considerations close to his heart and ponders spiritual questions sincerely and genuinely. Those three guys have fought inside of him for the microphone over the years.

ME: Prince believed he was chosen, but he wasn't going to let religion get in the way of him becoming a star. He was also a marketer who loved sex and fun and pushing people's buttons. He was also determined to not fail. He had to get people's attention now. He was at a critical crossroads.

BROWNMARK: He was afraid because he was on the last album on the contract. One of the first things he said to me is "Well, if this album doesn't work, I'm done." I said, "You're done? What does that mean?" He said, "They won't renew my contract." He was nervous and he told me that we had to make this album work.

BOBBY Z.: After "I Wanna Be Your Lover" became a hit, he got enough money from the label to put a studio in his house in Minneapolis. He takes his basement and turns it into the most unorthodox recording studio, with cords everywhere and a crappy drum set with cracked cymbals. It was weird counterculture deconstructive stuff. But he was looking at what was going on in London. He was looking at Adam and the Ants and Siouxsie and the Banshees and David Bowie and Freddie Mercury. He would interpret the Second British Invasion and turn it into sly funk. He'd add funk to it. It was his chili sauce, as he'd joke at the time. He could make endless rhythms—he was an incredible beatmaker before the term existed. And he was comfortable. There's a hesitancy in the first two albums that doesn't exist in the third. He knows who he is. You could see the confidence building.

ME: He was thinking about every aspect, like how the songs would sound for the average fan who was driving a car with crappy speakers.

JILL JONES: I always had a really shitty car, so he would always go out to my car and listen to the songs and then go back into the studio. He used to say he always wanted the songs to work for people who had Cracker-Jack speakers because not everybody can afford great speakers. My car was really good to listen to his mixes to see if it was going to fly. He would really pay attention to those kinds of little details.

ME: Of course, he was also thinking through the big details.

DEZ DICKERSON: We were in LA and we were in a break between shows. Prince sat everybody down and said, "Okay, here's what we're going to do. Everybody in this band is going to have a distinct personality and identity. I'm going to portray pure sex." Those were his exact words. "Pure sex" meant taking the piss out of every taboo, and it meant shocking people in every way he could come up with. He was kind of a precocious kid doing things to get a rise out of the adults. So I wasn't surprised when I heard "Sister" for the first time. That was his volley in trying to push that envelope further than it ever had been pushed. In terms of marketing and strategy, he was very calculated, wise beyond his years, and pure genius.

MATT FINK (Keyboards, the Revolution 1978–1990): I thought "Sister" was clever. He knew full well he was creating a controversial song. You're definitely going to jerk some people's chains with that one.

MORRIS DAY: *Dirty Mind* is not R&B;[10] it's rock 'n' roll. If you think of Rolling Stones records like "Miss You," and the rawness of it, I think that was Prince's headspace. He was writing rock 'n' roll music. That's the direction that he was heading in.[11] That's why he wanted so badly to be on the stage with the Rolling Stones, because that's the kind of music he was writing.

DEZ DICKERSON: The *Dirty Mind* record was the energy I wanted to bring to the band. It was the creative collision of where Prince had come from musically and the new wave and punk that I was actively exposing him to, because musically, that's what I was into.

ME: Prince knew he needed some controversy to become a super-star, so, in a time-honored rock 'n' roll strategy, he started flagrantly transgressing social norms. He made "Head" and "Sister," titled his album *Dirty Mind*, and went on stage wearing lingerie, heels, and trench coats, stoking intrigue and revulsion as he evoked subway flashers and perverts and men who were, back then, called "cross-dressers." It was an aggressive sexual aesthetic, a package that could not be ignored.

ALAN LEEDS: It's whatever you have to do to get attention. Distinguish yourself from everybody else. Don't look like Rick James, don't look like Roger Troutman, don't look like Mick Jagger, and whatever you do, don't allow yourself to be typecast in the R&B ghetto. Make sure the audience can't compare you to anybody else.

DEZ DICKERSON: The transition to punk rock/women's underwear/trench coat man was because he just made up his mind, "This is what needs to happen." The label freaked out and tried to get him to take his contract back, but they had an ironclad deal. They couldn't do it.

MATT FINK: I thought the whole *Dirty Mind* album was a big risk to take in the music business. There weren't many things out there that were as controversial as that. It wasn't my record deal I was just there to be a keyboard guy so I never protested, I never said, "Hey, I think this is the wrong direction for you to go." I just thought, *Boy, he's really pushing the envelope.*

BOBBY Z.: They got *Dirty Mind* in London and Paris. He was bigger there than he was in most of America. In America, it was shocking to a lot of people. Either you loved it or you were freaked out by it and didn't know what to think. The label didn't get it because he was challenging the system. He was like, "I'm not gonna be pigeonholed by the evil record company. I'm not gonna be constrained to the Black department." It was an f-you to the R&B department, and they heard it. The R&B department rejected the album in a lot of ways. They were pissed off, but he was determined to cross over.

ME: *Dirty Mind* was controversial, which made him bigger. But if you're controversial, then you're divisive and if you're divisive, that means there are people who are against you. What happens when you run into people who are on the wrong side of the divide? What if those people feel threatened by your transgressions? At a critical moment, Prince came face-to-face with people who were really angry about his transgressions. And those people attacked him physically.

5

Why You Wanna Treat Me So Bad?

The Worst Show Ever (1981–1982)

MATT FINK: Mick Jagger and Keith Richards were enamored with Prince. They felt he was someone who should be introduced to a huge audience, so they requested his presence as a warm-up act. It was after *Dirty Mind* came out. They wanted to give his career a boost and introduce him to mainstream rock 'n' roll fans, people in their circle of fans, and see what would happen. So we were brought on board to do the first two shows at the LA Coliseum. Ninety thousand people, sold out. It would be Prince, then George Thorogood and the Destroyers, then J. Geils Band, and then the Stones in that order. We were also set to play several more shows with them after that in other markets. We were supposed to play big dome stadiums in four other cities.

ME: There was a lot of pressure on Prince and a brand-new member of the band.

MATT FINK: André had left the group and Mark Brown had just come on board. This was Mark's first show with the band. It was pretty heavy for him. We were on the plane going there and me and Bobby Z. spoke to Mark and said, "How does it feel to play in front of ninety thousand people ahead of the Rolling Stones for your first show?" He said, "I don't even know who the Rolling Stones are." "Really? You've never heard of the Rolling Stones?" He goes, "No." I go "Who were you listening to growing up?" He says, "James Brown." And I go, "That shows you right there the disparity between white and Black people in music at that time." Even people like Mark didn't pay attention to the Rolling Stones. He didn't know who they were. Me and Bobby were a bit shocked by that, thinking, *Wow how could you have missed out on that?* I said, "Did you know who the Beatles were?" He goes, "Yeah, I've heard of them." "Did you ever listen to their music?" He goes, "Not really."

ME: That same lack of awareness existed on the other side. For example, Prince was becoming a star among Black music lovers, but most Rolling Stones fans knew nothing about him and they probably knew or cared little about some of his core influences—Rick James, Sly Stone, James Brown, Carlos Santana, George Clinton, Bootsy Collins, the Reverend Al Green, Curtis Mayfield, Joni Mitchell, Nikki Giovanni, and Little Richard. They might have cared a little about Jimi Hendrix because he was marketed as rock 'n' roll, but some them would've hated him, too. Without knowing and respecting any of that background, seeing Prince might have been a little like seeing an alien. Or, worse, seeing someone say, "Your traditional brand of masculinity is over." If you were the sort of person who was deeply invested in a very traditional brand of masculinity, Prince might seem offensive. Anyway, Mark joined the band a very short time before the Rolling Stones shows, and Prince had to get him up to speed quickly. In his first rehearsal with the band, Prince had to engage in some old-school corporal punishment, or as my father used to say, put his foot in that ass. Literally.

BROWNMARK: I come from a bar band and we're programmed to play a certain way. When you play in the bar, you're playing cover tunes all the time.

ME: Prince found Mark when he was playing in a tiny Minneapolis bar band.

BROWNMARK: I knew he was scoping me out, but I didn't know why. He was coming to see my little band all the time. I would see that little afro up in the corner. He'd be hiding out in the corner and peek his head around. He would watch us for a while and then just disappear. We all knew it was him. We'd be like, "Did you see Prince up there in the corner?" "Yeah, I saw him." He was definitely locally famous by then, but I had no idea he was there looking at me and studying me. Next thing I know, I get this phone call from Prince. "Come by and audition." That blew me away! I told the guys in my band and they were like, "Oh, you know what your initiation's going to be. He going to get you!" People were whispering that Prince was gay. I was like, "Man, come on man, shut up. It ain't like that, man." Even still, I'm scared to death because of all the talk. I'm scared like, *This dude's going to hit on me, man.* So I met Bobby Z. and he told me he would drive me to Prince's. We're in the car and Bobby Z.'s talking about, "You sure you want to do this?" I was like, "What do you mean am I sure I want to do this? What kind of question is that? He says, "Man, are you sure you know what you're getting yourself into?" I'm like, *Whoa, what is this dude talking about?* So we drive out to the house and it's dark and way out in the boonies. Prince opens the door and he's dressed like a rock star. Hair done, everything. I was like, *Oh, snap.* We went downstairs and had this ten-minute audition. I'm like, *What kind of audition lasts ten minutes?* But he already knew he wanted to hire me before I even showed up. The audition was just a formality. We jammed on a couple of songs and I guess he was just trying to look at how I played to see if I understood the feeling and the theory behind his music, and if I knew his music. He randomly picked songs from his albums and we'd jam on them for a few seconds and then stop. Then he looked at Bobby and said, "You can leave." I was like, *Oh no, no!* I'm nervous. I was like, *Man, don't make me have to beat you down, dude.* You know? Then Prince disappeared and I'm down there in the studio for at least thirty minutes in silence. I'm like, *I don't even know where I'm at. I can't run. I can't get away. I can't do anything.* All of a sudden, I hear him coming down the steps and I was like, *Oh man, here he comes. I'm going to have* *to bust him up*. He was all dressed up, smelling all good with perfume on, ready to go out. I looked at him and now I was really freaking out. He says, "I'm going to take you home, we can talk on the ride." We get in the car and he's got this bad stereo system, man. I mean it sounded like we was in the club. This dude had every kind of speaker up in his car, subwoofers and everything. This was before car stereo systems were like that. I'm surprised the fenders didn't fall off from the bass rattling so hard. He's playing his new album *Controversy*, which wasn't out yet, and I was like, "Man, this is going to be busting." He's talking to me and he's like, "So, I just want to let you know that if you want the job you have it, but I want you to take the weekend and think about it." I was like, "Ain't nothing to think about, bro, I'll let you know right now, I want the job." He said, "No, no. I want you to think about it because this is a band. I want you to become part of my band. So, I want you to really think about that aspect of it. It ain't a job, it's a band." I was like, "If you want me to take the weekend, I can do that, but I can let you know right now." I said, "I'm in, bro, but I'll let you know Monday."

Me: In his first rehearsal with the Revolution, things got crazy.

BrownMark: We were playing "Head." I had just listened to it and was playing it how it sounded to me, which was a mistake. He turned around, started walking, and did a circle around to the back of me. Then I felt a hard bam, right in the crack of the crack. I thought, *Did he just kick me?*

Me: Prince had kicked him. In his behind. Hard. With a pointed-toe boot.

BrownMark: I kept playing but I'm baffled. Ain't nobody ever kicked me without a fight happening. I was like, *Did he really just kick me?* I wanted to bust him up because now you're messing with my manhood and I'm six feet tall and he's five-foot-two. I was ready to beat him down. But then I thought, *You really wanna throw this away?* Because if I fought him, I'd be right back working at 7-Eleven. I had to really think about it. Do I need to beat him down or do I need to figure out how to deal with this once-in-a-lifetime opportunity?

ME: That is exactly why Prince loved to hire people who were green—if you needed Prince, then you were more likely to go along with whatever. The less experienced you were, and the more you felt you needed him, the more power he had. As the lone gigantic fish in the small pond of Minneapolis music, he could get people to put up with anything.

JILL JONES: He loved people who were new to the game so there was no friction with his vision. A more accomplished musician might come in and be like, "Do we have to keep playing the same riff?" When you're new, you're not as pushy about your credits, or "I came up with this" or whatever. It's less agita. You just do what you're told.

PEPE WILLIE: Prince could call his musicians up at three o'clock in the morning and get 'em over there to work! If that woulda happened in New York, they'd go like, "Muthafuckuh, I'm asleep! I'll see you later!" But because Prince was the talk of the town, Minneapolis totally supported him.

ME: They even accepted him being a little violent.

BROWNMARK: I stepped back and said, "Why would he kick me? What is he doing? What am I doing wrong?" Then he came back around again, but this time he whispered in my ear, "You better play that bass, motherfucker, or I'll find somebody who will." I was so mad. I was just sitting there steaming. I was boiling. So I left. I went home and told my mom.

ME: Mark was just nineteen and still living with his mom, who was his manager.

BROWNMARK: My mother has walked me through a lot of heavy lessons in life and I always listened to her. That day, she explained to me what had really happened. She said, it was kind of like with a prisoner of war. When you get captured, they have to break you for you to be obedient to what it is that they're trying to do. She told me, "He's trying to break you. He's trying to break you from all your old habits and your old patterns. And how he does it is he's taking away your dignity and your pride. He's stripping you down. If you fight him, then you just lost. But if you take what he's trying to do and you run with it, you're gonna learn something." I had to really think about It. *Do I really want to just walk away from this or do I want to explore a little more?* She said, "No matter what goes down, no matter what happens, always look at the prize." I knew he could get me to where I wanted to go. I sat down and I was like, *What is it? What's he trying to teach me? What is it he's trying to say?* Then I started listening to his records again and I started replaying them on my own and that's when it clicked. I was like, *I'm playing the notes but I'm not feeling it.* When I went back to rehearsal the next day we started playing and he came walking around to me and I'm looking at him like don't do it, because I won't deal with it again. I was like, *If he does that to me again, it's gonna be lights out.* But he came up to me and whispered in my ear, "That's what I'm talking about." I was like, *You couldn't have just told me that, bro? You couldn't have just told me you need to play with some feel? You gotta kick a brother and break him down to get him to find that?* He was weird like that, man.

ME: Once again, Prince was having a hard time relating to people in a simple, direct way, because he's hyperfocused on himself and his music and his interpersonal skills are so underdeveloped he can't easily communicate his feelings. Sometimes he was just disrespectful to people.

BROWNMARK: One day in rehearsal, he stops in the middle of a song and he's like, "Hold up, hold up. Everybody has a nickname. We need a name for this brother." He points at me. "What are we going to call him? Wait a minute," he says, "We're going to call him Brown Mark," and he hits the floor laughing. I'm like, "What's so funny?" He's like "That's your new name! We're going to call you Brown Mark because you're brown!" I was darker than everybody else in the group, but I didn't think he was serious. He was laughing at the top of his lungs, one of them gut-wrenching laughs. I was like, "You making fun of me? Of my color? Are you laughing at me?" He was laughing, but he was dead serious. That's how I got the name BrownMark. It grew on me.

ME: As they prepared for the Rolling Stones shows, Prince knew these dates were critical to him gaining visibility, winning new fans, and moving up to the next level.

BROWNMARK: He laid out this plan for how we were going to open for the Stones, go on tour with them and get this new audience. He said, "This could be really big." He always wanted to cross over and if one hundred thousand people see you every night on tour with the Rolling Stones, you can only imagine what it would have done for his career. Even though it was a Stones crowd, if you got 10 percent of them in each city, you're building your base.

MATT FINK: We went on when the sun was still up. We hit the stage around six or seven. We were supposed to do a half-hour or forty-minute set, tops.

BROWNMARK: We walked out there and you could hear the crowd roaring, man. It was nothing like I ever heard before.

MATT FINK: It was a Rolling Stones crowd, which, at that time, had a hardcore Hell's Angels-ish biker-crowd mentality. We get on stage and here's Prince in high heels, bikini briefs, thigh-high stockings, no shirt, and a trench coat—singing in a falsetto. He was just something that they didn't understand and he frightened them. Within two minutes, they were enraged. They're like, "What the fuck?"

MORRIS DAY: I was out at the sound board. I got the camera set up and aimed at the stage and you could kinda just feel the climate because you look out in the audience and everybody's there to see the Rolling Stones. You got bikers, you got some rough-looking cats out there in leather jackets and beards and long hair, and they're drinking beer and shit, and here comes Prince doing his *Dirty Mind* thing with a trench coat and some hot pants and leg warmers on.

BOBBY Z.: He loved wearing leg warmers with shorts. It was odd. And he had these gold and silver boots from Fred Segal.

MORRIS DAY: They're just like, "What the hell is this?" I'm thinking, *I don't know how this is going to go over right now.* So, he comes out on stage and does his thing. He whips the trench coat back behind him and his legs are showing with the leg warmers and all that and the next thing I know, I heard boos, a ton of boos, and then I started seeing beer bottles and shit getting tossed up on the stage. I said, "This can't be good."

ME: Two minutes into his set, Prince went into "Jack U Off."

BROWNMARK: When we went into that song Prince said, "Guys, this is what you do with your girl." I remember cringing when he said it. I was like, "No, that's not what you do with your girl, that's what your girl does to you." I was like, "No, no, don't say that!" Man, I never seen so many middle fingers.

MATT FINK: I'd say out of the first sixty rows of people, 80 percent of them were flipping us the bird and throwing whatever they could get their hands on. So, here we are being pummeled with food. I got hit on the side of my head with a crumpled-up Coca-Cola can. I saw a fifth of Jack Daniels whizz by Prince's face, must've missed him by less than a quarter of an inch. That scared the bejeezus out of him.

BROWNMARK: They went into a frenzy. Food was coming from everywhere, man. It looked like clouds. And people was booing. It was bad. Then more stuff started coming. I was like, "Wait a minute, was that a bottle?" Then it started coming faster and faster and faster. A big old grapefruit got lodged into the strings and threw the whole bass out of tune, so I'm up there playing out of tune, but you don't hear nothing because it's just chaos, total chaos. I'm there trying to play the song and tune the bass as I'm playing, trying to get back on track while I'm dodging flying chicken parts. I got hit with a bag of Kentucky Fried Chicken. I'm not sure it was Kentucky Fried but it was a big old plastic bag of chicken. Then Jack Daniels bottles are flying up on stage and people were throwing quarters, everything. And then Prince got hit upside the head with a quarter or something.

LeRoy Bennett: Watching it go down was just crazy. They were throwing shoes, sneakers, chicken, everything. It's heartbreaking to see him getting hit. And you could just see it was freaking him out. It was a pretty devastating thing to see.

Matt Fink: Three songs into his set, Prince walked off stage in a bit of a panic. He did not signal us to stop playing, he just stormed off and left us, so Dez had to signal the band and get us to leave the stage.

BrownMark: I'm looking behind me and everybody is running off the stage. I started running with my bass. I just started booking. It was still coming from everywhere and I looked like I was creating some more choreography the way I was jumping and dodging everything. I was the last one out.

Morris Day: I said, "I better hightail it to the backstage area." Prince is standing on the side, humiliated. Didn't really have anything to say. He's like, "I don't want to talk. Let's just get the hell outta here." So we jumped in the limo. Next thing I know, we're on a plane back to Minneapolis. This was the first and the last time I've ever seen this dude so humiliated. I mean he was super humiliated. It was tough to see.

Matt Fink: After we got off the stage there was some confusion. We said, "Where did Prince" go?" They said, "He took off." He got in the car and he left. He flew back to Minneapolis and said not to continue on with any more shows with the Rolling Stones.

Alan Leeds: It was as brutal a rejection as an audience can give an artist. After that first show, he was so freaked out he just got on a plane and went home. They were supposed to do two nights.

Matt Fink: Mick Jagger was disappointed by all this and called Dez at the hotel and asked him to call Prince to convince him to come back and do the next show, which would have been that Sunday.

Dez Dickerson: I told Prince I'd played in racist biker bars and had been attacked even worse. I said, "You can't let them run you out of town." He didn't care.

Matt Fink: Prince wouldn't listen to Dez. He said "Absolutely not. I'm not going to put us in harm's way. That was dangerous." So, Mick called Prince and talked to him

Me: Jagger told a reporter, "I talked to Prince on the phone after he got cans thrown at him in LA He said he didn't want to do any more shows. God, I got thousands of bottles and cans thrown at me. Every kind of debris. I told him, if you get to be a really big headliner, you have to be prepared for people to throw bottles at you in the night. Prepared to die!" Prince flew back to LA for the Sunday-night show.

Matt Fink: He came back and we tried it again.

BrownMark: The second show in my memory was worse than the first one. It was hot. I remember they had a water hose, just spraying people like cattle. All I saw was pink and red bodies, because nobody had a shirt on, and they was just spraying them down with water hoses. It was the weirdest thing I ever seen.

LeRoy Bennett: Before the band went, out Bill Graham [a legendary concert promoter] basically yelled at the audience and told them that they were idiots and they'd be paying a lot of money to see Prince in the upcoming years.

BrownMark: Then Mick Jagger came out because he was mad at the audience. He went off. He was kind of yelling at them like, "That wasn't nice. These are my friends," and blah, blah, blah. And they were like boo and started throwing stuff at Mick Jagger!

Me: Prince and the band went on and bottles and food came flying at them, but this time, it seemed like the crowd had been lying in wait for them. It wasn't spontaneous, they were prepared.

Matt Fink: This time, in spite of all the stuff getting thrown and the contempt of the audience, Prince stuck it out. I think we managed to get through four songs and then we left the stage but we walked off together with Prince. He was like "That's it guys, we are out of here and we're never coming back. We're done. I'm not going to do this at the other venues. This is too crazy. It's dangerous and I don't want anybody to get hurt. Why should we put up with that? Those are not our fans."

ME: Prince told a reporter, "I'm sure wearing underwear and a trench coat didn't help matters, but if you throw trash at anybody, it's because you weren't trained right at home." He said, "There was this one dude right in front and you could see the hatred all over his face. I left because I didn't want to play anymore. I just wanted to fight. I was really angry."

BROWNMARK: I think I was more confused than anything, like, *Is this what we're doing? Is this what I got myself into? I hope that ain't normal, because that was a disaster.* When I spoke to Prince, he was embarrassed and he asked me, "How are you feeling?" I think he was really concerned. I was like, "This ain't for me, bro." He said, "This isn't our crowd. You're going to see our crowd when we get to Pittsburgh."

ME: The horrific Rolling Stones shows were not merely a bad bump in the road; they were a transformative moment.

MORRIS DAY: The whole Rolling Stones situation was a growing process for him. I feel like if he wasn't determined, that could've discouraged him permanently, but I think he came away from it with a stronger determination to make it. He said, "I'm going to force feed what I'm doing on the world. They're going to love what I do." I think he had that type of determination coming away from that. That Rolling Stones thing was the end of the whole *Dirty Mind* situation. He came away from that like, "Okay, I'm going to switch gears a little bit and try this shit again."

LEROY BENNETT: That was when he started to change the way he dressed. That was kind of the end of the bikini briefs and the leg warmers. After that, he wore more clothes. He wore his very stylized pants with the buttons down the sides and things like that.

ME: But there was a much deeper impact on him, too.

LeRoy Bennett: It definitely had its toll on him as far as how open he was. I think he started to isolate himself more to where he was around just his immediate people, his family, his band members, and anybody that worked directly with him. He kind of isolated himself so that really it was more about his team and not really exposing himself much anymore.

ME: Once again, Prince responded to the pain of rejection by closing his world—just like after his parents rejected him and he pushed people away and obsessed over music. Now, after being cruelly dissed and humiliated by an audience he craved, he again shut down and consumed himself with work. This was the central emotional pattern of Prince's life—he struggles with how to deal with people, they hurt him, he isolates himself from the world and goes deeper into his music and becomes even less able to deal with people. He was able to use music as a refuge to protect himself, but could it save him forever? Wouldn't there be some time when he would need to connect with people, share feelings, and communicate? Up to this point in his life, everyone around him says his feelings only came out through music. Of course the trauma of being violently rejected by Stones fans was reflected in his music.

Bobby Z.: He went home from the Coliseum and started recording ferociously. He said, "If I want to achieve the stardom I want, I have to win over those people who booed me off the stage." *1999* is definitely a response to that terrible show. He went back to his home studio to record that. Before that, with *Controversy*, he was in Sunset Sound in LA. Back at home, he had more freedom, but it's a dark sound. He was always trying to fix something in that studio. He recorded a ton and he probably would've done five albums if he didn't have to stop. By then, you could see he was done screwing around. He stopped wearing used clothing, the old trench coat, the modified alternative clothes, and he got the custom shiny purple trench. As soon as I saw that I said, "Now we're really going for it. Now we're showbiz." Purple because of

"Purple Haze" and royalty and that's like the color of Minnesota: the Vikings are purple. So he divides and conquers, making "Little Red Corvette" for pop radio and "D.M.S.R." for the clubs and "1999" for his funk audience. The way *1999* came about is kinda crazy. We're on tour somewhere in the south and we pull into a motel where there's free HBO. That was a big thing back then. Everyone goes in their room and watches HBO. They show *The Man Who Saw Tomorrow*, a documentary about Nostradamus and how he predicted Hitler and JFK, and he says the end of the world is coming. Crazy. The next day, we get on the van and Prince is already at the venue and the song is done. That's how fast he could take stuff in and spit it back out. He watched the doc in the evening and the next morning, he's got this song that's cool as hell. It's the end of the world. It's Nostradamus without saying it, with a funky edge.

ME: Prince wanted desperately to cross over because he wanted to be a megastar and he knew he had to change to appeal to the maximum possible audience. He also knew that he had only failed to expand—he still had a base that loved him madly. When he was opening for the Rolling Stones, wearing women's clothes elicited laughs and scorn, but when he was headlining in Pittsburgh, he caused pandemonium.

BROWNMARK: We went to that show in Pittsburgh and that curtain opened up and the sound was piercing my ears. I was like, *Woah, I never heard anything like this*. Lighters lit, people screaming, floor stomping like thunder. We walked out and I took my position on stage and Bobby starts kicking the kick drum, steady beat, and Prince starts talking on the mic and I remember just looking over at him and being like, *Look at this dude*. I'm standing behind him, everyone was screaming and hollering, and Prince's little foot was tapping. He had this funky little rhythm and he was just cool. I ain't never seen nobody that cool. I was like, *This dude is in full control. This dude is just bad.* He's got that pimp walk going as he's walking back and forth on the stage and then he goes up to the mic and says, "Pittsburgh," and the whole audience went into a frenzy. They went nuts, and this dude just handled it. He controlled it, all them people, he controlled everything. When I saw that I was like, *I'm dealing with a musical genius*. I mean this dude was from outer space. He wasn't from here, I'm telling you. I always called him the Mozart of our time. Actually, when *Amadeus* the movie, came out, he blocked out a whole theatre and the whole band went to see it. I remember saying, "Yep, he's a Mozart." The way his mind worked in music, the things he would come up with, and the way he understood how to control people with his music, he knew exactly what to do to get them where he needed them to go.

ME: The Lonely Guy was a musical genius who was lost off stage. As so many people have said, he didn't even know who to be off stage. And he longed to have a family—he wanted connection and camaraderie and communion—but he was on a virtual island. Then his father came back into his life.

6

Papa

Dad Returns as a New Best Friend
(1982–1983)

ALAN LEEDS (Right fielder): It was the first warm spring day of the season and we were rehearsing for some tour in a warehouse. This was before Paisley Park was built. In Minnesota, the first warm day is like currency. You can trade it for anything on the planet because the winters are long and fierce and frustrating, and as soon as it warms up, everybody kind of goes berserk. On this day, when everybody showed up at the warehouse, Prince said, "Let's play softball!" Everybody kind of looked at each other like, "Huh? What? Softball?" Prince had already gotten one of his guys to buy a ton of bats and balls and gloves, and so we went into an empty lot and played softball for a couple hours. It was a great morale booster and a nice break for the musicians. It was a huge release, a release from the long winter, but also a release from rehearsing over and over, day after day after day. Meanwhile, with Prince, everything's still about music. He'd get to first base, having just hit a single, and he's talking to the first baseman about an arrangement for a song. Then, he gets to second base, and he's talking about the wardrobe for the band on the next tour. Then he's yelling at me, "Hey, Alan, make sure so-and-so is booked for the next rehearsal!" Or it's, "Hey, Bobby, did you fix that drum machine? That noise that was in there last night?" And he's just as competitive as everywhere else. Of course, he insisted on being the pitcher and being the umpire, too, and, of course, he insisted on winning. He had to be the star of the show. He was going to be A-Rod and yeah, he was pretty good, but he made sure you noticed. Then he'd yell at the crew. "Is the video camera working? Are you taping the ballgame? You're supposed to tape everything we do! Then he gets to home plate and looks at me and says, "See, you should have told them to tape the ball-game. This is great B-roll footage! You never know when it could come in handy!" You're just like, "Dude, do you ever stop? Can you ever take a break?" But he lives and breathes music. He doesn't have normal relationships. He doesn't have guys he hangs out with on Friday night. He's not one for small talk or casual conversation. There's no small talk. Never. No social niceties, he gets right to the point of whatever it is he wants done and if you're not part of that equation, he doesn't see you. There's no room for people just because they're friends or have memories or they're cool people. There's only room for the people that are serving his vision. He's a very distant personality. He isn't close to anybody. He's a very emotionally aloof person. I don't know anybody who's ever gotten past that wall. He can be demonstrative but it's all superficial. In the years I was with him, almost everything was somehow about the music or the show. He's so strictly defined by his career that there really hasn't been a normal life away from that.

BROWNMARK: Connecting with him one-on-one was very difficult because he would just not let you in. That wasn't his MO. He wasn't going to do that. You want to connect with Prince, you got to connect with him musically.

ME: There was no significant relationship in his life that was more broken than the one he had with his mother. After their rupture in his childhood, they never reconciled and he clearly stayed angry with her throughout his life. Most people who knew him said he rarely dis-cussed her and the times he did, the pain she evoked was clear.

ERIC LEEDS: His mother was a subject that you never wanted to bring up to Prince. It was a sore spot with him. You knew not to bring it up.

DEZ DICKERSON: He didn't talk about his mom much, and when he did it was a short conversation. There were issues between him and his mom. He didn't talk about them a lot. In the five years I was in the band, he brought the topic of his mom up four or five times. I got the sense that part of why he was so focused on his career was because he put that stuff in the rearview mirror a long time ago.

JILL JONES: He would do impersonations of her, and everybody who's gone out with him knows the one where he did her drinking and holding a cigarette. For him, it was just the worst thing ever, like she was cheap.

ANNA FANTASTIC: He hated alcohol because he said that's the image he has of his mom. She would hold a drink and a cigarette in the same hand, and he was grossed out by that. He hated drinking because his mom was quite a drinker and he even did an impression of her holding a drink and a cigarette in the same hand and taking a puff and then taking a sip. It was kind of putting his mom down. It was kind of degrading her a bit. It was obviously a bad childhood memory for him.

SUSANNAH MELVOIN: If he saw you with a glass of white wine in your hand, he said it to me one time, he was like, "Don't. That was my mom. Just don't do it."

ME: A few people in Prince's world met Mattie Baker, as she was named after her second marriage. She came around a few times.

BOBBY Z.: She would come by and watch our shows. She was kinda powerful in her way, but reserved. Definitely quiet but pretty blown away that her kid had pulled this off. She was like "Wow, he's got a record deal."

JILL JONES: His mom was very remote and distant.

A FRIEND: When I met her, you could tell right away that she was adoring him for who he became. You just know when it's not the real deal. She was kinda like, "I'm here only because you managed to squeeze out of the life you had and you've become something, and hey can you now get me out of the hell that I'm in? Like, come and rescue me now. Although I treated you like shit." That's like Abuse 101 with parents whose kids make it, you know? It's like, "I know I was terrible to you, but can you buy me a whatever?" He bought her a house, but it took years for him to make that decision. Years. He didn't want to give her anything. Nothing. But he did. And then he was like, here's your house. Stay away from me. I never want to hear from you again. But then he invited her to the premiere of *Purple Rain* and his first wedding. That would have been his way of saying, you know, "See, Mom, see, Mom? You know, you can't have a relationship with me but you can see what I've done." That's kind of how it was. And I never respected it from her, on his behalf.

ANNA FANTASTIC: Once, maybe twice, she came to the studio. I seen his dad loads of times. His dad was always around at that time but with his mom, it seemed like a very cold relationship, like fake-ish, but he wanted to show her how successful he was. That's how it felt. Like, look-at-me-now kind of thing. Prince said that she always asked for money. That was another thing. He told me a story about when he went and had dinner with Michael Jackson. He said the first thing Michael said when Prince walked in was, "Do your parents ask for money?" And Prince was like, "Yes!"

ME: The few people who could glean a little insight into his pain around his mom said that her marriage to Hayward Baker loomed large.

JILL JONES: Prince made it seem like she shouldn't have been with Mr. Baker. He made it seem like she had a choice to stay in this relationship with his dad, but how could she? That relationship clearly didn't work. It always seemed like he never got over his mom and dad's divorce. That's what was really clear to me. I used to say to him, "Everybody's parents' divorce." Like, who hasn't gone through it? It really seemed to affect him.

ME: It seems telling that in some ways, Prince tried to almost erase his mother from his life story. He told a few early interviewers that his mother was Italian. Then, in *Purple Rain*, he cast a white woman, Olga Karlatos, to play her. Yes, this was a clever marketing move—in the '80s, being biracial came across as edgy and interesting—but it also represents a sort of erasure of his real mother. Where the character of Prince's father in *Purple Rain* is said to be fairly accurate, the character of Prince's mother is quite distant from the real Mattie. Contrary to rumors set in motion by Prince, she was not white.

ALAN LEEDS: That was the biggest distinction from real life in the movie. She was quite yellow, light skinned, but absolutely Black. Both of his parents were Black. No question. I suspect it was just part of his whole gambit towards crossover and trying not to be pigeonholed by an industry that loves to pigeonhole you. It served a purpose. It was all part of his vision. Everything had a reason.

ME: The pain Prince felt and the void he experienced from not having her in his life was a core part of him.

SUSAN ROGERS: When I was a kid, my mother died after a long battle with cancer and I think one of the reasons that he and I were bonded and sympathetic toward one another was that we recognized something in each other. We related to each other as young people in search of healing, in search of something that would make us right, something that would give us what we didn't have. We knew that about each other and it kept us together for a long time. I know that losing his mother was tough for him.

ME: Although Prince clung to his anger toward his mom, when he reached stardom, he built a new relationship with his Dad.

SUSANNAH MELVOIN: He never spoke with his father at all until, out of the blue, it was all about John.

ME: They acted more like brothers than father and son and they made music together—John L. Nelson is credited as a songwriter on *Purple Rain*, *Around the World In A Day*, and *Parade*.

ALAN LEEDS: It was a relationship that hadn't been there when Prince was a kid. It was probably John's happiest years because, for the first time in his life, he wasn't stressed over money and he was excited at the people he was able to meet through his son's celebrity. When Miles Davis came to Minneapolis, he had dinner at Prince's house, and Prince made sure his dad was there. The idea that his dad could go to his son's house and have dinner sitting across the table from Miles Davis, who's mad at that? Prince loved including his dad in all kinds of glamorous situations, taking him to premieres, fancy restaurants, clubs, all of it. He introduced him to hot girls, got his wardrobe department at Paisley to make him clothes, gave him a purple BMW to drive around, and moved him into the purple house when Prince moved out and into a larger home. All of this was perhaps trying to give him what his dad's career failed to provide, but also perhaps trying to give Prince the father he wanted to have. So, you ask yourself, how much of this was for John and how much was for Prince?

JILL JONES: Prince loved having that relationship with his Dad. I don't know who was whose wingman at some points. It was funny because I once ran into Prince at a club in LA and he was with Devin DeVasquez, the Playboy Playmate. I said, "So, who is that?" He's like, "Oh, this is Devin. My dad's going out with her." I was like, "Your dad? Does she know she's dating John L. instead of you?" It turned out that she wasn't with John L, but they did that kind of stuff together. John L would keep Prince-like hours. They played pool and would do music together. He doted on his father. Prince would play his music for him and he got inspired by him. He would imitate his dad playing the piano, which was amazing. He adored his dad. Prince was a lot more humble around his father and there was this bit of wonderment when he looked at him. He really enjoyed his time with his father. John L. was a lovely character. I loved him so much, but he was a bit set in his ways, and his ways were very eccentric. He was a genius, so he was operating on a different wave and in a different environment. He really embraced his hermit qualities. He could be a complete recluse and sometimes he was very hard on Prince. They would go through periods of time of not speaking.

WENDY MELVOIN: John Nelson was cold. He seemed detached. Didn't talk much. You could tell Prince was intimidated by him.

JEROME BENTON: I was able to sit back and watch Prince just enjoy his dad. Mr. Nelson even dressed like Prince. Prince had made him some suits and he's walking around with his little purple flute. He even has some of the same poses and stuff. I saw this man, knowing that their relationship hadn't been the most soundest, enjoying his son. And the pride he had in his son, man, what an amazing thing to see. We'd be in Brazil, in Rio de Janeiro, just standing on the balcony looking out. And Mr. Nelson's like "Look at all that. You know how lucky you are?" "Yes, Mr. Nelson. And do you know how lucky you are?" He would just laugh.

MORRIS HAYES: One time, I had a rough day with Prince, like he was real hard on me and John L. came through and saw me down. He was like, "You alright, son?" I said, "Yeah, Prince just goin' in on me today." He said, "Well, let me know if he gets out of line. I'll get him back in check." I said, "Yes, please." Like yes, could you beat his ass please? It was cool that he said that.

ALAN LEEDS: In my experience, John was a sweet guy. Now, I've heard other things, that he was difficult, he was moody, but by the time I knew him, his son was a rich celebrity and he was enjoying some of the spoils of that. He and Prince had patched things up and were spending more time together, even working on some musical projects together. I had the opportunity to hear John play on countless occasions, either at his house, or at Prince's house, or horsing around in the studio. He had a very eclectic style. If you were jazz savvy, it put you in mind of Thelonious Monk, but perhaps without the pretty melodies that Monk would counter his weirdness with. I got the impression that when John was younger, he probably wasn't taken too seriously in the local scene. He was a good musician, but when it came to his own material, he was out there. He was a little odd, but it didn't sound that ridiculous. I think some of the people in Prince's band heard his stuff and were just like, "Holy moly, this is really, really out to lunch," but everything is relative. It depends on the context. People said some of Prince's music was crazy and then he got paid and all of a sudden it wasn't crazy. Maybe if John been successful, if he had had a couple albums on Blue Note, it would not have been so crazy.

SUSANNAH MELVOIN: John was really talented, but a really strange guy. I do believe that John had like, psychological, personality disorder stuff. I can't diagnose this man but he was not a well guy. He didn't know how to have a conversation. He was uncomfortable in his own space. At the time I met him, he was much older and Prince had just wanted to reconcile with his dad because he kind of felt sorry for him. His dad was a bizarre cat. He would sit down at the piano, and he'd play, and you'd think he was crazy. He'd be making a mess of the keyboard, just a total mess of it, like, just pounding on it and running his fingers up and down the keys. None of it made any sense. It was so avant garde, weirdly atonal and strange. Then he'd have some sort of melodic run with his right hand and then he'd play another chord and then it would go into sort of this nonsensical, crazy, weird part. You'd think to yourself, *Has he gone mad? What the fuck is he playing?* Then he'd get up, get some water, sit down and do it again. He'd get back on and play exactly the same thing. You were like, *He purposely wants to play like that? He can repeat it? How do you do that? Is that a savant thing?* It was both odd and really special. I was never a fan of the music. I thought it was pond water, but Prince dug it. He thought it was cool and weird. He emulated his dad. Prince would listen to him and he would howl with laughter and he would say, "I told you, I told you! It's crazy, right?" I think because of John, mistakes were really cool to Prince. Because who would ever do a mistake and then actually get out there and do it again? Who would ever do that? A big rock star would. You'd think he was an even bigger rock star for it. He would even say, "If you make a mistake, make that mistake huge. Make it big. Do it again." I'd be like, *Yeah, I get where that comes from.*

ME: Prince's music was deeply influenced by John's.

SUSANNAH MELVOIN: He looked up to his dad musically, big time. Prince loved that experimental side of his father, the atonal qualities of his music and the sort of experimental jazz nature of it. Prince loved the unpredictability of John's music. He loved his father for that, and he took that into his own music. He loved that his father was unpredictable and odd and committed, totally committed. That was definitely something Prince took. He learned that you have to commit to whatever it is you're doing, just make a big, hard commitment. Don't back out of it, even the mistake. Make the mistake. There's beauty in the mistake. I think you can hear that in plenty of things he's done. Sometimes, Prince would come up with something, he'd write something, and then he'd play it in the car, and you'd be like, "Wow, you got a lot of your dad in that." But inevitably, it would make a lot more sense musically than John's music.

JILL JONES: They figured out a way to work together, transferring tapes back and forth. Prince tried to incorporate bits of John's music into his own and while John's music was very abstract, Prince knew what pieces to extract and what to evolve and how to handle all of that in a way that wasn't offensive to his dad's ego.

ALAN LEEDS: You hear his father in him. His approach to playing the piano is reminiscent of how his dad played. If you listen to recordings of his dad's music, it's not that they sound like Prince music, but that there's a father-son thing there. I think deep down, Prince idolized his dad.

ME: But while John's jazz is embedded in Prince's DNA, the massive success of a rock record like "Little Red Corvette" made him think more and more about rock 'n' roll as the vehicle to mainstream success.

DEZ DICKERSON: There was no doubt that he had a strong desire to have a high level of pop success and, obviously, you weren't going to have that kind of success with "Head" or "Sister." I wanted us to be a rock band flat out. I'd been pushing for that. That's all I wanted. I was like, "You've got to check this out. You've got to listen to Generation X. You've got to listen to The Clash." And he got into those things enthusiastically. He knew that they didn't sign him to be a rock star, they signed him because they thought he was the new Stevie Wonder, but it was the punk rock thing [on *Dirty Mind*] that really broke it for him. The danger of that spoke to people. After that, Prince saw the opportunity to mix his over-the-top sexual thing with the danger of the British punk rock explosion.

ME: As they toured the country playing *1999*, they could see the audiences growing whiter.

DEZ DICKERSON: At the point where "Little Red Corvette" hit on MTV, there was a radical shift. You could see it changing really fast. From night to night on the road, you could see changes in the audience's demographic. It went from an arena being full of Black folks to being one-quarter white, then one-third, then one-half. This happened over a period of weeks. The thing that was interesting is it was happening in the deep south. The barriers first started to fall there. When you see it in Shreveport, Atlanta, and Dallas you're like, "Yeah, it's different now." Dallas was very divided when we first got out there. At first it was, man, I would really like to go but that's kind of outside the envelope. Then we saw folks get it in their heads that, it's okay for me to go to that show now. That changed. Really fast. I think that it was just time. I think there was a generational transition happening in that there was the trailing edge of the Baby Boomers, the youngest Boomers, who were looking at the world through a different window and were ready to start letting the genre barriers fall. It's almost like they needed permission, but once there was some sort of tacit approval for what we were doing, they came in droves. I remember doing a show in Jackson, Mississippi, and it was like, *Holy crap, there's a lot of white people in the audience.* And they're like hanging out in the tunnel behind the arena after the show. It was happening in some of the larger cities, too. When we first started doing Atlanta, there was a smattering, a splash of multiethnicities, but then it shifted, pretty radically, to being just a rock 'n' roll show. The real litmus test was our own hometown. We had this cult following there. We could first draw maybe twelve hundred folks, then fifteen hundred, then twenty-five hundred, but there was no radio airplay in our own hometown other than a very low-wattage R&B station, so we weren't on the radio in the place where we lived, but with the 1999 Tour, the show was moved from this twenty-five-hundred-seat theater to the arena. Then a second show was added. That was the moment we were saying, "Oh, oh. This has definitely changed." It was almost like when the Berlin Wall came down. It came down really fast.

ME: Success made Prince's confidence swell.

DEZ DICKERSON: To me, he was like an NFL quarterback in his third season. The game starts to slow down and you're seeing how all the pieces fit together a bit more and your game changes. I think that's just what happened. His game just changed. He was older and wiser and there were some very real ways that he was settling in. He was starting to master the process. I think he understood how the pieces fit together. He understood that he didn't have to prove that he could be more dangerous or more risqué than anybody else. He didn't have to prove that he could take musical chances that nobody else would take. He was able to sublimate those urges and work toward a higher and more central objective. He understood at that point what it was going to take. It's one thing to prove a point by going around stage in bikini underwear and leg warmers, it's quite another thing to prove a point by selling more records and having more hit singles and beginning to fill up stadiums as opposed to theaters. There was definitely a maturity aspect to it. Before that, he was trying to prove that "I'm the most daring artist ever. I can get away with saying things that other people won't say. I'm going to make the records that talk about having a dirty mind." It's almost that kind of Dennis the Menace thing, he was kind of being a menace for the sake of being a menace. As opposed to saying, "You know what? I don't have to prove that now. I just want to get on about the business of being big."

ME: Also: the crew around him was changing.

JILL JONES: During the *1999* album, so much changed for him. A lot of his friends that he'd grown up with had left. André had left, he didn't have Owen Husney, and he'd broken up with Susan Moonsie, one of his first girlfriends.

ME: He had also recently broken off a long, torrid affair with Vanity.

ALAN LEEDS: By the time I joined the 1999 Tour, Prince and Vanity had pretty much broken up. She still spent occasional time with him off stage, in his hotel room or on his tour bus, but he was spending more time with Jill Jones. He and Susan Moonsie[12] still had a deep friendship. There was nothing to make me think any one of those relationships were exclusive. On the other hand, the player in Prince made it clear that none of the harem were to appear friendly with anyone else. They were all expected to remain very low-key, and in their hotel rooms, unless they were with him. Once, when we had an off day in Denver, Denise [Vanity's given name; Prince gave her the name Vanity as a reference to her being the female extension of him] was sitting in a hotel room stir crazy. We somehow decided to go to a movie. Knowing that to be discovered by him would make her life miserable and me unemployed, we left the hotel by separate exits and met a block away. Nothing amiss was on the menu, just an urge to get away from it all for a few hours and breathe some normal air. She wasn't part of the Minneapolis mob that pledged obedience to Prince's personae. She was more experienced and more worldly than most of the youngsters on that tour. She also had a rebelliousness, a spirit for adventure, and a love of a good party that the others lacked or at least held in check. It didn't take long to discover that she was not shy about indulging at a party as opposed to the clean living that characterized most of the purple gang. She was very ambitious and quietly had her own advisors outside the Prince camp. Funniest thing was, at one point after I'd been in Minneapolis for a few weeks, Prince pulled me aside and said he was concerned about what he was hearing about Vanity and the people she was hanging out with. He asked if I would swing by her building some nights just to clock her comings and goings and see if I recognized any familiar cars parked nearby. I thought he may have suspected that Morris Day was hanging with her. Now, I would never agree to "spy" on someone, but the joke was that the people most often hanging out with her were Morris and me! Totally as friends, just casual, smoke a joint, watch a movie, laugh a lot type of stuff while we both missed people who were elsewhere. I'm sure she did have an effect on him and he did care for her as much as he was able to care for anyone, but he insisted on a quiet little woman. No matter how hard he tried, he couldn't break her. She probably scared the shit out of him.

ME: Friends say he dumped Vanity because she liked to get high. But he was then moving a lot of people out and resetting his life.

JILL JONES: When he was hiring people then, his thinking was more in the mindset of, "I'm a business and I'm going to expand." He started to take himself more seriously as an artist. His vision solidified during that time. I think he became even more visionary and was exploring new things and new thinking. I think he was exploring how to become an even bigger fish in the pond.

ME: The two most important hires of his life were just in front of him: two women who would help him find a sense of family and change his sound, ushering in the most successful era of his career.

7

Baby I'm A Star

Wendy Enters and *Purple Rain* Explodes (1983–1984)

WENDY MELVOIN: I was practicing guitar in Lisa's hotel room and Prince was walking the halls, going back to his room when he heard guitar coming from her room. He knocked on the door. He already knew me, but I'd never told him I played. He sat down on the bed and said, "Could you play me something?" I was so nervous. I was beside myself with the idea of having to play him something. I had this whole internal dialogue with myself that's sort of like talking yourself into diving into an ice-cold pool, right? It's like, *Just do it. Just dive. Just get in, get in, get in.* And I decided, *You know what? I'm not going to start soloing. I'm not going to do it.* I'm not going to be that guitar player because I never was. I just played him some big, fat, beautiful chord progressions that were gorgeous, and his eyes got big like saucers. He got that real wild look in his eyes that he gets where he doesn't say anything. His eyes were wide and they start darting. He left the room and about a week later, I was with Lisa in North Carolina and by that time, I guess Dez was not getting along too well with the rest of the band. He was telling Prince that he really wanted to go do his own solo career, and then he didn't show up to sound check in Greensboro.

BOBBY Z.: Dez couldn't take the sound checks anymore. They were brutal.

ALAN LEEDS: When I came aboard in the middle of the 1999 Tour, Dez had already somewhat segregated himself from Prince and the band off stage. His wife was on the road much of the time and Dez insisted on his own dressing room apart from the rest of the band. He seldom attended sound checks. I think he just felt out of place. He was a hard-core rocker, not a funk fan, and didn't really fit in. He used to bitch about Mark blasting George Clinton on the bus.

ME: Dez had always said he would not be in the band for long. And Wendy was hanging around a lot.

WENDY MELVOIN: I was standing next to Lisa and Prince came up to me and said, "Do you know how to play 'Controversy?'" I said, "Uh-huh." I didn't. I'd never played it before, but I knew what the fingerings were for that particular funk chord that's been used in many Prince songs. I knew that progression. So I started playing and Bobby looked over at Lisa and he said, "We have a new member." I flew home not hearing anything, but Prince went to Lisa and said, "How would you feel if I had your girlfriend in the band?" Lisa said it would be a dream come true. I always thought that that was really kind and generous of spirit for him to actually check in with her to make sure it was okay. She loved it, so Prince called me in the middle of the night and said, "How do you feel about joining my band?" I'm like, "Yeah, of course, I'm ready. Yes, yes!" He said, "Well, I've only got $300 a week, but you'll have a plane ticket in the morning. I need you to come out to Minneapolis now." Lisa called me an hour later and said, "Did Prince call you?" I said, "Yeah." I knew he was going to be massive. I knew it from day one. This was before *Purple Rain* started being written. Lisa and him and I enmeshed ourselves in each other and it became like a show-and-tell relationship that first year, where he showed us his closet and we showed him our closet and we tried to share each other's ideas, and the more he shared with us, the more we shared with him.

ALAN LEEDS: Wendy joining the band was a little controversial because the rest of the band felt like, okay, who's this eighteen-year-old kid? How's she going to work? How's this going to fit? But Prince had seen something in her. Wendy came from something other than the R&B world. She's the one who opened him up to Joni Mitchell and certain chord structures, and a sense of harmony that maybe he wouldn't have gotten from musicians who grew up just playing R&B or funk.

SUSAN ROGERS: Wendy knew every chord known to man and could really play. She brought a deeper rhythm to his music and she brought, just like Lisa did, different chords, more sophisticated chords that she would've known from all the musical training that she had had. She was raised on Stevie Wonder and the LA sound that includes the Beach Boys sessions that her dad played on and a combination of Joni Mitchell and James Brown. Wendy's always been so remarkable with rhythm. She helped Prince go in that direction he'd always admired, that Joni Mitchell direction, and still be able to couple that with that funk base that she had. The chords that she's fond of are very beautiful, sensitive, subtle, sophisticated cords. So Prince is able to expand his music in—I'm tempted to say feminine, which would be wrong— it's really a more harmonically rich direction. That was a welcome addition to his music.

BOBBY Z.: One member can change everything in a band and Wendy added tremendous color. Dez's style was more rock, like the band Cheap Trick. Wendy was more from the school of Joni Mitchell. It was a different input and a different band.

SUSANNAH MELVOIN: Wendy and Lisa together brought a more emotional component to his writing. Our father and Lisa's father were incredibly successful session players in Los Angeles. They were in the Wrecking Crew, so we grew up in that world. We had our own kids' band when we were little that was signed to A&M when we were like eight. We grew up with music around us everywhere.

ME: The Wrecking Crew was part of timeless songs by the Beach Boys, Frank Sinatra, Simon and Garfunkel, Sonny and Cher, Ike and

Tina Turner, and countless more. Wendy and Lisa felt at home inside of the music industry in a way that Prince did not.

SUSAN ROGERS: Wendy was the sherpa as he navigated the Mount Everest of showbiz. Prince was a shy kid from Minneapolis. You could see he was really struggling with having a public face. He was awkward in interviews and clearly uncomfortable with celebrity. He wanted to be famous, but linking with other celebrities was difficult for him. Wendy and Lisa showed him how to do it because they were from the LA music scene. Wendy and Lisa were completely comfortable with show business. They knew everybody. That was the school that they had grown up in so Wendy and Lisa helped Prince understand how you navigate LA.

BOBBY Z.: Lisa and Wendy brought sophistication. They were adults. Wendy's younger than Prince but, at that point, she was an adult and he was a kid. She brought a level of sophistication because they'd been exposed to showbiz on a huge level.

WENDY MELVOIN: I wasn't rattled by discipline or stardom or the pomp and circumstance of being rock stars. I had plenty of people in my house as a kid that were huge rock stars. Lisa and I and our families grew up together, so we spent a lot of time together. I fell in love with Lisa my last year of high school, which was a weird thing for our families. Cut to a hundred thousand years later, we're still partners. We're not lovers anymore, but we've been partners since that day. I had been a fan of Prince's. I had heard "Soft and Wet" in a nightclub in LA when I was fourteen and I went to a nightclub to go dancing. I heard it while I was on the dance floor and I ran up to the DJ because I was floored by what I heard. I said, "Who's that woman singing?" The guy was like, "It's not a woman, that's Prince. He's seventeen years old. He's from Minneapolis." I was hooked. I couldn't believe what I was hearing.

BOBBY Z.: Wendy comes along and she's not leaving. She's a lifer. Lisa wasn't leaving. Matt and Mark and I weren't leaving. We were a band that was committed. That made all the difference in the world to him. So he gave us the name the Revolution. He had been tentative about giving the band a name back in the *Dirty Mind* era because he thought the band might change right after you put up the poster. But when Wendy came, it solidified the unit. It meant the unit was supposed to be forever, and it made a difference in the level of trust level that he had.

ME: Prince was far more willing to listen to Wendy and Lisa because they were committed members of his musical family. With them in the gang, it became a family.

WENDY MELVOIN: The Revolution was like a family for him.

BOBBY Z.: It was a family. We were hanging out all the time.

ME: Prince had been craving family.

SUSANNAH MELVOIN: He had a strong desire to have family, to have that level of closeness, to have familial symbiotic closeness where you are not judged, and you were so close that you would never leave each other, even under duress. It was like, *Can we have a love so strong that we would never split? Can we love each other forever the way family does?* He longed for that.

ALAN LEEDS: That was his family. Those are the people he went out with, the people he partied with, people he invited to his house, people he broke bread with, people he worked with. It's like, no outsiders allowed, man.

BOBBY Z.: Wendy was the mom of the Revolution. Lisa was the mystic, our mind, our deep thoughts. Prince was the wizard.

BROWNMARK: We would bicker like family. From my earliest days with him, he told me how he wanted to form a group in the near future where we would all come together and we would all participate in writing this sound, truly developing and creating this new sound together. He didn't say a lot to me about the Revolution, but I had heard him use that term quite often. André and Dez Dickerson told me that he would constantly use that word. The Revolution. It's funny how that became the name of the group because, years earlier, that word was part of his plan to form this unit that he could work with. When we talked about that, I realized that I did not get hired as a work-for-hire. I wasn't a helping hand. I was a bandmate. He wanted a band. He wanted to be in a band that he could call his own band, so he picked us to form an actual band, which is probably why we fought a lot. If we didn't like something, we weren't afraid to speak our mind and he was very open to listen. The way a lot of the writing went with Prince and the Revolution was he'd slap a basic idea down and then bring us in to hear how we would interpret it. That's where that whole Revolution sound started to come from and eventually, by *Parade*, we had a really heavy influence on that sound. He listened to us a lot. He always won, but at least he gave us a voice. It was a real band.

ERIC LEEDS: Prince always looked at his band as being his family, but because he did not know how to express those feelings or have those relationships in a normal way, he became obsessively posses-sive about it. It wasn't that he wanted us to be his band as much as he wanted us to be his cult of personality. That's what he looked for. When there would be a rejection of that, he would respond to it in a very negative way. Normally, a relationship is based on a give and take. A relationship is dynamic in that both people get to have a turn controlling the relationship. But Prince is obsessed with always con-trolling the relationship entirely. At one point, he wanted the band to all be vegans. And they were vegans...when he was around. But when he wasn't, not necessarily. He attached some spiritual component to it, but I saw it as another way for him to exercise control. If you're gonna work for me, then you have to conform to my ideal.[13]

ME: Still, Prince and Wendy and Lisa all grew from their relationship.

WENDY MELVOIN: I learned so much by watching him carefully as a player. I'm so grateful that I came to the table with a certain ability on the guitar so that I could kind of keep up with him. But the thing that was great about our musical relationship is that we shared a certain sort of internal rhythm clock. My timing was always very good. Really, all you want with funk is to have good timing. If you're in front of the beat, then it's not funky. It was like watching a brain surgeon. I learned all my skills from him. I also learned how to be fearless with other instruments. I got my self-confidence from him. And we encouraged him to be whatever he wanted to be and we gave him space to find whatever that was. Watching Prince as closely as I've always watched him, I felt that he spent a lot of his childhood and his teens trying to prove something and prove it hard. By the time he was signed to Warner Bros., he was doing everything by himself and that came from this sense of, *I can do this, watch, I can do this. I'm more than what you think I am. Watch me.* By the time he had done *Dirty Mind,* he was like, *I'm going deeper into my self-expression here.* When I got in the band, Lisa and I both were really encouraging him to calm down, like, "It's okay, you've proven it, you can go any direction you want. With us, you don't have to be the kid from the *Dirty Mind.* You don't have to be the kid from 'Sister.' You don't need to be the guy who sang 'International Lover.'" He was forcing himself to be this character that pushed the boundaries of his insecurities. We were like, "You don't need to be that anymore. Let's figure out where you want to go now." When Lisa and I started playing in a way he hadn't been exposed to before, I believe his heart opened up and he got to explore more sides of himself musically. Before we came along, he had loved the musical athlete, but Lisa and I didn't really respond so much to that. We didn't try and play five thousand notes in five seconds. We were like, let's play one note really well. I think one of the reasons why the Revolution was the way it was is there weren't really any big-shot athletes. We became a great band by just being meat and potatoes, but it left a lot of room for him to do what he wanted to do.

ME: It became an intensely fruitful period for him. People said he made over fifty songs for that album.

SUSAN ROGERS: During *Purple Rain,* he was recording so much music I'm surprised it wasn't a double album. It was such a fertile period. He was recording like a fiend.

ME: But perhaps the biggest element separating *Purple Rain* from everything else Prince ever did is time.

BOBBY Z.: The main thing that happened with *Purple Rain* is it was forced patience. Everything else, he made rapidly. On *Dirty Mind*, he put a studio in his place and he made it quickly. *Controversy* he made quickly. On *Purple Rain*, the emergency brake was pulled. The movie took a long time to be written and shot, and he had to wait for it, so he had to move much more slowly. It was made over time rather than immediately and overnight like everything else. He went right back to that afterwards, but with *Purple Rain* he had to really think about these songs. He had time to experiment, to do stuff like take the bassline off of "When Doves Cry." To find new keyboard lines. There's more time to think about every choice that creates the presence of that music. And the pressure of *Purple Rain*, with the movie and everyone looking over his shoulders, that was like crushing coal to make a diamond.

ME: With time to think deeply, he was able to look at what he had and recognize that he was missing something. There was a part of this album's sonic puzzle that he wasn't finding. Around that time, his tour was following a tour by Bob Seger, who'd made the classic "Old Time Rock & Roll," which Tom Cruise danced to in his underwear in that iconic scene from *Risky Business*. Seger was then bigger than Prince and one day, Prince asked Matt Fink why he thought that was.

MATT FINK: I was with Prince after a show on the 1999 Tour and it was the night before we were going to play. We were hanging out at the arena where Seger was performing and Prince asked me what made Seger so successful. He was a very mainstream artist selling out arenas and Prince wanted to know what the appeal was. He didn't understand it, I guess. I said, "Well, he plays really straight-ahead mainstream white rock 'n' roll. If you created a song like that, you'd get over even bigger." That was my advice to him, and I think it influenced him to write a song like "Purple Rain."

ME: Recording artists are selling songs. Yeah, they're selling image and dreams and all of that, but you can't get to the mountaintop without unforgettable songs. Hits. Great artists make songs that appeal to a lot of people. They may or may not sing that well—Madonna sure didn't—they may or may not rap well—Hammer definitely didn't—but if they can create songs that resonate with a million-plus people, they can have the keys to the world. Madonna and Hammer definitely did that. There's lots of people in the music business who do not have the singing and dancing talent to win on *American Idol* or *The Voice*, but if they write great songs (or have them written for them) and they get in the booth and sell them in a way that makes those songs undislodgeable from our brains, then they can become megastars. Prince wrote "Purple Rain," a mainstreamy operatic rock ballad with a big arena rock chorus that a whole crowd could sing along with as they hold up lighters and have an epic communal experience while they're wrapped up in the music. It became a song that a whole generation could rally around. That song, and the album around it, transformed Prince from a big star to global elite. Well, the song, the album, and the movie *Purple Rain*. The first steps toward the movie came years earlier with the mid-1981 advent of MTV. In its now-quaint early years, MTV played music videos day and night, giving artists the space to make three-minute movies promoting themselves and their songs. Those videos showed music stars either performing their songs on stage or moving through a world of excess and fun or both. To many people, it was not immediately clear that MTV would last much less change the culture, but to Prince, the power of MTV was clear right away.

ALAN LEEDS: As soon as Prince saw MTV, he knew how to use it for his best interest. He began thinking in visuals right away. One day, I went down to the studio and he's playing me something, I don't recall what song it was, and then he told me the video vision he had for the song. I looked at him and said, "You just wrote this song this morning and cut it today and you already have a video in mind?" He said, "Alan, what you don't understand is people don't hear music anymore. They see music." That's the impact of MTV. He knew that MTV had radically changed how people absorb new music. He understood that this was a medium he could use to become who he wanted to be. That's why he had to do *Purple Rain*.

ME: Actually, Prince was trying to make a film before he made *Purple Rain*.

QUESTLOVE: There was a film done between *Controversy* and *1999* called *the Second Coming*. It was a concert film and narrative for the songs on *Controversy*, so it was of a hint of what *Purple Rain* would be. His first girlfriend, Susan Moonsie, was to play his girlfriend. The acting part was in black and white. The narrative was about a young musician who has big dreams, who's trying to make it out of the city. They recorded three *Controversy* shows at the Met Center, which was then the biggest venue in Minnesota. It's about an artist thinking about the struggle of what his life was before this big moment, this big homecoming show he's about to do. It's quasi-autobiographical, but because of the loose narrative and not having a director, they ended up scrapping the film. At the very best, it was a concert film, but Warner's wasn't excited. They killed it and he went about refining it. In that process, it became *Purple Rain*. But the talk behind his back was, "He's crazy. No one knows who he is. He's not big enough to carry a movie. No one's going to go see this thing." But he had to do it because he always had a plan to go further. He makes a big ultimatum to his management company, "You gotta find me a movie deal or you guys are fired." They were like, "We'll never find a movie deal. He's not big enough and he doesn't know that he's not big enough to demand a movie budget from someone." But at the last minute, they found a deal for him for him through Richard Pryor, who had a company that wanted to fund the script-writing and then Warner got interested and took it from there.

DEZ DICKERSON: He had made up his mind to make a movie. He said "If it's just you and me in the snow with a video camera, we're shooting this morning." He was just determined that it was going to happen.

They turned him down at first. It was his money and management's money that was the difference maker in terms of the deal. Between Prince and management, enough of their own money was put into it that Warner was willing to match it and go along with it.

JILL JONES: He had that movie in his head for so long. Every step he made toward becoming huge and famous, he knew every step of the way what he was going to do. The only thing that I ever saw really throw him off was when Vanity said she didn't want to be in the movie.

ALAN LEEDS: During the prep for *Purple Rain*, Prince had gotten frustrated with her ambition and was doubting her loyalty. She was equally frustrated and was talking to an agent about film opportunities other than *Purple Rain*. It became clear that she was over Prince and didn't share his optimism for *Purple Rain*. When [director] Albert Magnoli arrived on the scene, she made it her business to get close to him—trying to get a sense of what Prince and Magnoli had in mind for her in the film. Not long after that, she pulled up stakes.

JILL JONES: She was supposed to be the lead, the role that Apollonia got. Vanity dropping out messed up the dream for a minute. It was going to be a far darker character than what ultimately came out in *Purple Rain*. It was darker because with her in the role, you could really see the different archetypes that he worked with. Prince always worked with archetypes of women, of men. They were things that we'd all been indoctrinated with, so it was also quite familiar when you'd see it again. Everything was so strategic with him. Everything down to having me with the Marilyn Monroe-blonde hair, all of it. He thought it was a real laugh that a Black woman was pulling off this blonde hair. He actually cut my hair himself.

ME: They put out a casting call in magazines read by aspiring actors and the notice was spotted by a young actress-slash-beauty queen-slash-former LA Rams cheerleader named Patricia, who sent in a tape.

SUSANNAH MELVOIN: There were hundreds of VHS tapes on the floor and I remember him going through VHS after VHS, looking at women's audition tapes. When it came to Apollonia, he put in her tape and after a few seconds, he said, "This is her."

MORRIS DAY: He starts writing this movie and next thing I know, he's coming to me saying, "Uh, we're going to do a movie." I'm like, "Okay." I'd never done a movie before, and I had no reason to doubt it, but by the same token, I had no reason to really take it serious. But, before I knew it, man, we was doing dance classes and acting classes, and all of this shit, and directors and cinematographers were showing up. I was like, "This is real. We going to do this." I started going to the acting classes and I kinda made a joke of it. I was more comfortable making people laugh than trying to be serious, and they got pissed off. The teacher was like, "Don't come to my class anymore." He said, "You'd serve yourself better by going to the beach because you're disrupting my acting class." I got kicked out but some of that comedic edge I ended up using in the movie. They said I was clowning all the time, but it worked for me, so it was kinda like a slap in that dude's face. Then the director, Albert Magnoli, comes to me and Jerome with the whole script and says "I want you to make this yours." We'd go through it line for line, and he'd be like, "Okay, the script says this, what would you say?" We rewrote all our lines. That's a big help because when I felt like I was doing dialogue that I would really do, I was comfortable with it and I was able to do my thing. I was just being Morris, that's all.

ME: When the movie came out, Prince rapidly ascended to being one of the biggest stars in the world.

MORRIS DAY: *Purple Rain* just changed the game for him. He was on track to be a substantial pop artist, but then he went into the stratosphere. That's when he became the global household name and it was all because of the movie, which was a bold move, because who knew it would work? Almost no one thought that it would!

ME: Things got so big so fast that it was a little scary for him.

ALAN LEEDS: We were in the car, on the way to the premiere, which was at the Grauman's Chinese Theater in Hollywood. Of course, this was the biggest night of his career, the whole dream of making a movie that everybody was skeptical about had turned out right and the initial reaction to the film, the previews were off the hook. The music was amazing. We really felt that this was going to be his step into superstardom. MTV was following his every step. If there had been a TMZ, they would have been living in his closet. We're in the car, and we came out of the hotel, Prince and the band in full regalia, dressed for the premiere in outfits that they wore in the film. Prince picked a flower from the garden that surrounded the front of the hotel. We got in the limo. It was a parade of limos because Wendy and Lisa had their own car, Bobby Z. had a car, Matt Fink and his girlfriend in a car. I was in the car with Prince in the backseat. Chick [Prince's bodyguard] was in the front seat with the driver. There was a red carpet and the arrivals were strategically planned. First, the individual band members would get there and get their red-carpet moment. and then Prince would be the last to arrive. We have walkie-talkies with our security guys who were already at the theater and coordinating with us, telling us when to pull around the corner so that we'd arrive at the right time. We're in the car with Prince and we're in the backseat and he's holding this flower and gripping it with both hands the way you would a baseball bat almost. All of a sudden, Chick's walkie-talkie went off and it was one of our crew at the venue telling Chick to hold up because there are so many people there, so many fans screaming, that we've got to wait for the way to clear. Prince grabbed my hand, and his hand was shaking. He literally grabbed my wrist and his voice cracked, it broke. He said, "Wh-wh-wh-what did they say?" I honestly thought he was going to lose it. For that split second, he did. He totally, totally freaked out and lost control. I treasure that moment because it told me he's human, because this was the guy who basically tried to convince you 24/7 that he wasn't human, that he was somehow superhuman and had powers that God had bestowed upon him, gifts and powers that mere mortals didn't have. For this moment, he was one of us. Now, I've spent my life dealing with artists, some of whom had butterflies before they go on stage, and you learn what works. In the storm, you've got to be the voice of reason and have to calm his voice in the car. I drew in that experience and just very calmly looked at him and said, "He said there's a huge crowd, everybody is excited and we're going to slow down a little bit." He took a breath, exhaled, and then the moment passed. From that point on, his voice was back to normal, his look was back to normal. For that moment, he was that little kid rejected by his mother.

ME: Prince plotted to go back and see it with a real audience the next day.

ALAN LEEDS: At three or four in the morning, Prince says, "When we get up, I want to go to a theater and sit with regular people." I'm like, "Really? How in the world we going to do that?" He said, "I'll disguise myself." So, about eleven, he called and says, "I've got hair and makeup over here and I sent so-and-so out to get some clothes," and they went down to Melrose Avenue to one of the funky used clothing shops and bought an old overcoat and God knows what else. They had him looking like a young derelict who hung out on Melrose late at night. He had his hair tucked under a hat so you couldn't see the hair. He had sunglasses on, but goofy sunglasses, not celebrity sunglasses. So, he's got the disguise and we go to his room and make the plan. I explain to the bodyguard that I'll go ahead and reserve the back row of the theatre and set the timing. After the lights are down in the theatre and the movie has begun, we'll get him out of the limo and in there. Then Prince says, "Okay, now one thing before we leave the hotel. Call Gwen and tell her to go to the lobby and just sit in the lobby in those chairs near the elevators."

ME: Gwen is Alan's wife of many years.

ALAN LEEDS: It didn't take me but a second to understand what he was up to. I called her. I said, "Gwen, Prince wants you to go downstairs. I don't know if he's got something for you or what, but he said to meet him in the lobby." He looked at me and he says, "If she busts me, we don't go to the theatre. If she doesn't get me, we go." The bodyguard and I leave to go to the theatre to set things up. Now, Gwen knows we're going to the theatre so I'm not there for this part, but as Gwen tells the story, Prince came out of the elevator by himself in disguise, walked right past her, and she didn't even notice him.

ME: Prince loved dipping into disguises from time to time.

MORRIS HAYES: If he wanted to go out inconspicuously, he had a few outfits that he could put on, like he had a white beard and other funny stuff to make him look like some old aristocratic dude.

ALAN LEEDS: When Prince got to the theater, I came out to the car to get him and he said, "I know it's going to work. Gwen didn't see me." Meanwhile, his hairstylist went down to the lobby and told Gwen the whole story. She says, "You mean that goofy little guy? That was Prince?" The hairstylist said, "You've been duped." They decide, "Okay, wiseass. I'll show you." So, she and the hairstylist go to the theatre and they're standing outside telling people, "Prince is inside. Prince is inside." By the time we come out, there was maybe ten to twelve people gathered. Now, I don't think half the kids believed it, but five minutes later, who comes busting out running for a limo but the two bodyguards, me, and Prince. And she just looked at him and shook her head and he stuck his tongue out at her and jumped in the car and we all bust out laughing, but that was the kind of thing he liked to do. He was like, "Let me see if I can get away with this shit."

ME: Some who knew Prince well found the movie funny because of all the distortions of reality.

GAYLE CHAPMAN: I kind of giggled through most of it. It was a dramatization of his life. It was romanticizing how Prince thought people would resonate with the story of a poor Black child. He exaggerated everything. I don't know, maybe I'm cruel that way, but I watched it and I kept saying, "That's not right." I mean, the whole mother character is a fiction and then he portrays her as white. There were all sorts of things.

ME: Some of his friends understood what he was doing.

DEZ DICKERSON: He knew he'd have to be extreme in his presentation to get our attention. It's business. I have to be as extreme as hell to get attention.

BOBBY Z.: He was like, *I want something and I have to present myself in a way that makes me absolutely stand out. So this is how we're going to present it.* It makes a difference when you feel like it was a mastermind move to get attention.

ME: But some people saw through the dramatization and saw the story of the turbulent beginning of his life. In her memoir, Mayte says the movie is filled with allusions to Prince's "battlefield childhood." Whether the story was accurate is beside the point—Prince was mythmaking, letting us see him as a stage killer and a lady killer who was struggling through a lot of family strife yet the core of the film, the thing that elevated it from a kind of farce to something that was timeless and endlessly watchable, was the music—both the songs and the stage performances. Watching it felt like going to a great concert.

ALAN LEEDS: If there's any secret to the success of *Purple Rain*, it's that it was a brilliant performance feature, and that's because he saw what MTV saw.

ME: But as a massive star, Prince had even more reasons to shut the world out.

DEZ DICKERSON: After I left the band, Prince invited my wife and me out to his show in DC and after the show, he invited us up to the room. At this point, they're bringing in a grand piano to every hotel suite on the tour and his chef is cooking his food and it's a whole different thing. At one point during dinner, I said, "We're planning on going to Georgetown tomorrow." He and I had always loved having a day off and kicking it in Georgetown. I said, "You want to come with us?" For a minute, his face lit up, and then this sadness fell over his face and he said, "I can't do things like that anymore." That was a pretty stark difference. It was like, "Oh, okay. In a way, you got what you wanted, but it had a price that maybe you didn't expect, but you're willing to pay." He had to leave normal behind.

MORRIS DAY: When he made the transition from being the guy that I grew up with to being a star, he basically became untouchable. I mean he was kind of like the Wizard of Oz. He was the man behind the curtain, but he never came out from behind the curtain. You couldn't call him. I never had his phone number once he became the superstar. You couldn't have any contact with him. The only time I would talk to him is if he would call me. And he would call me at obscure times of the night, when I never expected it. He had a habit of calling me out of the blue at all hours of the night, so I knew if my phone rang at 3:00 am, it's Prince. That's just how he was. He was living the mysterious rock star life.

ME: The glamorous life. But, as the song says, "without love it ain't much." His connection to the real world was growing more and more distant. It was partly by design—fewer outside voices meant less of an intrusion on his creativity. Sometimes, he couldn't even trust his closest friends with evaluating his ideas.

MORRIS DAY: After he made "When Doves Cry," we were on the set of the "Ice Cream Castles" video, and he asked me to get in the limo so he could play it for me. Now, I was always honest with Prince. I always told him what I felt, even if it became confrontational. "When Doves Cry" was the first time I ever heard him do a song that had no bass. I was like, "Dude, there's no bass on here. It's not funky. Next time you play something for me, make sure it's funky." I got out the car and I slammed the door. Now, I was wrong about that shit. It might not have been the funkiest record, but it was a huge hit. Prince separated himself from people because he never wanted to let anybody get inside his head. I think keeping everybody at an arm's length was about letting him be the best artist he could be. Because how many times do you go through your day and allow somebody to say something stupid to you, and that just gets in your head. Prince didn't want to be in that space. He wanted to be like, "I am who I am and I don't want anybody's opinion of who I am." He didn't want to let anybody in his space who might dare change his thinking. You know, if I'm in the room with him, and we're talking, I'm going to get in his headspace because I'm going to say some shit that he might not want to hear. I think he'd separated himself from people for that reason.

ME: Some guessed that part of Prince's trouble in dealing with people and the wider world is what was going on in his mind—he told Michaela Angela Davis that he thought in music, but it seems like that's just a small piece of it all.

A GIRLFRIEND: There's so much going on inside his mind at once; it's like that *Beautiful Mind* movie and he's not going to let you interrupt his flow.

CHUCK ZWICKY: He sees a complete vision of something, even when there's only the bare, minimal skeleton structure, and anyone who has that kind of a vision and is trying to take this music that's in his head and get it on tape tends to not like distractions and things to get in the way of the process. You build up a bit of a wall around yourself to allow that kind of privacy. Some people are going to be a little put off by the seemingly aloof and terse conversation, but if you've ever seen astronauts or fighter pilots in their mode, they're very focused and the communication is very monosyllabic and to the point, and seemingly terse, but that's all of the information that needs to be conveyed at that moment to get the job done.

ME: The notion that Prince was only at peace when making music and lost everywhere else fuels all these stories of Prince fumbling through life's most mundane moments.

MORRIS HAYES: One day, Prince said, "Morris, will you take me to the hardware store? I want to get some chain for this back gate." I'm like, "What?" He said, "Yeah. There's somebody coming in." I said, "Prince, there's nobody coming in at the back gate, bro. You got cameras all over the place." He's like, "Are you gonna help me or not?" I said, "Okay, yeah. I'm gonna help you." I've got this Dodge Caravan that I used for equipment and stuff and I said, "I'll take you to the hardware store. No big deal." So, we get to Ace and I tell Prince, "Okay. I'm gonna go in and get the stuff. You wait in the car. I'm gonna leave it running," because it's snowing outside and it's very cold. I go in the store and I'm getting the chain and I'm about to look for a lock, but first the guy's got to cut this chain off. I'm telling him how long it should be, and he's doing his thing, and then, all of a sudden, I see this guy go cruising by in this turtleneck and these fluffy snow leopard boots. I'm like, *What? He's in here? Oh my God! He's in here!* I'm telling this guy at the store, like "Hey, man, just give me this piece, I gotta go. I got to get Prince." So, I go to the end of the aisle and I look for him, and he's disappeared. I'm like, *Oh my God. I've got to find this guy.* Prince had this really weird way of just showing up like vapor. Like he wouldn't be there, and then, all of a sudden, poof, like, *Oh geez, where'd you come from?* So, I finally find him and he's got an armful of stuff, like, a lock and a bunch of crap that he just grabbed from all around the store and I'm like, "What is all this?" He said, "Can we have this?" I'm like, "Yeah, sure. If you want." But I don't even know how or where he's gonna use any of this stuff. But whatever. We go to the counter to pay for the stuff, and by now there's people all around the store who are just frozen. They're like, "Dude, Prince is walking around through the hardware store. He's in here." It was all so weird. It was like something that happens in the movie but it's a wild, madcap satire and the guy who owns the place is standing there freaking out, they're all freaking out. He starts trying to talk to Prince like, "Um, my uh, my dad said that you used to come in here like back in the day." Prince is like, "Okay." Totally awkward but hilarious because of the looks on everybody's faces.

ME: Cue the music from *Curb Your Enthusiasm*. With a funky bassline, of course.

SUSANNAH MELVOIN: He's always been this little alien child who only wanted to play music. "I just want to play music. I need to play music." Bobby Z. has this great story where he and Prince went out at night and stopped to get something to eat at White Castle. Prince wouldn't get out to order by himself. He was Prince. He was like, "I'm not ordering these things by myself. Bobby, you do it." Bobby said, "All right.

Five cheeseburgers," and Prince would be like all happy that he didn't have to order it. He just had this otherworldly vibe of like, "I can't do the normal stuff, just let me play my music."

ME: Susannah became Prince's girlfriend back when he was still recording *Purple Rain*, and their relationship would become the most serious one of his life to that point. Of course, like every relationship in his life, it was a... strange relationship. Indeed, it was the relationship that he would write that song about. It would also spawn "If I Was Your Girlfriend," "Starfish And Coffee," and "Nothing Compares 2 U." In his long, complicated, epic relationship with Wendy's twin sister, Prince almost found a wife. She got a ring, and then, later, a proposal, but a funny thing happened on the way to the altar.

8

Forever in My Life

The Love of His Life

SUSANNAH MELVOIN: When I met Prince, I felt as though I already knew him because Lisa already had the gig playing with him. Wendy and I were still in high school, in eleventh grade, and even earlier than that, I was a fan. So when Lisa got the gig, Wendy and I were like, "We've got a family member that's playing with royalty!" We thought it was the greatest thing ever. I always felt I knew him through Lisa.

I graduated in 1982 and in '83, I got my first job, working for David Geffen as his receptionist at Geffen Records. At the Geffen Christmas party, there were people from all the labels underneath the family of Warner Bros. Little seventeen-year-old me goes and gets my first dress. I was completely awkward. It was a big party. I want to say that it was at Le Dome on Sunset Boulevard. I'm wandering the halls, thinking about whether or not I'm going to leave, just feeling super claustrophobic, not mingling with anybody. Then I see, over on the far wall, Prince and Vanity. I'm like, *Do I say something? 1999* was out and he was a big star. I thought, *No, I'm not going to say anything.* I didn't know how to deal with that at all, so I went to a pay phone. I put ten cents in and called Wendy and Lisa. "He's here with Vanity. He's here. Should I say something to him?" "Yeah, go and say hello. Go say hi."

Lisa was like my sister and he'd just met Wendy. I was like, *Okay, I'm going to get up the nerve. I'll go say something.* So I gingerly walk up and look right at him and he's looking at me with no expression. I'm thinking, *Is this not a good idea?* I'm getting this feeling, *Don't walk any closer*. But I just felt compelled, like, I've got family who you know so you should know me! I was seventeen and dumb. I say, "Excuse me, my name is Susannah, and you know my twin sister Wendy." He says, "Hello." And he's just staring at me, waiting for me to start, like, okay, fill the space, say something more. Vanity comes in and she's like, "Oh, look at how cute she is! Look at those chubby cheeks!" She touches my cheeks. "Look at how sweet and cute and chubby those cheeks are!" Of course, all I could think of is myself three hours earlier, looking in the mirror, going, *Oh my God, you've got cheeks out to here...*It was my worst nightmare. She was saying, "I'm big momma, here. Be careful." So I was like, "Really nice to meet you, I just wanted to say hello." I backed up and I was like, *Boy, that was a bad idea. Such a bad idea.*

But it wasn't a bad idea because within a few weeks, he was back in LA and he was calling Lisa and Wendy and we all were picking him up at the airport. He liked to stay with us sometimes. Wendy and Lisa had this great car we used to call Betty Flounder. It was a 1964 Mercury Montclair, this salmon-colored, beautiful thing. We get in Betty Flounder, drive to LAX, pick him up, and bring him back to our place. He stayed on our couch, and we had many funny nights where I'd be in my room, which was right off the living room. There's the couch, five feet from my bed, and we had two Persian cats and they would jump on him in the middle of the night and you'd hear him like, "Lisa? Wendy? Can you come get the cats?" I would be in my bed like, "Oh, my God. The cats." It was very funny. So, he was coming to California a lot, and he wanted to stay with Lisa and Wendy a lot and I was there. I was just around him more and more because it was an incredibly intimate space, like, a tiny, tiny, tiny house. It didn't have real doors, it had saloon doors. You'd just look under and say, "Oh, there's a naked person under there." No privacy, just silliness. One day, we were all hanging out and he needed to use the restroom. The restroom was in my bedroom and there's saloon doors in the bathroom. There's no privacy. But he comes in, does his business, comes back out, and he's standing beside my bed sort of looking at the bed. There's this huge dip in the center of the mattress. I walk back in and he says, "Do you sleep in this?" I said, "Yeah, I sleep in that." He said, "Do you have a job?" I said, "Yeah." And he goes, "Can you buy yourself a mattress?" I was like, "Well, I only sleep on one side, so..." He kind of patted the bed, got up, and walked out. The following day, he had a mattress and a box spring sent to me. It was kind of stunning that he did that. He was like, *I've got to get her a bed*. It was waiting for me when I got home from work the next day. Those kinds of things start to happen. He sent flowers to my door every fucking day. At one point, our house looked like a funeral parlor. We would just giggle and howl at how hysterical it was, but he just kept them coming. *I want her. I want her*. And he did. He wanted me.

He would call and we would talk for hours on the phone. Those conversations were really sweet and unique. I had never had conversations with a man who could be so gentle on the phone. But it was strange because he really wasn't that interested, but he knew how to seem interested. He wasn't really even asking about you. He was creating an environment that you wanted to be in. Whether he was present emotionally, it almost didn't matter, until he became a bad guy. When he was, we would say, like, bipolar! Like, what happened here? How do you get on these high highs for days and then become someone else entirely? I cannot diagnose this man but he'd go forty-eight hours without sleep or even seventy-two hours, and then he would crash. That's not a manic episode? Come on. There's stuff going on in the family, in my opinion. I saw it. Wendy saw it. Lisa saw it. Like, something's up. We knew it. He knew it. And he, in every possible way, was hiding it with his genius. And it was getting worse. It progressed, which was really sad. We could see it happening. We almost thought, *Is he getting ill?* Like, *What's happening to his brain?* But he managed to hide all that stuff. I don't think anybody ever saw him that way except for us. But there was a relationship building with all three of us, with me and Wendy and Lisa. I don't think he had ever met people like us that he related to so deeply on an emotional level. I think that's one of the reasons, if not the most important reason, that we became muses to him, particularly Wendy and Lisa. Musical muses. It was the first time he'd actually trusted himself emotionally with somebody. It was a very unique relationship that we all had with him.

Meanwhile, he was starting to record the *Purple Rain* soundtrack. That was done much earlier than even the rehearsals for the film. He would be at the studio and he would call and say to the girls, "Can you come down? I need you to add guitar, add keyboards, or to sing on this. I need your help, you've got to be in the studio." I found myself going with them. Either I'd be like, "Can I come down to the studio?" Or he would say, "Bring Susannah. She can come down." I felt as though there was a tension between me and Prince, something was heated, and I was certainly following that energy. It was clear to me that this is a person that doesn't just give attention to somebody for no reason. He wasn't super emotive or easy to communicate with, so if he wanted you there, it meant something. I found myself going down to the studio a lot, and one particular day, I went into the bathroom and was finishing up my business, and I hear click, click, click—heels coming down the hallway toward me. Knock, knock, knock, on my door. I open up the door and he just barrels in, closes the door behind me, pushes me up against the wall, and he just starts to kiss me all over. All over. He says, "I can't stop thinking about you." I'm like, "Wow!" I was like, "Can I wash my hands?" Good thing I had my pants up. We kissed, he walked out the bathroom door, and that was it. He just walked away. And I was left with that. I was like, *Wow, okay*. And then, I was like, *I don't even know if I like this. I'm not so sure just what happened.*

A few days later, when he was staying in a hotel, we were all at home asleep when the phone rang in the middle of the night. We all knew who was calling. Of course, the girls were like, "Don't answer it. We don't want to go to work, just don't answer it, we need to get some sleep." But I had this feeling it was for me. A voice in my head said, "Pick up the phone." Prince said, "Can we hang out? Can I come get you?" I said, "Sure." It was like two or three in the morning and he'd just finished at the studio. So, he comes and gets me, and we're in the limousine and he's very sort of sedate and reflective. He almost looked sad. I felt like, *Wow, you just asked me to go out with you and go to your hotel and you don't seem very into this.* So I said, "Okay, I'll just go for the ride." We get to the hotel and he gets out of the car first and goes up into the room. I follow him but he has completely just stopped speaking. It was as if I wasn't even there. I thought, *Well, this is weird.* I was like, "Are you okay?" Nothing. Then he gets on the couch, and he lays away from it. I sit on the coffee table and I'm just gently saying, "Are you okay, Prince? Is there something you want to talk about? Are you alright?" Nothing. This went on for like twenty-five minutes. I'm looking around like, *Hmm. Okay.* I didn't have the tools to be like, "Well, you take your time, I'll be in the other room. I'll watch some TV and be a grownup about this." I didn't know what to do. Finally, I get up and walk out. I get in a cab and go home. *If you're not going to talk, I'll just go home.* The second I'm in the house the phone rings. "Hello?" I never heard anything like it in my life. Screaming, cursing, yelling. He was so mad that I walked out, that I didn't stick it out. It was some test like, see how long you're willing to be uncomfortable. How uncomfortable can you be in front of me and not walk away? There was something really going on, and that was a theme throughout my knowing him. He could be completely cut off and quiet and you had to navigate that with him without saying anything. Like he was saying, "Don't talk about it. Just be here with me." I didn't get that until way later. That night when he called me, I was like, "No one's ever spoken to me like this." No one had ever cursed me out. I had never experienced it in my life. I was like, "You can't do that!" And I hung up. A second later, the phone rings again and now he's even more irate. He's like, "How dare you hang the phone up on me!" I was like, "I do not know what you're doing. I don't know what you're trying to say to me." Then he hung up because he wanted to be the one to hang up on me. That was my way into understanding that he had a temper. I was like, "Okay, tread lightly here." Because I was smart enough to know that ultimately, he was saying, "Can you stick around?" I was like, "Yeah." I went along with that, with all of it, because I was being lured. He was coming after me, and making a real effort to put himself out for me, and I pushed him away at that moment, but he didn't stop. He came back for more. And I was perfectly happy to indulge it.

ME: There were also moments of connection and beauty.

SUSANNAH MELVOIN: I remember once while he was recording *Purple Rain*, we were walking down Melrose Avenue. He knew that I was a dancer when I was younger, that's what I wanted to be, and he asked me to show him how to do a pirouette. So, it was just the two of us on Melrose at one o'clock in the morning and me teaching him how to do a pirouette. For me, to be with a man who's asking me to teach him how to do a pirouette, that was something I had never seen, or seen since. That's about holding on to your masculinity while embracing your femininity. That's who Prince was.

ME: But, even in a romantic relationship, it was hard to communicate with him.

SUSANNAH MELVOIN: If he's having a really difficult time, just saying, "Tell me about it," that wouldn't happen. It wouldn't be, "Let's sit down and have this conversation about this stuff that connects us." His feelings would come out in other ways: they would come out in the music.

ME: Prince couldn't communicate deep feelings through talking. His love language was music. In some ways, his only real language was music.

SUSANNAH MELVOIN: I grew up with a young girl who I still know named Cynthia Rose. I told Prince on many occasions the story of this girl I went to school with from second grade up to sixth grade. She was extraordinarily kooky, lovable—a beyond sparkly creature of a girl.

ME: She was autistic, but that term wasn't used much back in the '70s.

SUSANNAH MELVOIN: I just thought, *This is just an unusual person.* She's on the spectrum, and she's a musical savant. Every single morning on the way to school, we'd be on the bus together. Often, she'd be behind me, sitting in her chair. You could hear her saying, "Twenty, twenty, twenty, twenty…" I'd say, "What are you saying?" She'd say, "My favorite number is twenty. You know why?" I'm like, "I don't know why." She goes, "There's an even number." This was every day. She had this Groucho Marx like walk, and she would always say, "You know what I had for breakfast?" I'd say, "What did you have for breakfast?" She'd say, "I had starfish and pee-pee!" Every day. "I had starfish and pee-pee for breakfast." I told Prince about her, and sometimes he would ask me, "Tell me the story about Cynthia. What ever happened with Cynthia? That's such a beautiful name. She was so kooky. What was up with her?" He was so attracted to that story. I would get all animated and act all the parts out. I would act like Cynthia and do what she would do. I would show him who she was and we would laugh and laugh and laugh. Then one day, in 1985 or '86, we were in the studio at our Galpin house that we had just finished building. The studio was finally up and running and he was recording as much as he could, like, every moment of the day. I was sitting at the kitchen table and he said, "Can you tell me the story of Cynthia Rose again? Can you write down the details?" I spent the better part of an hour writing it all down, and he looked at it and he was like, "Starfish and pee-pee. I don't know if I can sing starfish and pee-pee. There's no way I can sing pee-pee. Can you imagine singing pee-pee? Do you mind if I change it to coffee?" He goes down into the studio. Ten hours later he comes up, and he says, "You want to hear it?" I walk down there and he's standing at the board. He presses play, and he says, "Here it is. I'm going upstairs. You can put the background vocals on it." I just thought, *It's beautiful. It's beautiful. It's beautiful.* He even weaved in the actual names of all the kids in my class, including our teacher, Miss Cathleen. He says the second child in line was named Lucy. Lucy was Miss Cathleen's daughter. That's who he was. That's how he could share himself and have a moment with you, by taking imagery and story and making it into something. That's where he felt his most honest place as a writer and as a creator. That's the place where he could share with you and have an experience of you.

I was beyond blessed to be with him, where he could be inspired enough to say, "This is how much I hear you." But we would be lacking in all the other intimate stuff, like communicating. His love had to come out in physical ways; it had to come out in the music. That can be super complicated and weighty. And he wasn't monogamous. He was with many, many women. I was a willing participant in that, I was okay with that a lot of times. I turned a blind eye to it. I knew when he was monogamous and when he wasn't. I was used to the spontaneity of our relationship and the tentative quality of it. So, being in a relationship with him was complicated. When it came to our musical life, it was really clear and straightforward, but when it came to our intimate life, it was complicated. My experience with him was beautiful at times and really hard in other ways. It was always his way. Everything had to be his way. I'm surprised we got through it. But that was the kind of a relationship we had. Now, as a sexual man, that was totally different. His sexuality is super complicated but I don't even want to get into that part. He wasn't what one would think Prince would be.

9

Anotherloverholeinyohead

What It Was Like to Be with Him

ME: What was the sex god like in bed? Was he the international lover who was freakier than you could imagine? Did he really have a dirty mind? There's lots of women who know, and several who were willing to kiss and tell, but only anonymously. There are several different women talking here.

A GIRLFRIEND: Once, he showed up in front of my apartment. He said, "I'm downstairs. Can you come down?" I said, "I'll be right there." I got in the car and he smelled incredibly good. He was fully done up. He looked incredible. He had on a turtleneck sweater, this beautiful, fluffy thing, that sat right under his beautiful face. He looked at me and said, "You look like a doll right now. Come closer. Come closer." I got as close as I could but he wouldn't say anything. He just started the car and revved the engine like we were about to go, so I'd move back. It was awkward, like I didn't know what he wanted, like he kept playing a joke on me but it wasn't funny. He wasn't saying anything. I'm sitting there like, "Where are we going?" I keep asking. Eventually, he says, "Somewhere fun." Finally, he starts driving and we go to his house. This was my first time there, so I'm nervous. He gets out and gives me the key to the house and says, "You open it." I do and we both walk in. Suddenly, he pushes me up against the wall and he's rubbing up against me and he's smelling me and kissing me and all I could think was, *This feels too choreographed.* I couldn't fully get into it because it seemed like a dance or a performance. It was not him letting loose and us really being there with each other. That night and every other night I was with him, for as long as we were together, he would never come. It was like that was way too much information for someone to have on him. He couldn't get that loose and free and real to let you see him come, to see him release, to know what he looked like when he was totally vulnerable. Actually, he came one time, when I wasn't looking at him, which made me feel weird and distracted while we were doing it. We weren't really connecting during sex.

A GIRLFRIEND: Let me put it this way: the foreplay was great.

A GIRLFRIEND: The foreplay was unreal and it wasn't like, oh, he could give great head or whatever. It wasn't that. It was the psychological aspect of getting you there. It was the way he would smell.

A GIRLFRIEND: Being with him was always intimidating for me because it was Prince. He was creative but he's not as wild as everyone thinks. I heard that he was with other women, but with me, he was very gentle. Very gentle and thoughtful. He was the closest thing that I'd had to having a woman.

A GIRLFRIEND: He makes you feel safe and protected and taken care of and he makes you feel girly, like a woman, but he's also in touch with you in a way that's very feminine while simultaneously making you feel girly.

A GIRLFRIEND: He was the most patient man I've ever been with. And the most complicated in terms of being in bed with him. He was the most sensitive, the most androgynous, this perfect balance of male and female energy. He's a true Gemini. He's masculine but he's in touch with his femininity. It's complicated.

A GIRLFRIEND: He was a lot like the "If I Was Your Girlfriend," song. He's the sensitive guy whose female side really comes out with women. He wasn't just trying to fool around. He appreciated your femininity. He worshipped women.

A GIRLFRIEND: He has great respect for women on one hand, but on another, he has a blatant disrespect and disregard for women. You don't see it when he's speaking to you; you see it in his actions. They're not genuine. He's not honest. He gets bored easily. He's not monogamous. He's very controlling. And he's not that sweet to women.

A GIRLFRIEND: It wasn't like having sex with a man. It was bigger than that. It was erotic and unique and very androgynous, if you know what I mean.

A GIRLFRIEND: Most guys don't pick up on small things or details or pay attention to little things. He reminds me of a woman or of being in a relationship with a woman in that every subtle action you do is noticed without having to be explained. He gets the way you gesture or the way your eyes move down or he can sense insecurity. He's also very masculine but not in a dude way. In a man way, like strong.

A GIRLFRIEND: He wanted you to bathe him and he wanted to bathe you. He loved to take baths. You would be pouring a bunch of stuff in the tub and then we'd get in and it was just great. Have a glass of wine. Not much went on. He didn't want to do anything else. It was like you could kind of tell, oh, this guy just wants to hang out in a tub with you like a girlfriend. He doesn't want to do anything. He just wants to be a girl. I thought that was adorable. I felt safe with that.

A GIRLFRIEND: He bathed me. He brushed my hair. He likes baths and bubbles and products.

A GIRLFRIEND: He ran the bath, he put the bubbles in, he took your clothes off, he washed you, he washed your hair, it was a whole procedure and process. He put lotion on you after. He'd give you a robe. It was worshipful, sweet and sensitive. I don't mind if someone wants to wash my hair.

A GIRLFRIEND: He was into girls having experiences with each other around him. He would send a girl over to talk to me while he was watching from upstairs, to watch the interaction. Or he'd say, "She has a beautiful body, doesn't she?"

A GIRLFRIEND: He had threesomes. He liked that quite a bit. He had girls have sex in front of him and he liked that a lot.

A GIRLFRIEND: He was very soft in bed, like he was a coach. I would do something to him and he would show me the way he wanted it done if it wasn't the way he wanted it.

A GIRLFRIEND: The act of it was not as freaky as you'd think. It was not wild. It wasn't *Dirty Mind*, "Erotic City." The actual act itself was kind of romantic. It was more loving than freaky and gross. He never made you feel gross or cheap or that you were one of many. I never felt unimportant. He always made you feel beautiful and perfect.

A GIRLFRIEND: We're not talking about the kind of sex that one would think. It was super, super normal, super loving, super give and take. More normal than what you would think.

A GIRLFRIEND: There were times when I would see him, who he really was, if he was sleepy. If he was awake, he was on, guarded about showing too much of himself. He didn't try that hard to give you any clarification about what he was going through.

A GIRLFRIEND: During sex, he's still performing and his expressions are overt, thought out, and not natural. He'd be composed, dressed to the nines, and his actions were intentional. I felt like he was performing. Even when he's light and easy, he's controlling himself.

A GIRLFRIEND: Even during sex, he was closed off and not giving you his real self, but, like, acting.

10

Let's Work

His Work Ethic Was Superhuman

SUSAN ROGERS: Prince was shy. He needed to be protected from certain social engagements so that he could stay himself. We were on the Purple Rain Tour, and he had been nominated for an Academy Award. The album was taking off, the movie was doing great, and he was on the cover of *Rolling Stone*. He was a big, big star, and he was about to do a show in LA. Elizabeth Taylor wanted to meet him. She was one of the biggest stars in Hollywood history and he wanted an Academy Award. She was the sort of person he needed to win over. Usually, after a show, he didn't want to hang around backstage and do the meet and greet. He did not want that kind of attention. He was very uncomfortable with it. He liked his privacy. "Purple Rain" was always the last song and as soon as it was over, he left the stage—shower, change clothes, then play an after-party, some little club until five or six in the morning, or we'd go to a recording studio. That's what we did every night. But this one night in LA, his management told him, "You have to do the thing you hate to do. You have to go backstage afterward, and hang out with Elizabeth Taylor and these celebrities. These are the people who've nominated you for an Academy Award. These people want to see you." Reluctantly, Prince agreed. I was on tour with him as his technician, and my sweetheart, my former boyfriend, the technician John Sacchetti was there, too. He wasn't working for Prince, but he was the one who had first told me about the job. He said, "Your dream job is waiting for you, Sue! Your dream job! Prince needs a technician, Sue!" He essentially got me the job. John was kind of tall and thin. He looked a little like a young John Travolta. I'd managed to get him a comp ticket, and John was really, really excited that he got to see this Prince show. John was an electronics genius. He got a patent for a digital telephone in the early 1980s. He was from an Italian family in a rough-and-tumble neighborhood of Quincy, Massachusetts, and he had this really strong Boston accent. He would say, "huspital" instead of hospital, and "mayan" instead of mine. John had come out to Minnesota to help me a few times and Prince adored him because John understood equipment and he was a good man with a heart of pure gold. Both Prince and John are working-class people. All three of us came from parents who struggled. That's the cloth we're cut from. Life is a struggle for many of us who work really hard. But that's what we respect. So, Prince is backstage after the show in the green room, standing there trying to talk to Elizabeth Taylor. The room is packed with Hollywood celebrities, and they're having this conversation, which I imagine was pretty one-sided. They're surrounded by bodyguards and you can imagine that all of these Hollywood folks are probably holding their breath and pinching themselves because at this moment they're backstage with two of the biggest celebrities in the world. Everyone in the room must've been thinking, *I'm doing great because look at me. I'm backstage with these people.* But there was one person in that room who saw something different than everyone else—John Sacchetti. He was there in the green room, waiting for his girlfriend, Sue, to finish wrapping up the cables and putting the tapes away. When he looked at Prince and Elizabeth Taylor, he saw a brother in trouble. He saw Prince standing there, catatonic, trapped in a conversation with this woman wearing a white mink coat and diamond earrings, her shoes worth more than John's whole life. He said, "I have to help the poor guy." John threw himself on the grenade.

An avid and enthusiastic drug user, John elbowed himself in between Elizabeth Taylor and Prince and stood with his back to Elizabeth Taylor. He got right up in Prince's face because this was the Boston way, and in his thickest Boston accent he yelled, "Prince that show was wicked awesome! I dropped two tabs of acid before and I smoked a big doobie during the show and I was drinking beer out of my eyes and Prince, that show was awesome!" That gave Prince a chance to escape. Prince's bodyguard, Gilbert Davidson, who, of course, knew who John was, grabbed Prince and whisked him away like, "Who let this nutcase backstage? Sorry, Elizabeth. Gotta go." I bet the whole room was thinking, *Why did this crude, uncouth, ruffian ruin our good time?* Prince told me that story and he was laughing the whole time. He said, "That guy saved me! I love that guy!" He saw that John had taken a bullet for him. John had seen Prince as he was—a kid who didn't want to be in that situation, a man who didn't want to be around people who saw him as a celebrity. He saw himself as a working man and he just wanted to be around people who facilitated his work. That's what he was all about—the work. Not the money or the fame or the celebrity. He was a working man whose work just happened to involve fame. That was one of his tools; it wasn't something inherent to who he was. Prince always had this blue-collar work ethic. Deep down, he didn't see himself as a celebrity like Elizabeth Taylor. He saw himself as like John Sacchetti, a blue-collar working man. Prince clocked in at the studio every day and started a new song and stayed until it was done, even if it took twenty-four or forty-eight or seventy-two hours. He was a worker.

ME: Prince routinely had studio sessions that lasted for days.

CHUCK ZWICKY: I had more than one forty-hour day with him. I've always admired the diligence and discipline that Prince has, and his work ethic. He just kept going and kept working until he had it.

SUSAN ROGERS: Imagine you're in the studio. You've been at Sunset Sound with Prince for twenty-four hours. You've just done something amazing and you know it's going to get heard. Work is really difficult when it's unrewarded or when it's thankless, but when you've just done a song that you know millions of people are going to listen to, that's some pretty good fuel. That gives you energy. It's thrilling. So, let's say you've just finished, it's six o'clock in the morning, sun's coming up, you're kind of delirious, you're wrapping cables, you're filling out the tape box labels, he goes and brushes his teeth, then he turns around, he comes back in, and he says, "Fresh tape." Fresh tape means, "I've got a song in my head, we're starting all over again." If he starts a song, he won't leave the studio until it's finished. Suddenly, we've got another twenty-four to go. It would make me laugh with joy and with excitement like, "Come on, let's do this." I found it thrilling. The things that were asked of us who worked for him were incredible. Staying up for twenty-four hours was just routine. There's so many times that I was up for forty-eight hours. There were times when I would do three days in a row. On one special occasion, I did four days in a row, ninety-six hours. The work was punishing and difficult. It was also very, very rewarding. He was good to us. When you did those exceptional days, those forty-eight-hour days, there'd be a little something extra in your paycheck. That was his way of saying thank you. But it was so much fun.[14]

A GIRLFRIEND: He had to finish because each song was in his head so clearly that if he didn't get it out, he'd have multiple songs going at once.

ALAN LEEDS: You can talk about Prince's work ethic, but sometimes there were occasions where what we saw as a work ethic was really just him trying to occupy himself because he couldn't sleep. He couldn't turn off his tapes in his head. Is that because he's just so bloody creative? Sure, that's part of it. Because there were always ideas floating in his head, ideas for songs, ideas for videos, ideas for movies, ideas for how his band should dress, ideas for how he should dress, ideas for what girl he would take to the gig next week. He couldn't turn it off. Sometimes, you could even see him struggling to do that where it might be late at night in a studio and you could see him physically starting to wane a little bit. Maybe he would start to talk about something trivial like, "Hey, have you seen me at basketball games this year?" Out of nowhere, he would change the subject to something that really wasn't of any major significance. You saw he was wrestling with trying to figure out how to just calm down and maybe call it a night. It didn't always work. As a result, he expected everybody to indulge his ideas. He wasn't a person to write the idea down and save it. It was like, *Okay, it's on the list, now I got to check it off the list as quickly as possible because the ideas are piling up*. It might mean him going home to bed at three and then getting up at four in the morning and going back to the studio to either finish the song he started earlier that night or start a new one from scratch. He was just a machine that wouldn't stop. His engineers said their hours were too long and they'd be working when they were just dead asleep at the board. But during the course of creation, there was no second-guessing. It just flowed and he didn't interrupt the flow. His biggest complaint in the studio was that the tape exchange never rewound quickly enough to suit him. He would be so impatient. If you lay down a track and then you're going to lay down a second track on top of it, you've got to rewind the tape back to square one. He would literally stand by the tape machine and try to egg it on to go faster. It felt like Carlton Fisk directing his famous home run, his body language trying to keep the ball fair as it flies through the air. He's trying to will the tape machine to move quicker, to rewind quicker. He used to talk to Susan Rogers and say, "Isn't there some way you can oil it or do something to speed it up? I get so tired of waiting for the tape to rewind." Nobody else is like that. It was like he was a conduit of music coming from somewhere else and I know that's been said of other artists who have been quite prolific, but the speed at which it came out of him was remarkable. He made a song a day. I really never saw anything like it. He would come in the building in the morning with a notebook that had lyrics and some music ideas jotted down and he'd go in the studio at one or two in the afternoon and by early evening he would have a rough mix of a finished song. And we're talking about a song that might have umpteenth parts. Two or three guitar parts, a bass part, a drum part, perhaps percussion, various keyboard parts, lead vocals, and sometimes background vocals that were stacked and you'd sit there and say to yourself, "How much time does it take to do what he did?" This was one person creating and still it was done so quickly that you couldn't imagine it'd be technically possible, let alone creatively possible. It was just mind-boggling. Then I'd go home because I'm off of work and the next morning, I'd come in and he'd done another song that night. There might be two, three, maybe four versions of the same song, done at different tempos with different arrangements, like, he would lay down a song and then decide to redo it a certain way, but the mountain of work, there's really no words. You just shook your head. It was staggering, it was astounding. Even those words pale. It was supernatural. He went through so many engineers because nobody, nobody, could physically keep up with his pace.

Susan Rogers: How did I keep up? There's the exhilaration of knowing you're working with this artist who's amazing, I was a fan of his, that helps a lot, and this is your dream job and I couldn't wait to hear what we were doing. The other thing is you learn certain tricks, you learn to drink a lot of water or you brush your teeth, which is a great way to trick your body into thinking it's morning and you've just begun the day. Or I'd drink coffee but not too much. You'd just train your body how to do it. But it was easy because I was very happy to be there. It's like Christmas Eve for little kids who are just too excited to sleep. I don't think I thought about myself. I don't think I thought about what I needed or what was good for me. I was a soldier who had a job to do. That was the mentality, like this was important and this needs to happen and I was very much a part of the machinery that was getting it done. I felt like we need to get these records made. We need to facilitate this man's work. I had the engineering and the audio technical skills that he didn't have, and I could facilitate recording him and I could be part of this assembly line that got all this work done. I was his hands. It was really rare for me to have a day off, so I knew that I had to stay well. Like anybody else, I got sick from time to time, but I did what he did. I took the DayQuil, drank a lot of water, brushed my teeth, and kept going. I felt very grateful to have that job. I loved the work we were doing and there was nowhere else I'd rather be. Like a good soldier, I didn't want to let down the team.

ME: When Prince was in the studio, he was working rapidly.

MORRIS HAYES: When he's playing in the studio, it's all one pass, done. I've never seen anybody that could go in there and knock stuff out so fast. He came to my house and he asked for a clean sound. I gave him a clean sound on my amp simulator. He played the part, one pass. He said, "Give me a dirty sound." Dirty sound. Played the part. One pass, thank you, good night. No red-light syndrome where the red light goes on and you mess up and it's like, "Oh, give me another take," none of that. He just hit it. He would do that all the time. It just was freaky. But he's working on a genius level, like working on a frequency that nobody else is working on and using a part of the brain that other people are not functioning with. He was seeing it finished in his head first and then playing.

SUSAN ROGERS: In the studio, it was never stop and wait for this guy to play this right. That never happened. He was such an expert. He was like Michael Jordan playing basketball. He was as good as it gets. So, anything he can imagine in his mind's ear, he can play. The execution's going to be perfect almost every time.

ALAN LEEDS: When you watched him work, you saw so little hesitation. While he was recording a drum track, he was already composing the bass track in his head. Then, he'd record the bass track while he was composing the guitar track in his head. You can talk about multitasking, but this is ridiculous. Some people take weeks to do one song because they concentrate on the drums for a couple of days and the bass for a couple of days. He's doing it all in one day and he's basically writing it all while he's performing the other. It was inhuman.

SUSANNAH MELVOIN: He moved around the studio in a blur. He was always like, "I know how to make the song work. I know how to create perfect drum tracks." He'd go in and pull out the LinnDrum or he'd get on the drums, but mostly it was a drum machine, and he would find a beat first. He'd find this amazing pattern, then he'd pick up the bass, lay down some bassline. Then he'd play guitar. Then there'd be keyboard overdubs. If he hadn't walked into the session with lyrics already, then you'd have to leave so he could sit on the floor with a big pad of paper and write lyrics. Then he would say, "Okay, set me up for a vocal." Then, "Okay, everyone out. Give me a minute." The studio would have to be empty for him to sing. He would never do a vocal in front of anybody. It was very rare that he would ever sing in front of anybody. Very rare. When he was singing "The Beautiful Ones" for *Purple Rain*, he's in there screaming and howling. It's take after take, after take, after take, and I was just like, "What is happening in there?" Once he was in the booth singing a vocal, it would take about three or four hours. Then he'd do some overdubs, mix it, and it'd be done. He loved the studio. He was always saying, "What am I doing in this moment that would inspire the music? When's the next moment I can be in the studio to record?" Every moment was about the music.

CHUCK ZWICKY: At the start of a session, he would have three ideas for songs and he would end with three mixed, completed songs. Pretty intense. He never spent an inordinate amount of time on one song. I've certainly worked with artists who will agonize over a single song for many, many days. I never saw Prince do that. He had a very clear idea in his head about what they needed to do, what it needed to sound like, and he could make his ideas come to life very quickly. He never second-guessed himself and he never scratched his head. He never said, "I wonder if this is good or not." If you had five kids on the playground with popsicle sticks and glue and you said, "Make a house," he's the one who immediately knows what the house is supposed to look like and puts it together quickly and it's done, where other people might spend hours trying to make the front steps. He's got vision and he knows intuitively what makes something work and what prevents something from working so if he leaves in something that seems a little odd, he knows intuitively whether that is going to help the overall impression or not. I mean, nothing he puts on his records is a mistake, although a lot of it sounds unusual.

ME: If he wasn't at home, he was on tour, and if he was on tour, his daily schedule was insane.

ALAN LEEDS: When we were on the road, he would be at a venue early. If sound check was 4:00, he was likely to be there at 3:00 or 3:30, sitting on the piano, or playing with his guitar, or trying to change something in the music, either fixing a part that he didn't like or inventing a new part or maybe writing a new song. The band would show up for sound check at 4:00, and sometimes they'd run through the show, but sometimes they'd just jam. There were certain songs he loved to jam on at rehearsals. One was "Body Heat." It's a relatively obscure James Brown track, but he loved "Body Heat," and he would have that band playing it over and over and over for thirty minutes straight. Sound checks usually ended between 5:00 and 5:30, but it might go on until 7:00 if he liked the groove, which would mean there's thousands of fans piling up outside the arena waiting to get in. Then they do the show and the band is on stage playing for three hours, then they'd go back to the hotel and two or three nights a week, Prince has me or the production manager or the promoter find a club in whatever town we're in to do a club show at one or two in the morning. Some of the band would be like, "Yay, that's exciting!" and some would be like, "Man, are you serious?" Maybe they were exhausted because they'd put in eight hours of music that day, but Mr. Music didn't care. He expected everybody to have that same capacity for working on music that he had, that same bottomless pit of energy, focus, attention, and interest that he had. But nobody else was capable of it.

WENDY MELVOIN: He had more stamina than anyone you could imagine. I think part of that was pathology.

BROWNMARK: Sometimes, people got to a point where they couldn't stand it anymore. You could just tell that they were hating sound check that day and we might be in the middle of a groove of a James Brown song and you'd be like, "Dude, we're not even playing this in the show!" But Prince is just feeling it and he's just like, "Turn this up. Give me some more piano. That sounds a little boxy. Put some EQ on it." Then, all of a sudden, he'd say, "Alright, see you guys in a few," and leave. We're all tired, hungry, and we got to go through hair, makeup and the whole shot because in the Revolution we had the big hair and the fancy outfits. For me, it took an average of two hours to get ready for a show with everything that had to be done, especially the hair. I had a little micro-curling iron and I'm curling each little hair like a Shirley Temple curl. It was an ordeal every night, and then after the show Prince is like, "You guys want to go play a club?" "No, Prince. We don't want to go play the club." But there's no such thing as the word no to Prince. So we'd go do a concert, only we wouldn't do our set: he would just call out songs. We did so much sound checking he could call out anything and we could keep it going. We'd tear the stage down until two or three or four in the morning and then you might get a call at 4:30. "I need you in the studio." It's like, "Dude, do you ever sleep?" And don't not answer because he'll send the bodyguards to knock on the door. He used to do that to me all the time when I wouldn't answer. I'd be pretending the ringer was off and then *ding-dong*. "Mark. Prince wants you at the studio." I'm like, "Goddamn." You had to get up and go. That was normal life. That was a continuous pattern. My running joke with him was, "Do you sleep like that?" Because he would be on all the time. Hair, clothes head to toe, everything just perfect. I'd be like, "Do you go to bed in your heels? Do you sleep?"

ALAN LEEDS: This was a guy who couldn't sleep.

GREG BOYER (Trombone, NPG 2001–2009): I never saw him sleep.

JEROME BENTON: I've never seen him sleep.

ME: Jerome met Prince in his teens and was close to him throughout his adult life, so that "never" is doing a lot of work. It appears Prince was a lifelong insomniac. He'd stay up for days at a time, working feverishly, then crash for half a day, and get right back to it.

JEROME BENTON: Even when we were traveling, I'd go to sleep, he's awake and when I'd get up to get some cereal, he's already up at the table working on music. I don't know how I did it. I really don't know how he did it.

MORRIS HAYES: This may be like breaking news right here, but I have to keep it real with you: Prince was a day-walker vampire.

MORRIS DAY: I would tap out at two or three in the morning like, "I gotta go." I'd go back to the hotel, come back the next morning, song is done. When we would tour, he always wanted us to show up at the venue at like three o'clock for an eight o'clock show. I could take issue with that except when I got there at three, this dude's already been there for hours and he's dressed up and made up and he's got the golf cart and he's riding around the venue like the arena was his home. His energy was incredible.

GREG BOYER: Being in his band is the musical equivalent of being in the fire department in the respect that you had to be ready to really, really play at a moment's notice. He would wake you up out your sleep in the middle of the night and say, "Hey, we're going to do a recording session," or "We're going to play at some club," or "We're doing an after party, be downstairs dressed and ready in fifteen." And you're like, "It's 3 a.m.!" He's the only person I ever played for where sleep wasn't guaranteed.

WENDY MELVOIN: It was insane. You had to have a lot of stamina. There were a couple gigs where thank God we were in good shape, or one of us would have been dead. I think we were in the south of France and we'd just finished shooting *Under the Cherry Moon*. We did a show in a circus tent. It was the dead of summer and it must have been 110 degrees in that tent. We did a full-on show and Prince and I had to get off stage and go right to EMTs with oxygen tanks because neither of us could breathe.

ME: How did she keep up?

WENDY MELVOIN: I had my girlfriend with me. I loved him. I loved Bobby. We were like Apollo 11. We were in a capsule together and we had to fly the machine, get off the moon, and get back to Earth together. That's what it was like. We were in a little capsule. And we were motivated because we knew that we were doing something great.

ME: Prince's aftershows were legendary. They were stripped-down affairs, just a man and his music, no artifice, just jamming, almost like we were watching him practice. I caught one of those at a Manhattan club called Club USA and another in Hollywood that went until dawn where there were like twenty people, and another at a club in Manhattan called Tramps. These were shows you had to just know about. There was no advertising, just a whisper campaign spread by people in the camp. In 1997, I was walking out of a Prince concert at Jones Beach in New York when one of his publicists touched my shoulder, pulled me close, and whispered, "He's going on at Tramps, around midnight." I said, "I'll be there." The show started after one. It was Prince on guitar, Questlove on drums, and D'Angelo on the keys. Whoa. They played for a few hundred people—I remember seeing Claire Danes there. We could hardly believe our luck when this soul funk supergroup walked out on stage. They jammed through "The Ballad Of Dorothy Parker" and "Brown Sugar," turning it into an amazingly funky groove that blew everyone away. This was a time when Prince was refusing to play any of his old, nasty, erotic songs, but after about fifteen minutes, Questlove—oh impish, irascible Questlove—looked at D'Angelo and even though he knew he shouldn't do it, he couldn't help himself. He called for the band to go into "Head" from *Dirty Mind*. As soon as they started, Prince was gone. He disappeared like a magician, poof. But it was magical while it lasted. Knowing Prince, after he left, he probably went straight to a rehearsal.

MORRIS HAYES: We rehearsed every day like people go to work every day. You punch a clock, you go in, and you rehearse.

ME: For Prince, rehearsing meant doing it 100 percent.

MORRIS HAYES: The kind of energy Prince brought in rehearsal was amazing. He didn't use half gas like, I'm gonna do a little bit here and turn it on later. Prince would come to rehearsal and be in full show mode. He came in calling out cities that we were gonna be going to like "LA! Tokyo!" He would be in full regalia, dancing, doing his whole thing. That was part of his conditioning. He did long rehearsals so he could perform for hours and be able to maintain that level the whole time. It was important to him to work out the way you were going to play and have everybody have to hit it hard all the time. He always said, "The way that you do it at rehearsal is the way you'll do it at the show. And you do the same show whether there's a crowd of ten or ten thousand. You play the same way. You do your very best every time you pick up your instrument." That's what he was about. I don't know how he could sustain that level of energy all the time, but that's how serious he was about music and about doing his best. Even if it was just me and him, he was adamant. "If you're gonna play, let's play it right." I remember once, we were at his house in LA, just me and him hanging out, and I'm playing drums. We're grooving. Prince can play like that for hours, but I don't even play drums. I can kind of play, but I can't go for like two hours just playing drums, bro. I got tired and started switching up the groove and he got all frustrated and furious like, "Why are you doing that? You had a groove!" He put his guitar down and said, "Morris, if you're gonna play, play for real. Play it like we would if there was an audience." He was so pissed off that I didn't take it as seriously as he did. He was just like, "You have to respect it. If you're gonna play, then play, or don't play at all."

BOBBY Z.: We did one groove for fifty-seven minutes. The guy was relentless.

WENDY MELVOIN: We spent twelve hours a day together working out songs. We did one groove in a song for eight hours. There were days where we could play one sixteen-bar groove for hours on end, just mastering the groove because the groove sounded good. That group of people, we were all totally into doing that. And maybe Prince would be going around to different instruments and trying different things or dance moves. Every rehearsal was videotaped, so he'd be testing his moves to watch later.

JEROME BENTON: We would do one song for eighteen hours. You would play it over and over and over and Prince would add little parts here and there. Then you'd play it over and over and over and over. The whole day on one song. It was an amazing process. It gave us a work ethic that allowed us to be second to none.

BROWNMARK: I hated those rehearsals at first. Like, "Come on, man. How many times can you play the same thing?" But he told me his philosophy once. He said, "The more you learn it, the more it becomes who you are. And then you don't have to practice it. You just play it. It becomes who you are." So we played 'til we developed that sort of deep feel. When that happens, when the song becomes second nature to you, you hit the stage and your concentration isn't on the musician-ship, we already got that, it's on the dancing, the choreography, the energy. It's on everything else. Because the stuff was so ingrained and embedded in our heads, he could switch stuff, he could add stuff, he could do all these little tricks and signals and we'd be ready because we're not thinking about the music. We got that in our soul.

JEROME BENTON: After the band finished rehearsal, he would leave and go to his own rehearsal.

ME: Or he went to the studio. How did he keep up this superhuman pace? To anyone who knows anything about the 1980s, to hear of someone in the '80s working intensely for days on end without sleep-ing says "cocaine." But Prince was not using cocaine.

JEROME BENTON: I'm just putting it out there for everybody: he didn't do no drugs when I was around in the '80s. I did not see it. I did not hear about it. And I was looking. I was looking in his eyes, I was looking for that demon because I don't need to be around when you go into a seizure and you want me to give you mouth-to-mouth. Honestly, God strike me dead right here—I've never seen him do drugs and I never heard about him doing drugs. How was it that he stayed up for three days in a row? I don't know.

SUSANNAH MELVOIN: In his marathon sessions, he would eat cake. He loved, loved, loved cake, mostly vanilla with chocolate frosting. I would make that for him on a regular basis and that would keep him going. He would come up from the studio, take another slice, go back down. That's how he kept going.

ME: Prince prized sobriety and absolute self-control. He was the guy who told others to not drink or do drugs.

BOBBY Z.: He didn't drink. He was never a drinker.

JEROME BENTON: We'd be hanging out at Studio 54 or one of those places with Grace Jones across the room, where all the great white artists are trying to get behind the rope. We're sitting back there and I'm getting my drink on and I wouldn't get to three drinks before he would slide my drink away. He'd be like, "You cool." He didn't want us getting drunk. He said, "You're cool. You don't need that." Not only was he not getting drunk, but he didn't want people around him getting drunk.

MORRIS DAY: If I felt like I needed to get high, I'd split and go do my thing because he just wasn't the person to do that around.

JILL JONES: I never saw him using drugs. I never saw anything. As I think back now, I would say, probably, drinking DayQuil or NyQuil in the middle of the show while you're on tour may not have been a good thing, but this is guy who if he even heard about people doing drugs, he'd just slag them off completely. And I would not have missed an opportunity to call him a hypocrite. So I didn't know about him using drugs. Not at that point.

ALAN LEEDS: During the Purple Rain Tour, he somehow caught drift of the fact there were people on the crew who were using cocaine.

MORRIS DAY: I heard that during the *Purple Rain* time and thereafter, there was coke amongst the crew, security, and even some bandmates. There was a lot of coke floating around.

ALAN LEEDS: Prince called me and his manager Steven Fargnoli into his dressing room and wanted to know about it. Steven had to run around and ask everybody if they were abusing drugs, as if anybody was going to confess, like "Yes I'm using drugs. You can fire me today." The whole crew was using blow. It was the '80s, it was rock 'n' roll, and it was a schedule that was inhumane. The people who were moving our gear around from show to aftershow to the next town worked their butts off and hardly got any sleep. I suspect that whoever was dealing coke to the crew had a very lucrative franchise for about six months, but it didn't touch the performers. That band, as bands go, was amazingly clean. There was a little weed smell in the hallway of the hotel every once in a while, and maybe on an off night, somebody might know somebody who had a little bit of blow and took a sniff for the party, but this band was clean. There were no druggies. Prince would not have put up with it. The atmosphere around him was spooky clean and in rehearsals, you better not show any evidence of the crew or anybody doing anything. If he saw two crew guys in a corner looking suspicious, he'd have me check on it. He had a borderline paranoia about having anybody around who was into drugs.

ME: All of that is why it's so tragic that, according to several people, Prince began using opioids in the 1990s.

ALAN LEEDS: For the majority of Prince's career, he was in discomfort and I'll use that word instead of pain because I'm sure there were a lot of nights you would call it pain and other nights, it just an annoying discomfort. You're talking about a guy who dances up a storm in high heels.

ME: For many years, Prince suffered with chronic pain in his hips, knees, and hands. This may have begun with a huge hit his body took during one of the rehearsals for the Purple Rain Tour.

ALAN LEEDS: The Purple Rain Tour had the famous bathtub scene where he would climb up into a bathtub. At the end of the song, it would go to dark. We were rehearsing that part in a local arena in

Minnesota and the tub fell apart. It broke and fell ten or twelve feet to the stage floor with him in it. I never moved so fast in my life. I was on the sound board with the stage manager and we were just looking at it from a geometric point of view just to get an idea of what the scene was going to look like and, suddenly, we saw that the tub hadn't been fastened properly. We saw it ever so slowly start to tip, knowing full and well at one point he's going to slide out and down and hurt himself. We started running and yelling but it was too late. He and the tub crashed to the ground. We all went straight to the hospital with fears that something bad could have happened to him. It looked bad. There was a certain amount of panic. It turned out that he had just gotten some bumps and bruises, but after that, his back hurt day after day. He started the tour with a really sore back and it never really went away. He's doing all this dancing and jumping around in high heels and then in LA, he slipped and hurt his knee. I had to get a doctor because it really, really hurt and this was only adding to the problem. He got some meds and manned up and finished the tour, but I don't think his hip and his leg were ever completely normal after that.

Susannah Melvoin: He saw the tub falling as a sign from God telling him he needed to repent and change something. He went to Wendy and Lisa, apologized for something, and told them what had happened, that he felt it was a sign from God, because he actually thinks that God's talking to him.

Me: Prince's chronic physical pain, his need to perform, his aversion to doctors, and his willingness to use opioids made for a dangerous cocktail that would lead him down a dangerous path toward addiction far earlier than fans realized.

11

Let's Pretend We're Married

Prince Pops the Question (1984–1985)

BOBBY Z.: *Around The World In A Day* was in the can before we played the first *Purple Rain* show in Detroit. He was ready to release that and we'd just started the first of 105 shows for *Purple Rain*. He couldn't wait to get *Around the World In A Day* out.

SUSAN ROGERS: It is my favorite of the records we did together because it was the last time he was innocent. This was Prince before Prince. We were at home in Minnesota getting ready for this movie to come out, getting ready for the *Purple Rain* album to be released, preparing and rehearsing for a big tour. It wasn't clear that he was about to become a star. This could've gone either way. He was releasing a semiautobiographical movie about his life. What if the critics didn't like it? What if his R&B/soul audience didn't like the big rock ballad that's reminiscent of Journey or Bob Seger? What if this didn't work? It could have killed his career. But while we were making it, Prince was happier and more optimistic than I ever saw him. After making it, really, after releasing *Purple Rain*, everything changed. But, while we were making *Around the World in a Day*, he was still innocent, still a kid. Songs like "Raspberry Beret," "Pop Life," and "Around the World in a Day" have an exuberance about them that's easily felt. It has that gratitude. "Tambourine" has an unabashed admission of self-satisfaction. It's about masturbation. And "Condition of the Heart" is one of my favorites because it's one of his most honest lyrics. Prince rarely admitted that he was in pain. Rarely, rarely, rarely. He never wanted to admit that he was hurting, but on "Condition of the Heart" he's saying, "A sometimes lonely musician." He was hurt, and it's a vulnerable moment for him. Those moments were rare. That's perhaps my favorite album.

SUSANNAH MELVOIN: After *Purple Rain* was done, Prince had this moment like, *What do I do now?* He was recording a lot of music, but nothing had really congealed. He's just recording, constantly recording. He's at the warehouse, behind the console, tape is up, and he's endlessly recording, not sure where he's going. Then my brother Jonathan and Lisa's brother David came to Minneapolis for a visit. Dave was the most interesting, cool person ever, a great poet, an amazing musician. He had taught himself how to read and write Arabic. My brother was the same. For fun, he would read the string section for "The Rite of Spring" [by Stravinsky].

SUSAN ROGERS: Jonathan and David brought this song called "Around the World In A Day."

SUSANNAH MELVOIN: Wendy said, "We've got to play this for Prince; he's here. Let's play it for him." Wendy gave him the tape, he went into the car and put it on, and the first thing he said was "Can I have it?" David and Jonathan were like, "Sure."

SUSAN ROGERS: Prince loved it.

SUSANNAH MELVOIN: Prince barely changed the song. He put a new verse in but the rest is Jonathan and David's. I don't think Prince had ever even heard Arabic music before. He'd never heard finger cymbals. He didn't know that any of that even existed. That song became a huge influence on him and that's how that whole movement started. It was inspired by the song "Around the World in a Day." It was not, "I want to do a Beatles, *Sgt. Pepper's* record." All the critics were wrong. He said, "They're wrong about that. That's not my psychedelic record." You have to understand that Prince had this ability to be inspired. His big moments in his musical life were inspired by songs. This one song in particular, "Around the World in a Day," became the foundation for this new period.

SUSAN ROGERS: The message in this record was, "There is an 'us'. We have created a world." *Purple Rain* is one man's masterpiece and it's about one man's most artistic thoughts. Other musicians played on it, but it's close to being a solo album. So, after you've conquered yourself, what do you want to do? You want to be able to say, "The world that I'm creating includes all of us and we're all different colors and we're all different ages. Look at the cover and you can see that. We have different abilities and disabilities. We come from different backgrounds. We might take drugs, we might not. We might be bold. We might be shy. This is an 'us'," and that's why there's the rainbow color palette on *Around The World In A Day*. That's why *Around The World In A Day* is the way it is. Prince was saying, "Now I'm going to show you the depth of my musicality and my artistry. Now I'm going to show you my breadth." He was also getting closer to Susannah, even though their relationship continued to be a rocky roller coaster.

SUSANNAH MELVOIN: Being in a relationship with Prince wasn't easy. He hated the fact that Wendy and I needed to be with each other. I mean, you can't break that bond. You can't stop how Wendy and I are together. That's from the womb. He did not like that. Wendy paid for it and I paid for it many, many times and it was not fun. He hurt my sister deeply with trying to keep me away from her. I was the bird in the gilded cage sort of thing and I didn't know how to get out. I would literally sneak to make a phone call to my sister. Somehow, he'd fucking find out and I would literally be frozen in fear. I was like, *Why am I so scared of this dude? What is happening to me?* This was something I'd never experienced. I'm afraid that this guy's going to catch me doing something that's completely natural and normal. Anyone in their right mind would walk out and say, "Are you kidding me? I can't call my sister?" But I didn't. It still pains me to think that I was that young and dumb. I allowed a lot of his bad behavior to sort of slide. But he did not buy into people's relationships. He didn't understand anyone having an intimate connection. His intimate connections were his made-up connection to God. He never had any sort of quiet time or internal time ever. He was very disconnected from personal relationships. And he got worse and worse at this over time. We were very, very, close but there wasn't that ability to be honest with difficult feelings. For me, those difficult feelings could be, "I don't like the way you treat me," or "I don't like being alone, Prince. I want to be your one and only. You say I am, but I'm not."

ME: Somehow, things kept moving forward.

SUSANNAH MELVOIN: It's summertime and we're in Minneapolis. Bobby Z. and his now wife Vicki Norby were having their wedding. Prince and I had gotten into a tiff. It's hard to say an argument because I wasn't arguing with him. He was pissed about something, something about me, and I didn't know what it was. I was like, "Okay. I got to get to the wedding." So we're all at Bobby's wedding, it's a beautiful day, and these two beautiful people are getting married. Vicki is sort of an honorary band member and Prince loved her. I'm sure he wanted to be at that wedding, but whatever. I'm at the wedding and at the end, after they've done their final, "You may kiss your wife," I get a tap from someone. They say, "Prince is here." I turn around and he's standing at the back of the wedding hall. He's watched the whole thing. Then he leaves. Then we all hear, "Meet at the warehouse. He wants to record." Bobby and Vicki were like, "He wants to record? We're leaving!" "No, he needs to record." Everybody was like, "Okay, this must be super important." They get to the warehouse, and there's this song to record, "Empty Room." It's a tearful, beautiful song. My red hair is on the mirror and he's just bereft that I'm gone. He's so sad. He's got to have everybody playing on this song now. So they do it, they finish, and he leaves for New York. The following day, I get a call from Alan Leeds saying, "Prince needs you to come to New York." I thought he wanted to just get away. I said, "I'm tired." Alan insisted. "He needs you in New York." So, I get on a flight and go. At the hotel, we have a beautiful reunion. He's a different guy. There is something that's shifted. I sensed the shift. I'm not sure if it was the wedding, or that he got the music out, or maybe the music was like his apology, and we can start over again. I don't know, but I was all for it and we had a beautiful night. The following day, he said, "Do you want to go shop?" Yeah, what girl doesn't want to go shop? We get in the car and he says to the limo driver, "Do you know any jewelry stores nearby?" The guy says, "Yeah, as a matter of fact, just up here on such-and-such is Van Cleef & Arpel's." "Okay. Stop there." We stop right in front of the store, get out, and open the door. They're all waiting for us like they knew he was coming. All the carpets rolled out. "What can we give you?" and "Which diamond do you want to see?" He said, "Show me your biggest diamond." I'm looking at him, like, what are you doing? They take us back down these hallways to this little room and they bring out boxes of these beautiful rings with lights that are being reflected off of mirrors and velvet and all this stuff. I'm looking like, "Wow, that one's pink." Then I said, "Oh, a friend of mine, when I was growing up, she worked as a jeweler and there's such a thing as a canary diamond." Poof! Here come the canary diamonds. They start bringing out engagement rings in all various sizes. Then we see this beautiful white diamond. "Oh, wow that's, lovely." Prince said, "Will you try that on?" I try it on and it fits perfectly. It's six carats. It was enormous. It was beautiful. I was like, "Wow, that's beautiful." I was not thinking anything larger was going on. We had had such ups and downs. We'd been together three years off and on, maybe more, but he'd seen many people in between and I'd seen somebody so who knows where we are. I take the ring off and give it back but Prince said, "No, no, no. Put it back on." I looked at him like, "It's got to be really expensive." He said, "Just put it on." I did, and he was like, "We'll take it!" I said, "You're gonna what?" It had a $90,000 price tag on it. I said, "You're kidding me." He said, "No, why not?" We walk out, and that's it. There's no, "Will you marry me?" There's no proposal. And I wasn't going to be like, "You just bought me this beautiful engagement ring, where's the proposal on your knee?" I wasn't going to make him say it. I wasn't going to do that. That's not me. I wasn't going to spoil what I knew he was trying create in that moment. But I am thinking, *Good Lord, you just spent a shit ton of money on a ring.* It's a beautiful ring and he's super excited and he's all sparkly about it. Then he says we're going to fly to Paris the next day.

ME: They were preparing to film another movie, *Under the Cherry Moon,* which they would shoot in Nice, France. Susannah was going to be the female lead.

SUSANNAH MELVOIN: We spend a week in Paris. We're staying at the Crillon, which overlooks the Arc de Triomphe. We had a beautiful week together. We played guitar, we walked the streets, and I saw a side of him I had never experienced before. That week, he was completely and totally devoted to me. For once, no recording, no studio, just me and him. At some points, he would say, "Let's call Wendy and Lisa and play guitar." We would call them and we'd have our acoustic guitars and we'd be playing stupid, silly songs. That meant so much. We became the four, that group of four again and in my mind, I actually thought, *He sees me. He's seeing me. He's seeing my closeness to my sister, he's accepting our bond, he's normalizing it,* which is something that I hadn't seen him do before. Before, he sort of pushed the world away from us. He kept me hidden a lot. All of a sudden, he was bringing all of us together. Me, Wendy, Lisa, him. Even though we were in Paris and they weren't, we were all this unit. It was wonderful. I was so happy. Then, one morning at like 5 a.m., he comes into the hotel room. He'd been up all night. He has the balcony doors open, and he says, "Susannah." I'm like, "Yeah, what?" He's like, "I've got to talk to you. I've got to talk to you." I sit up and I look at him. He's pale. Chalky white. He looks frightened. I was like, "Are you okay? Did you see something?"

He's like, "Just come here." We go stand out on the balcony, and says, "Come sit up here." So I sit up on the top there and I'm looking at him and I said, "What is it?" He said, "Well...I don't want you to be the lead in the movie." I said, "Oh? Okay." Then he said, "I want you to be my wife." What? Then he said it again. And he meant it. He said, "I want you to be my wife. I want to marry you." I said, "Yes. Of course. I want to be your wife." And, we were engaged. After that, we flew to the south of France, to Nice, to do more location scouting for the film and spent a few months there. It was all really wonderful until shooting was done. Because he was also recording the *Parade* record and Wendy and Lisa were flying from Nice to London and writing tons of material and he was saying, "Write it all. You do it. Can you do the string arrangements on this? Lisa, can you do the arrangement on that?" That whole record is Wendy and Lisa. It really is. Not that they wrote it all. They didn't.[15] I mean, they wrote "Mountains," but I mean there was a real collaborative thing with the three of them then.[16]

ME: But collaborating with Prince is far harder than it sounds.

BOBBY Z.: The girls would send him things and he'd go, "Nah." They'd work their ass off and he'd go, "I want it more, I don't know, more something." The girls were looking for things that didn't exist and Prince wasn't explaining himself at all. It was very stressful. But it's a beautiful record and that's them, that's their influence. Their music was always so beautiful. It's about being stuck in France and about Prince thinking more deeply about musicianship and percussion.

SUSANNAH MELVOIN: Between him and me, things were starting to change. Once again, Prince did not feel comfortable with my relationship with Wendy. It was like, somehow, he said, "If you're going to be married to me, I'm not going to have my wife have a relationship with her twin sister." He was compartmentalizing. Music here, relationship there. But it started to really get bad. Like Eric Leeds says, is this a bad guy with good moments or a good guy with bad moments? I think it's got to be close to fifty-fifty. And I would know when it was coming because there was a look he'd get in his eyes. *Holy shit, he's going to that place. The bad guy's coming.* His eyes would change color. They'd turn really lucid and green. Like really, really, really lucid and shiny when he was in a really bad place. And he'd get very aggressive in his demeanor. He was really, really frightening.

ME: She went back to Minneapolis.

SUSANNAH MELVOIN: We bought a house in Minneapolis right near where we were building Paisley Park, right up the street. Bought like two hundred acres of land on this beautiful property and while he was filming, I was in Minneapolis gutting the house, getting the studio together, working on furnishing it, and making it our home. But we never got married. There was not even talk of a wedding. We never planned anything. I wasn't the kind of girl who has dreams of wedding dresses. I never thought that way. My version of planning was the house. In my mind, that was my wedding. That was my future with him. I was creating a home. The hoopla of getting married was not the thing to define me and my relationship with him. What I remember is talking to him on the phone and saying, "The house is done, the house is done! I can't wait for you to see it," and then him walking in, and seeing the house. I was just like, "This is our house. This is where we're going to start it all." To me, that was my moment with him. That was the wedding, for me, seeing him walk into the space that I had created for us.

ME: Several women said that when Prince gave you a lengthy task like choosing or making a home, that was a bad sign.

JILL JONES: I knew when he would give you busy work to do, like, go find a new apartment or go fix up a house or something like that, that meant you were out. You were like, *While I'm here, what's happening on the other side of the world?*

ME: As Jill said elsewhere, "When you got an album completed, you were done as a romantic interest. Some guys send you flowers, Prince would give you an album." She also said he separated women from the rest of his world and from the rest of theirs, giving himself total control.

JILL JONES: He created a sense of isolation around the target. Isolated from their surroundings, from their friends, their family. You become incredibly vulnerable. We were all moved to Minneapolis, where we all were away from our friends, and then sort of thrown into this pit with a bunch of other women vying for his attention. He brought me in to work with Vanity 6 and he put me on their payroll. They paid for me on the tour. They did. Vanity was not cool with that because everybody wants to pick their own background singers, but no, Prince threw me on the same bus with her when we're all kind of dating him. You feel like Prince's cargo, Prince's chattel, his property. I guess you find some kind of solace in thinking you're in some special league, but it's really dehumanizing after a while. He loved to put people in the same room just to see how they would react to each other or treat each other, but it was incredibly difficult seeing the insecurity that reeked from every single woman. I couldn't imagine someone that famous wanting to settle down at the height of their fame so I was realistic about that but, it hurt to see a ton of different women coming through.

ME: He kept a vice grip on the ones he liked most.

ANNA FANTASTIC: He was controlling. I had gotten an offer to do a movie in Europe and he said, "Well, if that's what you want to do, then you need to be there." I knew what that meant. It's either you do that or you are with me. He liked his own way. It was my way or the highway, but in a very kind way. It was an unequal relationship. Some relationships, there's a give and take, but with him there was no give and take. It was what he wanted all the time.

JILL JONES: Sometimes, I thought he was paternal. He wanted me to explore the world, and I did, but it was also incredibly difficult to leave without him becoming incredibly angry. He kept me on the label until their contract expired, so it wasn't like he would let me go.

ME: He always kept the revolving door turning.

JILL JONES: He'd tell me about him and one of his girlfriends and then within an hour, I was on a plane to Minneapolis or Paris or wherever to see him. When I was leaving, Sheila was on her way in. It was strange. Every girl was aware of the other girls. When we were all on the bus together, you'd be sitting there going, "Okay, if she's not with him and she's not and I'm not, then who the hell is he with tonight?" It was really hurtful at times. The thing that really started to mess with me was that he was physiologically confused. I once told him that. I said, "You're becoming physiologically confused because there's just too many people, too many bodies, too much." By that, I mean our bodies are maps. There's a sense memory attached to sex. If there's too many people, you can become confused. There was a sadness to a lot of things around me and him but then there was this primal thing, this physicality, and I think that got in the way all the time. A lot of our songs are a little bit primal, not so love song-y.

ME: Remember, they did "Lady Cab Driver," a lusty, carnal record that breaks down to Prince giving his reasons behind each pump.

JILL JONES: We did a song called "4 Lust," very wanton stuff. It was difficult to work together without being physical.

ME: But no matter how close you were, you were always sharing him.

JILL JONES: Everybody just adored him and found him kind of irresistible. He made you feel like you could do anything. Plus, he had this bizarre habit of, I guess, there were the elite ones and then there were just the one-nighters. And I guess maybe there was some solace for those of us who felt like we were in the elite group, I don't know. But it became a little cheap after a while to see what he entertained and sometimes it became a little bit disgusting. I could tolerate the girls from the earlier days. But the girls that started to traipse in and out, or even walking in a room and going, "Who is it?" That was something I just couldn't live with. It was too much. My mother used to always be like, "I can't believe you girls at your age are going through this shit." And she was right, I mean, we were. I don't even know what to say. It was really difficult to just see girl after girl after girl and some-times the same girl over and over, because a lot of things that maybe I thought were special, suddenly didn't seem special if I knew that ten or fifteen other people had experienced them. Those were the things that our arguments would consist of. And I almost had to compart-mentalize people, things, settings. My mom always asked, "Is his attention sincere?" I don't think she really thought it was. Otherwise, he wouldn't have tried to destroy me as much as he did when I tried to leave. But there was a point where I just couldn't take it anymore.

ME: But when she was upset, he knew just how to reel her back in.

JILL JONES: During the Purple Rain Tour, we had a big blowout. It was pretty critical. It was bad. I didn't talk to him for the rest of his tour, but I would show up to gigs. I remember one night at the Forum, he had one of the bodyguards bring me to the front of the stage and he sang some songs directly to me. I was just looking around like, *Oh my God. This is so embarrassing.* He was, basically, apologizing. After that tour, I had to go into the hospital for surgery. When I woke up, this other man, who owned a yacht company and was trying to court me, had sent a roomful of flowers like an adult and my mom was rooting for him, but Prince had sent all these children's toys and balloons, and candy necklaces, every candy you could think of. It was like Dylan's Candy Bar, just everything, and I was like, "This is so nice!" I felt like I was ten years old. You go, "Wow, who does that?" My mom's sitting in the corner going, "Oh my God, she's going to make the wrong deci-sion again." Right after I got home, Prince called and we didn't really talk about the surgery, nothing about me at all. But we picked right back up. I think Prince had the ability to make every girl feel special, from the numerous ones he was dating to those who were listening to his records. Plus, he always created this unpredictability. He always kept a door open that he could come back in through, whether it's two weeks later, two months later, or two years later. Many of the women I've met, he just waltzed in and out of their lives. He could make women feel that they were the only ones, even though, in reality, they knew they weren't.

ME: She was surprised to find herself in the painting that was the cover of *Around The World In A Day* among the many musicians in Prince's life.

JILL JONES: He showed me the cover and said, "That's you." He told me I was the old woman who was crying in that green dress and those ugly little boots. They were these boots I used to wear in the '80s when Prince and I went thrifting a lot. But I'm crying. I said, "There's Sheila [E], she's like a cat and there's Susannah playing the violin. Why am I crying?" He goes, "Because I'm gonna know you forever." And I was like, "Wow. But why's a sister gotta be so broke down? Why am I always crying in everything? I'm crying in *Purple Rain*. I'm crying in everything we do." And he goes, "Because I'm gone." I said, "Well, where are you gone to?" He said, "I'm up the ladder." So, that was kind of strange.

ME: Prince wrote "She's Always In My Hair" about Jill.

JILL JONES: He brought it over and gave me the cassette. He was trying to make up for an argument that we had had. I remember listening to it and I was like, "He wants to make up with me." But I had an issue with the lines in the third verse about maybe he'd marry me, maybe not. I was not comfortable with that depiction. I was like, *Really? So, no matter how many women, I'm going to be there?* That fell right into my mom's concept of him and pimpdom and me being the bottom bitch. That was just a little too deep for me. Also, when he was going out with Kim Basinger, that was a little bit like, *Oh my God, how many of these do we have to keep going through?* I had boyfriends intermittently, in between being with Prince, but there was always this tension between us, and yet he was always still my best friend at times.

ME: Through all the craziness and the pimping and the toxicity, she still loved him. But once the wild roller coaster of dating him was truly behind her, nothing was ever the same.

JILL JONES: It was very difficult to find anybody who matched up or was even interesting. Going from him to a regular guy who was taking me out to dinner and a movie was not gonna cut it. That was really difficult. I ended up dating people with even more dysfunctional personalities.

12

Manic Monday

He Could Be Amazing,
He Could Be a Terror

MORRIS DAY: Alexander O'Neal was supposed to be the lead singer of The Time. Alexander's a great singer, but he was just in a different headspace. He said, "I got to have more paper." He wanted more money than we could cough up then. We didn't have it. And after we went through a series of singers and nothing worked out, Prince said to me, "Why don't you do it? Why don't you sing?" I said, "I don't want to do that. I don't want to sing. I'm a drummer. I'm comfortable behind the drums. I want to play drums." He said, "You could do it, man." Back in Grand Central, I used to come up and sing a couple songs in front of the band, so I had done it. He'd seen me do it. So he kept saying, "You should sing." I said, "I don't know what to do as a lead singer of a band."

ME: Morris Day became one of the baddest, most compelling front men of his time, a man who commanded the stage so deftly that he almost stole *Purple Rain* from Prince. He would strut on stage in full pimp mode, the epitome of cool, flirting with the audience while letting them know that he was in love with himself. It's amazing to think of him being afraid to sing lead and wondering, *How the hell do* *you even do that?* But even though he was inexperienced and nervous, Prince saw something in him and gave him an opportunity and gave him confidence and gave him time to grow into the role.

MORRIS DAY: He said, "Just be cool. Put your hand in your pocket and be cool." And that's what I did. So, if you notice in the "Cool" video, my hand never comes out of my pocket. I'm strongly taking his advice at that point. The whole song, I'm leaning forward, I'm walking, hand in the pocket. He definitely pushed me out there to be the lead singer and I'm glad he did.

ME: Prince put Morris through years of tutelage that Morris called boot camp, which meant recording, rehearsals, choreography, everything.

MORRIS DAY: We just ran it and ran it and ran it, uh, to the point where you could do the show in your sleep. By the time we got to '84, once we started going on tour with him, the rehearsals were rigorous.[17] We would rehearse around the clock and then go out and do the shows and come back and rehearse some more. We did that for months at a time. And each time we went out on tour and every time I stepped on stage, I realized something different in myself and how I wanted to convey myself and come across as an artist. I just kept adding to my repertoire and doing the little things and seeing what people liked and putting that in the spank bank and saving it for later and doing it again.

ME: Prince, as a teacher, could be rough on students.

MORRIS DAY: He never bit his tongue. If I'm in the studio and I'm doing a vocal track, sometimes he was like, "Man, that was really good, let's do that again," but he might say, "You know, if I had Charlie Wilson in here, I wouldn't be having that problem. He's a real singer." Just saying the craziest shit to the point where you would want to retaliate. When I sang "777-9311" he went out to dinner with some chick while I was there for hours working on this vocal. I layered it; I did everything. He comes back. He's like, "You wasted all this time. I don't even like it. You don't even sound right on this." I left the studio with that thought in mind. I had to hear all of that shit and internalize that and I went to bed thinking, *Damn, I got to attack these vocals again.* I come back the next morning and he's a whole other person. He's like, "Man, I love it! You sound young. I love the way you sang this." So we kept it. You never knew what you were going to get with Prince from one day to the next.

ME: The Time started as an outlet for Prince, a place for him to put his musical ideas that were too hypermasculine for his own brand, but it was also a way for Prince to motivate himself.

JILL JONES: A lot of times, he saw that he was giving The Time something that was so great that it was in competition with his music, so he'd go back and write something else to compete. He was essentially competing with himself—that was another bizarre thing about him.

ME: The Time was also Prince's way of reflecting what he loved about Morris.

MORRIS DAY: The Time was an alter-ego band for Prince. There were songs that he had cut for himself and set aside that we ended up using. We had always hung out, André Cymone, myself, and Prince. The three of us, in the early days, we went everywhere together—clubs, all of that. Prince and I started to get tight because he noticed a crazy side to me. The way I laughed, the kind of shit I would talk, and so when we started putting the band together, it was his alter ego in one sense, but it was also him extracting from me. He would gravitate to things that I would say and he was like, "We got to put that on the record!" Like the way I laugh—he was like, "We got to put that on the record!" So he was bringing forward a lot of my personality and putting it on the record. It started it was an alter-ego situation for Prince and then it turned into a Frankenstein-monster situation. And it was just from years of boot camp.

ME: Over time, thanks to Prince's encouragement, his lessons, and his influence, Morris grew. He became a worthy extension of Prince's persona, the badass macho pimply stud who lived at the far edge of his masculinity.

MORRIS DAY: I don't think I ever would've been front man without Prince's help and advice.

ME: What Prince did for Morris he did for lots people—he had a strong desire to help people and an ability to see more in them than they could see in themselves and a willingness to giving them the opportunity and the confidence to help lift them to new plateaus. So many musicians said he helped them be better than they ever had been.

ERIC LEEDS: Prince was very good at being able to reach inside you and bring things out of you that wouldn't be what I'd naturally pull out of myself. One time in a recording session, he told me, "I want you to play a solo on this song, but I want you to approach it as if you just picked up the saxophone for the first time in your life." Now, I was a huge fan of Miles Davis and I related it to the same thing Miles used to tell Herbie Hancock and Wayne Shorter: he'd say, "I don't pay you to play for me what you know. I pay you to play for me what you don't know." I would try to look at it in the same way. I could bring whatever I knew about the saxophone and my musical experience to the table, but he was really looking for something more than that.

ALAN LEEDS: He's saying, "Forget everything you know and just let it flow and give me something as emotionally honest as possible."

ERIC LEEDS: I really enjoyed going in the recording studio with him, and it wasn't about whether or not the song we were working on was something I would want to go home and listen to. I was there because his ability to get things out of me as a saxophone player was bigger than what I might've done for him if left to my own devices. Being stretched like that is what I appreciated. Those are experiences that I treasure. You don't get an opportunity to work with somebody on that rarified level of music very often.

ME: Prince did that sort of lifting up for all sorts of people.

STEVE PARKE (Photographer): With Prince, you got chances that nobody else was likely to give you. He would see your creative brain and your creative abilities and challenge you and push you and bring out what you could do that you wouldn't do for yourself.

ME: Prince changed Randee St. Nicholas's life just like he changed Morris Day's.

RANDEE ST. Nicholas (Photographer, video director): I photographed him and then he called me over to look at the pictures and he goes, "I want you to direct my next music video." I said, "I'm not interested in being a director. I'm a photographer. I don't really want to direct a music video." He goes, "Yes, you do." I go, "I do?" He said, "Yeah. I think you're the one to change the way I'm perceived visually." Now, he's not a guy you say no to, and he's not a guy you question, but I said, "You can have anyone. I don't know why you want me." He said, "I think you see me." I went home and I thought about it and I thought, *You just can't say no to him.* He's not that guy. You want to please him, you want to do whatever he wants you to do, and you want to excel at it. So, I agreed to do it, but I was booked for three weeks. He's not a guy who has any patience at all. It's like, "Let's do it now or we're never doing it." I was booked on other jobs and I couldn't get out of them. So he had to wait three weeks for my schedule to open.

ME: The video was "Gett Off," a raunchy, orgiastic clip.

RANDEE ST. Nicholas: The job began with him saying, "You need to speak to this person at the record company about when we need to do it and about the budget." I'm like, "I don't talk about budgets." He goes, "Yeah, but I need you to." So, I get on the phone with the record company and the person promptly says to me, "Let me be clear when I tell you this: we are not doing a video for that song. There's no way we're releasing it. It's not coming out. So, let's not even have this conversation." Prince calls me and goes, "So, how'd your conversation go?" I told him the story, he goes, "Uh-huh." He clears his throat and he goes, "Excuse me, I'll call you back in a few minutes."

A few minutes later, the same record company person calls me back and goes, "Correction, we are going to do that music video. When are you available to do it?" So, Prince calls me and he goes, "I want it to be kind of like that movie, *Caligula*." And I'm thinking, *Okay, it's going to be a wild, sexual orgy. I can do it*. I watched the movie several times and we went back and forth. I chose a cinematographer, and I sent my whole crew ahead of me because I couldn't be there until the day we started shooting. On the first shoot day, I took the red-eye to Minnesota and went to the set and when I walked into Paisley Park, I had all these extras come running up to me going, "We'll get naked on camera." "We'll have sex on camera." "My sister and I will make out with each other if you want." I'm like, *Whoa. Am I in LA making a porno? What am I doing?* It was so crazy. There were 150 extras and a huge crew—we had about two hundred people in total on this set. Now I'd done big advertising jobs, but with a crew of like twenty people. This thing was huge. And the set was already built, and the band had been rehearsing and the dancers, Diamond and Pearl had been rehearsing. So, I walked right onto the set and instantly started directing. I had my monitor on my side of the stage and Prince had his on the other side of the stage. There was maybe twenty feet between us. We start filming and on the first take, I must've been dancing in front of the monitor. I don't know what I was doing: I was completely lost in the moment; it was an amazing experience. Prince called cut, which I didn't even hear because I was just so excited. He looked at me and he said, to everyone on set, "And she didn't want to do this. Look at her. She's having the time of her life." He started laughing, and everyone started laughing. That was the first take. And it just kept on like that. It was three weeks of being in the most amazing film school because you had all the bells and whistles, all the stuff you needed, no financial restrictions, and, of course, no sleeping or eating. All you did was work around the clock. It was a really amazing experience and obviously, one that I loved, because I've done about 350 music videos since then. It changed my life completely.

ME: One of the sweetest stories from Princeworld is that of a clothing designer from Chicago named Debbie McGuan who, because of Prince, got to live out her dream.

MICHAELA ANGELA Davis: Debbie McGuan was like a super fan. She had been drawing him since her teens, but always around fashion. She'd been drawing him in different outfits and having dreams of him and visions of him.

ME: Michaela came to know her in the '80s, when Michaela's sister and Debbie were roommates.

MICHAELA ANGELA Davis: My sister was living in Paris at the time. She was a background vocalist and she was singing with all these big people. She had this great apartment and people would come and have dinner, and [the designer] Patrick Kelly would come, like, there was very few American Black folks in Paris in the '80s, so their apartment was a scene, a fabulous scene. Debbie was adopted into that group and she would just draw Prince all the time. Like her whole sketchbook of designs were all Prince. All she did was draw Prince. Everybody knew she was obsessed.

ME: Someone in that little scene got some of Debbie's sketches delivered to Prince.

MICHAELA ANGELA Davis: A week later, she was at Paisley Park, and she stayed there forever. A lot of what you saw him wearing in the '90s and '00s, she was dreaming, like literally dreaming, and drawing. I feel like they were communicating on this other level. Debbie was connected with him spiritually. That was her only dream and there it was. She was just so grateful that he had made her dream come true.

ME: McGuan worked for Prince for fourteen years as one of his in-house designers, sketching ideas and handing them off to his in-house tailors. Prince never wore anything off the rack—he had his own fashion company inside Paisley Park, designers and tailors who worked for him alone, making custom clothes. Sometimes, he would send Debbie a song and let her pull inspiration from it and think of what looks would go with it. Sometimes, he would send her tear sheets from magazines. Sometimes, she imagined something new and presented it to him and it worked because she had an almost telepathic connection with Prince. He loved it when people he worked with could have that sort of connection to him, where he wouldn't have to tell you what he wanted.

GREG BOYER: There's what I like to call a wavelength. Something that you can't really put your hands on, but you can feel it. He would create a very strong wave and it was easy to latch onto because he just made the feeling, the vibe, very definite. If you fail to grasp on to that, it was very obvious that you weren't with everyone else. Kind of like I'm running after a garbage truck and if it pulls away too fast, you can't jump up on the back of it and ride it. He just made it very, very strong. He was an excellent quarterback musically. All he had to do was just give you a look, and you could know what it was. Well, you had to figure out what it was, but it didn't take long to figure out what you had to do when he gave you a look. You knew what to do—play a solo, come up with a horn line, change keys, whatever. It didn't take a lot of words 'cause he made his intentions very clear. After playing with him a little bit, you had to understand what to do when he gave you a look, or you wouldn't be there much longer. He wouldn't ask you to be in the band if he didn't think that you had that kind of ability to communicate with him without words.

STEVE PARKE: I felt like that's how I maintained doing so many projects with him over time. I sort of got into his headspace and said, "I'm thinking this will work for him." But at the same time, when he moves around, it's just up to you to capture it. Like, if he turns, take a picture. If he turns the other way, take a picture. It wasn't a whole lot of communication. There was never a lot of communication, it was more in the moment, and him signaling through his body language and his movement the feeling he wanted.

ME: If you could get in that flow, you could get into his inner circle, but if you were in his inner circle, you had to be ready to run because he was always on. Even photographers had to be ready to rock at any second.

RANDEE ST. NICHOLAS: I was driving down the street one day at like 9:30 in the morning and I looked over at a stoplight and I saw this building that had smoke wafting off the roof and I thought, *Oh, that must've just been on fire.* I got out of my car and walked into the building through this little opening, and the whole thing had just been on fire and it was all charred. Just then, my phone rang and it was Prince and he goes, "What are you doing?" I go, "Well, I saw this building that must've been on fire in the wee hours of the night and I just walked in because it's so amazing." He goes, "Where is it?" I told him the address and he goes, "Okay, call studio instrument rentals and get a piano over there. I'll meet you there in an hour." So I hustled to get my assistants, my gear, the rented piano, and I got a model down there just for entertainment for him, and he showed up and we did this amazing photo shoot. I went back the next night because I thought it'd be great to shoot it at night, like, lit with moonlight, but the building was completely locked up. If I hadn't done that shoot at that moment, the picture would've never happened: it was now-or-never kind of thing. That was a metaphor for how Prince lived his life, because if you could be spontaneous in the moment and hang with him no matter what, you got to capture him, you got to be in, and you got to be part of this incredible journey. He was really spontaneous and he forced you to think on your feet and always give your all, never let your fear or frustration stop you. It was kind of just his incredible time capsule of creative energy happening pretty much twenty-four hours a day.

ME: Prince brought that same spontaneity to his film projects even though film, unlike music and photography, generally requires a lot of planning.

AFSHIN SHAHIDI (Photographer): I worked with him on a film that he made called *3121*. It was actually a feature-length film and it had multiple filmmakers, but I think I worked on the majority of it. It did not have a script. Often times, I would walk in and he'd say, "Okay I want to film here." I'd say, "What's happening?" and he'd say, "Just get the space ready and we'll film and you'll see." At one point, he called me at home and was like, "Hey, what are you doing tomorrow?" I thought he wanted to get together to take some pictures. I said, "I'm free." He said, "Okay, come to Panama." "Panama City? What are you doing in Florida?" He's like, "No, I'm in Panama. Come to Panama." I flew all the way down there only to find out he wanted to film down there. I had to go to Miami to pick up equipment. I was producing at the same time as shooting as the same time as directing portions, but we made a feature-length film that I never read the script for. It was all in his head. We'd drive around Panama City, Panama, in a van with a couple of million dollars' worth of film equipment and just stop anywhere that inspired Prince. He'd hop out and we'd be filming on the streets of Panama even though I would have no idea how that scene related to the overall story. We also shot in Morocco, and LA, and Minneapolis. I've seen a couple of cuts of the film, but I don't know if it will ever see the light of day, but it was quite the experience making it with him.

ME: Prince could sometimes be really loving and affirming with the people in his orbit, especially when it was on his terms and he was in charge.

SUSAN ROGERS: Around '85, we were working at Sunset Sound in Los Angeles when I left the control room for a minute. I was buying a house and I told Prince I need one minute for this call, "I'm buying a condominium on Lake Harriet [in Minneapolis] and I need to talk to the realtor." Prince called in Gilbert, his valet, and whispered a few words to him and Gilbert left. Half an hour later, Gilbert came back with a bottle of champagne and Prince said, "When I was a kid, I used to dream that I was living in a house on Lake Harriet and now I have people working for me who own homes on Lake Harriet." We clinked glasses. It was so great. It was one of those moments where you look at each other and say both of our dreams have come true today. That victory for me represented a victory for him too because he made that possible.

ME: Prince loved to be the one to make wins possible for people and he loved to make people look big. When the band was touring, if they stopped in the hometown of a band member, Prince gave that band member money to give away so they looked like a big shot.

MORRIS HAYES: Prince would ask, "Where did you go to high school?" And then he'd get one of those big, giant paper checks and make it out for a hundred grand or whatever and you would give his money to your school. It was really cool. I used to live in Chicago, and when we were going to Chicago, he called me up and said, "I want you to find three places on Chicago where we can give some money. Find three charities." That's the kinda thing he would do. He'd say, "Find a place and we're just gonna give them a bunch of money."[18] It was just so awesome that he would do that in everybody's city. Once, we went to South Carolina, where our old drummer John Blackwell was, and we went to his school and Prince had given him this crazy check and John went back and he was a hero, man. The whole school turned out like in this rally in the gymnasium and all of the students came and we had on our garb and he comes in and he's got this check and he talks to the kids and it was phenomenal. It really made John look like this hero. For them, he was. The whole atmosphere was incredible because of the generosity and it made him look so wonderful because it was like here's John Blackwell coming back to his school with this check; I mean, it was amazing.

ME: But Prince could also be very hard to work for.

LEROY BENNETT: Prince was difficult to work with. He was a perfectionist. He had high standards and either you could follow it or you couldn't. And he was pretty ruthless with his public humiliation. He even did it during live shows. During one show, he said, "I thought I was working with a bunch of professionals." He would call people out if they made a mistake during the show. He'd turn around and say "Fifty dollars!" Meaning he fined them fifty dollars for messing up. He expected perfection from everyone. It was so intense that it put knots in my stomach, watching other people get berated in front of everybody. It would happen in rehearsals all the time. It's like every time I walked into Paisley Park, I just had this sick feeling in my stomach because I knew what was coming.

BROWNMARK: You had to watch him or you'd get fined. If he did something and you missed it and you kept playing, when everybody's stopped, he'd started dancing and saying, "I got some money! I got some money!" One day, my fine was up to $1,200. I was making around $2,200 a week during the Purple Rain Tour, so it was very annoying because you could lose serious wages in one day, mostly for missing cues. I was on stage dancing, playing, having a good old time, and all of a sudden everybody done stop and I'm rumbling. I'm still playing. I'm like, *Dang it*. He just looked at me and was like, "I got some money," and I knew what it was. He said, "Alan, Mark just made a mistake." He didn't do it all the time, but he did it a lot. I remember he said, "Everybody gimme twenty-five." Like "Twenty-five hits in a row?" "No," he would say, "Give me a hit on the twenty-five." That's what he would say. "Give me twenty-five," and I'm like, "Twenty-five? Okay." And we're going through the hits as a band and I'm sitting here trying to count, "Three, four, five six," but if I got distracted anywhere in there, I'm lost and be like, *Oh, shoot. I don't know what number we're on.* If I don't hit one, he would hear it and if I hit one more than everyone else, he would hear it, and so either way you're in trouble. I think "I got some money," was like his favorite line. "Alan, I think somebody messed up." Sometime I'd be like, "You ain't really going to take this money from me, are you?" But Alan Leeds would be taking notes and it would always be subtracted from my check. Whenever I got fined, he took that money. I would get so angry. I got angry because I heard a lot of the guys say he'd fine them, but never take the money. But he always took the money from me. He used to piss me off.

GREG BOYER: You had to be ready for him to call you out in the middle of the show and then just crank up and keep going like nothing happened. Then he'd send management after to say, "You've been fined $5,000 for something you did on the concert tonight."

ME: Throughout the '80s and '90s, according to sources, Prince paid the Revolution around $3,000 a week when they were on tour and $1,500 a week when they were off the road—a solid fifty-two-week-a-year job for musicians who weren't usually getting steady gigs. Of course, there was always a range depending on who you were and what you brought to the table. A star like Sheila E. might have made around $10,000 a week. In that period, Prince had a lot of money to draw his power from—his advance for each album was between $250,000 and $500,000, with each advance based on how much his prior album had sold, but it couldn't be less than $150,000 or more than $500,000. This, when he was putting out an album a year. And that's just album revenue—his take from touring was in the millions and he was touring all the time. Prince's musicians got paid well compared to other touring musicians and that gave Prince power over them. It made musicians beholden to him and forced them to put up with his relentless schedule and his temper.

MORRIS HAYES: When I would pull into the garage, if I saw his car, my stomach started hurting, like, *Oh God, he's here*. I've seen people break down in tears after he started getting on 'em and berating them for not getting it right. Prince told me, "You know how I am, Morris. I'm like a pit bull. When I get on you, I just stay on you until I get a result." I've had some real tough days with Prince. Some days, I just wanted to beat his ass for real. Like we actually came to a point one day where I had to let him know like, "Either I'm gonna go home or I'm gonna choke you and be on CNN." I don't know why, but it was like I'm gonna work on Morris day. Playing with him was like boot camp. I likened it to being in the Marines and on this day, he was like, *I'ma work on him*. And he was very good at knowing your breaking point because it was all about breaking you down to build you up. That's the way he looked at it and he would pound on you. This day, he was pounding on me. It's very difficult because once you get in a rut and he's yelling at you and everybody's there, it's really hard. So, he'd be there just killing you and everybody would have to wait while he kills you and it's like, "Okay,

Morris. Let's just play that part by yourself." So you're doing it over and over, and you're nervous because the spotlight is on you, and you want to do it right, so either you figure it out or you don't and if you don't, you'll get frustrated and he'll get mad, and then it comes to a head. When he had an audience, that was the worst, especially if there was a girl around. Then it was really bad because he's got to show this person like, "See what I can do? This six-foot-five soul brother, I had to work him over. I had to just let him have it, you know?" He would just get in that mode where he had to clobber me and I knew that's what he was doing. I wanted to kill him and knew I could do it if I could get my hands on him! I could pound him to pieces, but his thing was, psychologically, "I have to just mentally break him down," but he always had to walk the fine balance of not getting beaten up by a band member. That's where I was. There was those days. But there was definitely more good days than bad.

JILL JONES: How would you know who he was from day to day? That's a landmine for people who worked with him.

SUSANNAH MELVOIN: He could turn around on a dime and go from fun guy to the next thing you know, you were screwed. You were docked pay or you were out and you never heard from him, and you never even knew what happened or why. So there were those two sides to him.

JEROME BENTON: There was a desire to relate to and treat the people in his world like family and yet there were moments of being mean to people where it was like, damn! He was mean to people. I've seen him be mean.

BROWNMARK: I fought with him a lot because I did not understand the way he dealt with me a lot of the time. He was very hard on me and I didn't understand that. I didn't know why. To this day, it was one of the things I wanted to ask him. "Dude, why were you so rough on me?" Because I was loyal. I was a soldier. He was the commander in chief to us. He was the leader. I got that. But it didn't mean that I was going to take everything that he threw at me. Me and him fought a lot about how I dressed and where I could go on stage and so many things. A couple of times, it almost got to fistfighting. But I'm a lot bigger than him, so I'd always take a couple steps backwards and rethink my course of action. It was mainly verbal fighting, but you could never win with him. Never. You could argue 'til the sun comes up: it didn't matter. I remember once he said to me "Mark, I'm right, always. Even when I'm wrong, I'm right. So, stop arguing with me." Eventually, I learned that I'm not going to win so, why am I arguing?

WENDY MELVOIN: He mocked people a lot. If you came in wearing something that was not to his liking, he would mock you.

HUCKY AUSTIN (Security, 1984–1991): I used to wear bandanas all the time. One day, they were in a rehearsal and I came in the room and he stopped the music. He said, "Hucky, you know who you look like?" I'm like, "No. Who do I look like?" He said, "Man, you look like Harriet Tubman." Everybody busted out laughing at me. I left. He could obviously see that my feelings were hurt so the next day I come to rehearsal and he's got a bandana on just like I had worn it. I asked him, "Hey, I thought yesterday you said I looked like Harriet Tubman." He said, "You did. But I make it look sexy." Prince would never tell you that he was sorry, but he might show that he was sorry by his actions. That was his way of saying, "Hey man, I'm sorry. I'm gonna do it now, too."

BROWNMARK: One time on stage, this dude did a Bruce Lee flying dropkick dead in my chest and kicked me all the way back up onto the drum riser. He did it because we collided on stage. There was some choreography that we all did on "Why You Wanna Treat Me So Bad?" where me, Prince, and Dez came together, and he was so excited with adrenaline that he forgot that that's what we were doing at that moment, so he spun around and ran into me. I'm bigger than him so it was like, bam! He hit a brick wall. I just played it off and backed up, but he was embarrassed. And the way he chose to play it off was to back up and then run at me at full speed. I said, "Oh, this doesn't look good." He went way up in the air and he said, "Pow!" He hit me dead in my chest with his boot and I went flying back. I said, "What was that?"

I got up and he came at me again. This time, he kicked me and I flew back onto Bobby's riser. I was just lying there on my back. I'm trying to play it off because I don't want the audience to know what's happening here but I'm like, *What the hell is going on?* I shook my head, and I thought, *I've had enough,* and I took my bass off and started holding it like a baseball bat. I was running at him and his back was turned to me but I was coming at him. I was going to pound him right in the back of the head. Security was watching the whole thing like, "Oh, he about to snap!" They was just waiting for me to snap and they jumped in and grabbed me. They prevented me from hitting him, but after the show I did damage to that locker room. Broke stall doors, sinks, mirrors, everything, I kicked everything down. I was really angry. I tore that locker room up and he had to pay for that. After that, I said, "I don't want to do this no more. I'm done." I was going home. I was leaving. Later that night, Chick came knocking on my door. He said, "The kid wants to see you." I was like, "I don't want to see him." Then Chick came in the room and sat down. Me and Chick had become really good friends from hanging out on the road. He said, "You know man, he does some dumb stuff, man. But he cares about you. He really cares about you, man." I was like, "Cares about me? Did you see what happened? He did a flying dropkick on me. He kicked me like Bruce Lee dead in my chest. He embarrassed me in front of all them people." He's like, "Mark, man. Don't throw this away. Don't throw this away." I was just torn about it. I didn't go see him. I just stayed in my room and the next morning I got up and I got on the bus, and Prince came up to me like nothing had happened. He came up to me and he started talking like, "I was watching the video of last night's show. Man, that was pretty cool. Wasn't it?" I was like, "Pretty cool? You kicked me in my chest." He said, "Man, that was just part of the skit! We collided and that's how you play it off. We just had to make it look like we was slam dancing, like we were just being punk rockers, just going crazy on stage!" He was making all that crap up because he knew he messed up. He knew he did me wrong. But I was a nineteen-year-old kid and I wasn't used to any of this kind of stuff, so I just let it go. I thought, *I can throw it away or I can ride the wave.* Because we was definitely on a wave. I saw his success. I saw the way them crowds were and the way the album was doing, I thought, *This is going nowhere but up.* So I let it go. But it was fucked up.

LeRoy Bennett: He was intense because he was so brilliant and he was very hard on himself. He pushed himself constantly and he expected everybody else to work on that same level, and if he did that to himself inwardly, he probably thought he could do it to anybody. He would get frustrated if somebody didn't get exactly what he was thinking. He didn't want to constantly have to repeat himself, so you really had to be on the ball and be on the same wavelength with him. When I arrived in Minneapolis, the first five days were hell. He expected me to know every single song he had ever written. Prior to going to Minneapolis, I didn't really know who he was. So after I found out I got the job, I did a bit of homework but when I got into rehearsals, I found that he didn't quite understand that things take time when you're starting to program lights. He would humiliate me in front of everybody. Every day after work, I'd go back to the hotel and I'd cry and go, "What the hell am I doing?" But I wasn't going to give up. Fortunately, the band was very sympathetic because they had also received the same kind of treatment. After the second or third day, Bobby Z. came up to me and just gave me a big hug and said, "Don't worry about it, man. It's just the way he is." Then his manager Steven Fargnoli showed up and he told Prince, "Look, just calm down, he's doing a good job." At that point, he backed off and he started to understand that I was focused and doing my job the way he wanted it and he started to respect what I was doing. From that point on, we became really close. We watched the David Lynch movie *Eraserhead* three or four times. I think he was hurt sometimes. I felt that he didn't think anybody could live in his world. I'm sure it was really a very lonely world. He didn't trust people. He was also very fragile. I think that's what I saw more than anything else. I didn't focus in on the anger and the nastiness because with my job, I have to understand all the artists that I work with, I have to get inside their heads, but I don't think how he treated people was right. I know he felt bad sometimes. He would never say sorry, but you could just tell. I'm so blessed to have worked with him. He definitely made me see who I am. He had a way of looking into people and seeing that they could do more than what they thought they could do. That's part of why he was pushing people. I had a really good relationship with him, but I also understood that he was a complete asshole sometimes.

ME: If you got on Prince's bad side, you had to endure his icy cold shoulder.

ALAN LEEDS: His way of dealing with people depended entirely on how much he thought they would take. There were certain people in the band that were punching bags because he knew he could insult them. He could talk about their momma, do whatever he wanted to do, and they would still be there tomorrow, ready to go. There were other people, like my brother Eric, who weren't gonna take that. Sometimes, things happened. Once, we were somewhere in Europe, I think it was Rotterdam, and it was one of those nights where Prince called an aftershow. Eric wasn't feeling well, and, on top of that, it had been a long day with a long sound check, and we'd just traveled the night before. It was one of those grueling days where nobody was feeling it. The crew was worn out. The band was worn out, but Prince was insistent. "We're gonna do this club show." So of course, everybody sucked it up and did the show. Everybody except Eric. He said to me, "You tell him I'm sick. You tell him whatever you wanna tell him, but I'm not going. I'm just not going." I spent about ten minutes on the phone with him like, "Look, dude, you're putting me in the middle of a shitty situation. You're my brother. If it's somebody else in the band, I don't care. But now I'm caught in the middle of this." He's like, "I don't care, that's too bad." So we get to the gig and Prince is like, "Where's Eric?" I said, "He wasn't feeling well; he stayed back at the hotel." Prince said, "Call him and tell him I said 'Come over.'" I said, "He ain't coming." Prince said, "Oh, okay." We did the show and the next day Eric showed up at sound check with a great attitude, really friendly, saying, "I'm feeling better." And Prince said sarcastically, "So you feeling better? Good. Cuz you know I gave everybody a big bonus last night." It was true. Now most aftershows, nobody got anything extra. Prince paid his musicians very well, way better than anybody else in that era, because it was understood that if he wanted to record, or do a late aftershow, or rehearse for ten hours, you were there, no questions asked. So, his way of messing with Eric was simply to say, "Look, everybody else got like $500 extra last night and you didn't, na na nana na."

MORRIS HAYES: In 1996, I had a big blowout with Prince when we were in Japan. It was his fault. I can say it now. Back then, we would ship our equipment overseas, like it would go on a ship, and it would take two months for it to get there. During that time, we didn't do a whole lot. We didn't rehearse; we had time off. But when we got to Japan, we only had like three days before the tour would start. Typically, we would take those three days and rehearse, just run through the show. But, of course, in true Prince fashion, even though we hadn't played together in a while, he decided we're gonna jam. We're just gonna groove and not run through the show. So when we got on stage there were a lot of cues that he forgot, which made things impossible for the band because if we're supposed to be in the second verse and he jumps to the third verse and he starts singing the third verse, you have to make a split decision as an individual musician—*do I follow him as he jumps off a cliff, or do I play what I'm supposed to play?* Everybody's gotta make that decision in a millisecond and at the same time. What happens if two people decide to follow him and two decide to play what they're supposed to play? That's called a train wreck.[19] Well, the first couple of shows, we had a bunch of train wrecks because when he cut a verse, some of us decided to go with him, and some went, "No, I'm—that's not what's supposed to happen. It's gonna adjust the whole trajectory of the song." So then, we got to have a meeting in his office after the show. That didn't go well 'cause Prince was good and hot. He wouldn't talk to us. He would use our road manager, Ian Jeffrey, as his mouthpiece. You could be sitting right there and he wouldn't talk to you. He'd talk to Ian and Ian would tell you what he said. And it got real funny. He's sitting right there and he's talking to the road manager like, "Tell Morris this, that, and the other," and I'm sitting there, I'm like, "I can hear you, bro." And he was like, "Tell Morris I can't even talk to them if they're gonna blow it like that." But he was serious. It was bad. He reamed us out. I tried to explain that we didn't know what to do after he leapt over a whole verse, but it's not gonna be his fault, so he was like, look, "We can't be friends if you guys are gonna sound like that. These people paid money to come out; they need to see a perfect show. And we're not gonna be friends until we give them that." It was not cool for a few days. But I told the guys, "Look, man, just go with him. Whatever he does, we just go." So we go to Fukuoka and the show was just smashing and afterwards the manager came and said, "Boss wants to see you." We went in and he was speaking directly to us, saying, "Now, when you play like that, we can be friends."

ME: But what was perhaps worst was that sometimes Prince stole songs from the people around him and didn't credit them for their work, costing them millions.

BROWNMARK: I used to come in a couple of hours early because all the equipment was there and it was free session time. I would work on new material for my band Mazerati. Prince normally was late for rehearsal but every once in a while, he would pop in early. It happened just a couple of times, and each time it was like, *Dang it, man. I just lost that song.* Every time he would show up early, I was like, *Man, he's going to take this.* One day while I'm working on "Data Bank," he walks up to me like, "Oh, what's that?" I was like, "Oh, it's this group I'm working on." He didn't know about Mazerati. I couldn't just tell him I had a band, so I was like, "Oh, it's just this jam I'm working on." He was like, "Yeah man, hit that again." He grabbed his guitar and that was it. As soon as that happened, I knew I had lost it. As the rest of the band trickled in, he started handing out different parts and getting people jamming on their instruments. Next thing you know, he'd taken the whole thing over, and I didn't get a writer credit for it. There was nothing to show that I had even created the basic groove for the song. Another song, "Kiss," was started by Prince. He gave me a cassette tape of him singing the words over a slow acoustic guitar. I hated it because it just sounded like an old folk song, like some Bob Dylan type of thing. He said, "You should do this because it will give Mazerati a different feel." By then, he knew about Mazerati. I said, "Alright, man. I'll give it a shot." So me and my man Dave Ripkin went in the studio. I came up with the beat, then put the guitar part in. Then it was like, "It'd be cool if we put the Keypex Gain Brain Compressor on it. The Keypex will take a keyboard or any recorded sound and process it so it can be triggered by another rhythm source. I used an acoustic guitar playing basic chord progressions and triggered it with the Keypex. That's what gave it that choppy rhythm that drives the track. Then I was like, "Ooh, it needs some logs." We call them log drums, the DX7 log drums program. Now the song's coming together. I was using a DX drum machine. That song was written on a DX, so it had a whole different sound and feel than the stuff Prince was doing. Then we put the vocals on it and we gave them that whole gospel feel with the harmonies. Prince walks in just as we're getting ready to go to dinner and he was like, "Whoa, you should let me work on that a little bit. What time you coming back?" I already knew what that meant. I was like, *Dang man. He's going to take this*. When I came back from dinner, he said, "I want you to hear something." He came in singing with that falsetto and I was like, *Aw man, he done took the song*. Then he said, "Man, this would be a better hit on us, so I think we should release it on the Revolution album." Now, I'm thinking *Cha-ching!* "You mean I'm going to get a song on a Rev album?" He was like, "Yeah, man. You know how I take care of things." I knew this was gonna be a hit and, of course, it was a huge hit. I was driving down the street when I heard it on the radio. Didn't even know it had been released. I got to the hotel room and saw the video on MTV with him and Wendy and I was pissed. I was like, *Dude, you couldn't even tell me when it was coming out? Didn't tell me that they had a video? Couldn't incorporate me in a video?* I was heated. Then I got the album cover and it said,

"Thanks to BrownMark for handclaps." I was like, *Whoa*. That's when I found him. At that time period, he was hard to get a hold of, but I found him and I just went off, man. I was like, "Yo, dude, what is this? You promised this and that," and he says, "Oh, that must be a mistake. Man, don't worry about that. You know I'll take care of you." I hadn't learned all about royalties and all that kind of stuff yet but he said he's going to take care of me, so I was like, *Okay, I trust him. He's going to do me right*. Nope. I ain't never seen an ounce of change on that song. Not one penny. I was the cowriter of the whole groove. He wrote the lyrics and the melody, but I wrote that groove. That was all me, 100 percent. There's no ifs, ands, or buts about it. I could've retired off of that one song alone. "Kiss" has brought in millions, like heavy millions. We could be talking $100 million. I don't know. The publishing rights on that alone—that song is still being played and used to this day. But, you know, I can't cry over it. It's gone now. The statute of limitations ran out and I couldn't go back and fight it. Once I realized that I had something, it was too late for me. And that was a regular thing. There was a lot of that going around. "Girls And Boys" was my groove. Same story—I was in there early, working on a jam, and then Prince walks in like, "What's that?" You just have to hit yourself in the head 'cause right then, you know it's gone. You've lost it. That's the way it was.

PEPE WILLIE: "Do Me Baby" was André's song. Prince took that sucker and made it his, copywritten and everything. Prince was controlling and people feared him.

MORRIS DAY: I've heard that he's taken songs. He took one of my songs and didn't give me credit for it. It was "Party Up." I cut the song really slow and really funky because that was my thing. I was heavy into funk. Then he heard the song and he said he wanted it. He said he'd give me money or he'd help me get a record deal. I said, "I'll take the record deal." So he takes the song and puts his name on it, but I didn't have a problem with it because in one respect, I got paid.

ME: Prince gave great songs to others, to bands he was creating like The Time and Vanity 6—which were representations of his hypermasculine and feminine sides—as well as to people he liked, such as the Bangles, Chaka Khan, and Sinead O'Connor.

MORRIS DAY: There were a lot of songs where you would think that Prince should've kept them for himself because they were so great, but he had a major interest in growing some of the entities that he formed. He knew he had to give up some good songs because he really wanted to have a whole production company that was successful. Now, he did double back on some of the songs he wrote. He wrote "Nothing Compares 2 U" for The Family and he went back and did that one himself. And "International Lover" was supposed to be for The Time. I sang that song first, left, and when I came back, his vocals were on it. He was like, "You didn't sing it good. I'm keeping it." I sang it pretty damn good, you know.

ME: Prince had to be in charge or he wasn't interested. Even when it came down to being a part of something like "We Are the World." The song was a gigantic deal in 1985, when the whole world had been crying over Ethiopia and watching the children just wither away with sticklike arms and distended bellies. Millions had died, and now every major star in the music business was getting together to do one monster group song for charity that would combat the famine in Ethiopia. It was the brainchild of Hollywood legend Harry Belafonte, who recruited Michael Jackson, then the biggest singer in the world, and Quincy Jones, one of the biggest producers in the world, to pull in singers to help create a project that would raise money to help Ethiopia, the most noble cause anyone could imagine at that time. Every superstar singer they called said yes—Stevie Wonder, Diana Ross, Kenny Rogers, Bette Midler, Lionel Richie, Tina Turner, Ray Charles, Billy Joe, Bob Dylan, on and on. Of course, they invited Prince.

ALAN LEEDS: His management, his record company, everybody in his orbit urged him to go. Just the idea of so many superstars in one room working on the same project made it seem like he should be there for the history of it. Quincy Jones personally called him and begged him. He said, "We've got a special part in the song for you where you and

Michael will sing to each other. You'll be featured above and beyond most of the artists, right up there with Michael."

ME: The song was going to be recorded in LA right after the American Music Awards.

ALAN LEEDS: We were in Los Angeles on the Purple Rain Tour. Management begged him. We all begged him. I said, "Dude, it's going to look whack if you're not part of it. Everybody's gonna be there. This isn't about the competition, whose record sells better than the other, whose tour sells more, all that's gonna be left outside the doors of the studio.

ME: He thought about it.

ALAN LEEDS: The night of the recording, he was still hemming and hawing.

ME: But he would not say yes.

ALAN LEEDS: After the AMAs, we went back to the hotel and he was like, "No, no, no, no, no, no. That's a clique over there. Quincy and Michael, I'm not going over there and let them manipulate me and be a guest on their record. That's not what I do. I'm not going to be part of that like everybody else. I don't do things like everybody else."

ME: Prince could have driven a few minutes through LA and been a part of the biggest charity song ever, the biggest supergroup ever, the biggest moment of music industry charity ever. But no.

ALAN LEEDS: Quincy and Michael had scheduled the session for two in the morning, after the AMAs, so all the artists could leave the show, change clothes, go to a party or two, have a couple of drinks, and then go to the studio. Prince had just cleaned up at the awards and had a great night. He could have participated, but it's like if everybody else is doing it, then he wasn't going to be a part of it. If everybody's going right, I'm going left. It wasn't that he didn't believe in the cause. It wasn't that he didn't respect the artists. Many of them were amongst his favorite artists. If anything, he might have felt intimidated, but

I'm sure he would have risen to the occasion because he had that gift to overcome intimidation. It really wasn't about any of that. He just doesn't do what others do. If everybody else does it, he's going to do the opposite. That was a career strategy. He wasn't going to do a group jam. And he wasn't going to put himself in any situation where he was not in 100 percent in control. He considered walking on somebody else's stage as someplace where he's not in control.

ME: So while everyone in the music business was at A&M Studios recording "We Are The World," which would go on to sell over twenty million copies and become a national phenomenon raising tens of millions for the cause, while that was happening...

ALAN LEEDS: Prince was back in his hotel room hanging out. There were several of us there. Bobby Z., Wendy, and Lisa. I was there with my wife, Gwen. We had a few drinks and celebrated his success at the AMAs.

ME: He had won Favorite Pop/Rock Album and Favorite Soul/R&B Album and Favorite Soul/R&B Song.

ALAN LEEDS: All we kept saying to him was like, "Okay, dude, you cannot go out tonight." Prince famously liked to go out on the town and run the clubs. It was AMA night, a hot night in Hollywood, so, of course, he wanted to go the clubs, but we said, "No, dude, you can't. If you're not going to do 'We Are the World' along with everybody else in the business, if you're not going to A&M studios to participate in that, then fine, but don't go out because it's not going to look right if you're out hanging around while everybody else in the industry is donating their time and energy and creativity to a worthy cause." He said, "Yeah, yeah, yeah, I know. I know. I know." So we hang with him in his hotel until like 1:30 in the morning, until we finally felt like he was in for the night and it was safe to go back to our rooms. Gwen and I went to bed. Then, about three in the morning, my phone rang, and it was Big Chick, his bodyguard. He said, "Buddy, we got a problem." He tells me that they had gone out to a club, got into an altercation with an aggressive paparazzi, and one of Prince's bodyguards had punched him.

HUCKY AUSTIN: Prince didn't like to have his picture taken and when we came out of, I think it's El Privado Carlos 'N Charlie's, right off of Sunset, there was a bunch of photographers outside of the nightclub and they were taking pictures. Chick got Prince in the car, and then he said, "You guys got to go get that film." I'm thinking, *This is gonna be a problem.* So, two guys went back to the photographers to try to get that film and the photographers are like, "Hell no, I'm not giving you my film." That turned into a tussle and both of those guys ended up getting arrested.

ALAN LEEDS: The police were called. The bodyguard was locked up and this was going to be all over the press. It was the nth degree of everything we warned him about. Of course, the next day, the stories were right there in the papers. On each one was a story about this miraculous recording session where every celebrity in the world was in one studio singing one song and the other story was about Prince at a nightclub having a photographer beaten up. Not a good look.

ME: Flash forward twenty years later to a 2004 tribute to George Harrison at the Rock & Roll Hall of Fame induction ceremony and, this time, Prince shows up to show us that you can join the group without really becoming a part of the group.

ERIC LEEDS: Prince got on stage and performed with a whole bunch of rock 'n' roll icons [Tom Petty, Jeff Lynne, Steve Winwood]. It was not something that Prince would typically do, i.e., allow himself to be part of someone else's agenda musically. So they all did the song and Prince finished with a long solo. As soon as Prince started playing, you could see the looks on the other guys' faces: *We only hold this instrument; this guy actually plays it.* In thirty-two bars of music, Prince just wiped the stage. It was so unaffected and natural. I said, "Go ahead, Prince!" Because that's the Prince that I relate to—the exceptional musician. I said, "Prince did it again. My man." As soon as the song was over, all the other guys put their arms around each other to celebrate this performance in honor of George Harrison, except Prince. He threw the guitar up in the air, looked at the audience dismissively, and walked off. Here you have this wonderful performance where he steals the show and you wanna say, "Go ahead, Prince," but what he leaves you with is, "Oh my God, this is guy an asshole." That's the dichotomy. I mean, this is a guy who has done some exceedingly generous and thoughtful things for me and other people, but a day later he would turn around and say something to you that was so off the wall and offensive that you would say, "How do I reconcile these behaviors?" I think it's because he had the emotional maturity of a five-year-old. I think he never understood the value of doing something thoughtful for somebody on its own merits. He really didn't understand the consequences of doing something nice for somebody any more than he understood the consequences of doing something really nasty to somebody. Children don't know that. You have to teach them what works and what doesn't and how relationships work. Prince never understood that.

ME: Prince's inability to deal with people did show up in the music. He never wanted to share his deepest feelings with people, never wanted to allow himself to be vulnerable and create deep bonds because then he could be left and abandoned and hurt so he kept himself closed off. Even during sex, women said, he was not sharing his true self: he was performing. In music, he surely had the technical ability to write and sing and play any kind of song, but it seems like his heart may not have been open to diving into the difficult realm of truly sad songs because working with deep, painful emotions required a level of vulnerability that he was unable or unwilling to share in his music. Wendy says this was his biggest hole as a musician. Yes, he made some great sad songs, but there's a deeper level of musical sadness that he wasn't willing to visit.

WENDY MELVOIN: There are plenty of people in the world who listen to Prince play the piano and weep; that's totally true. But I'm talking about a certain kind of really trained musician ear that hears harmonics in a certain way. If you listen to Erik Satie, or Aldo Ciccolini playing Erik Satie, or Arthur Rubinstein playing Chopin's nocturnes, you're going to feel a crack in your being. Prince couldn't do that kind of crack. He could play soul and gospel and make you so impassioned that you're going to scream and yell and whoop and holler and maybe go into a frenzy with tears because you're so excited by what you're hearing. But the really quiet, intimate heartbreak stuff, Prince didn't do well. It was so hard for him to be totally brokenhearted without there being a sense of showbiz to it. That was too vulnerable to him. He could listen to Joni Mitchell and cry. I mean, there's serious heartbreak in the words and the voicings on her guitar or piano that she uses that just elicit you going deeper into a part of yourself. That's what that kind of music does. Prince couldn't tap that part of himself. It was too scary and it was way too vulnerable because he was way too self-conscious.

ME: People who knew Prince knew that he would avoid dealing with those hard emotions and in the rare moments when he didn't, they were confused.

JILL JONES: One time, I was out and when I came home, my house was burnt down. Everything was gone. This was after all the things that I'd been through, the hospital and everything, where I would think, *Oh, this is too taboo for him.* You know, real feelings, Prince doesn't want to talk about. And yet that night, in the wee early hours of the morning, he tracked me down at my best friend's house. He called and he was crying with me. I don't think a lot of people know that. That was a really poignant moment, but I just kept trying to figure out why.

ME: Prince turned himself into a great musician so he could escape the vulnerabilities and the pain that started in his childhood, and that meant that it may have been too much to reach deep into his emotional well and inject truly painful feelings into his music. After a traumatic childhood where he was misunderstood and unwanted, he needed a world where he was the king and he made the rules. He needed acceptance and affirmation and adulation. Several people close to him said that even as an adult, Prince was like a hurt little boy who wanted to make sure he was never again needy, never again outcast, and, especially, never again abandoned. As someone who felt abandoned by his mom, the thought of being left was far too painful. He could never handle being left. But then he realized his Revolution family was in crisis. People were tense, hurt, and unhappy. And some of them wanted to leave him.

BROWNMARK: Wendy and Lisa felt like they were being held hostage almost. He was having them work long hours and be at his beck and call 24/7, and they were getting tired of it. Plus, Prince wasn't being faithful to Susannah. So Prince and Wendy and Lisa had a big falling out two weeks before we were supposed to start a tour of Europe and Japan. The Parade Tour. Wendy and Lisa quit and walked out. They were driving to the airport to return to LA. Bobby Z. had to race to the airport and stop them from leaving and somehow persuade them to do the Parade Tour.

BOBBY Z.: I retrieved them from the airport at Prince's crying behest.

BROWNMARK: Bobby convinced Wendy and Lisa to stay because without them, Prince would have had to cancel the tour and there were a lot of people who were depending on that tour for their livelihoods. So we did the tour and I thought things that been smoothed over and forgiven, but...

13

Old Friends 4 Sale

The End of the Revolution (1986)

WENDY MELVOIN: I'm going to correct the record right here and finally forever—we wanted to stay. We were being paid a certain amount of money by the end of *Purple Rain*, which was not a lot of money at all. Lisa and I were being asked to play and write with a whole bunch of other people, and we told him about it. We said, "We don't want to do that. We want to be here. We'll stay forever and ever and ever and ever if we can find a way to get enough money where we could maybe get a house here in Minneapolis and not keep living in a hotel room here, like, get paid enough money to actually function." We gave him a contract that said, "We are yours exclusively for as long as you want if we make X amount and we no longer have to fly back and forth from LA to Minneapolis and stay at the Chanhassen Inn anymore." We wanted to be able to buy a house in Minneapolis. He said, "Okay." Lisa and I went to look at a house on Lake Minnetonka. We told him about it and he went, "Why are you looking for a house?" We were like, "Because we were talking about making this big change and you were okay with it." It ended up not being okay. He felt betrayed by the contract we had given him. And it wasn't that much money. Compared to what we were getting, it was nothing. But he felt betrayed by that. It was like,

"You should be here without having to need any of that. You know I'll be here for you." It just didn't make enough sense. I don't mean living high on the hog, I mean like, not in a hotel, not in a Days Inn. A few years of that was enough. Meanwhile, he was in a relationship with my sister. It was going terribly south because he was cheating on her and I was witnessing it all. I was tormented by it. I was horrified to see what was happening to my sister. He wanted it to be a big secret and it wasn't, and he wanted me to be loyal to him, and that became a problem. You can't ask me to choose between my twin sister and you. It's just not going to work. But he asked me to, and I wouldn't have it. He was like, "There's dissension among the ranks and I'm going to cut this off now." But he didn't tell us that at the time. Lisa and I were still looking for property, acting as if that was going to happen. Then we did this incredible tour, the Parade Tour, and everything was fantastic. Then when we got to Japan, there was some weird stuff going on, and his energy changed. He got really cold and really dark with all of us. We started having sound checks at Yokohama Stadium, and he asked me to not play during sound check so the warm-up band that was opening for us could sit in with him and play. That had never happened before. I was like, "He's going to fire us. Something's happening. He's going to fire us." At the end of the tour, in the last show in Yokohama Stadium, he turned around and looked at all of us, and he destroyed his Purple Rain guitar. I looked at Lisa and I gave her the slitting the throat sign. I said, "We're fired." Bobby looked at me and said, "It's over." We knew it.

SUSANNAH MELVOIN: When he broke his guitar, the one he used when he played "Purple Rain," it was this very aggressive moment. He never did that. He was not some rocker who broke guitars. That was a loaded gun. That was the guitar that he'd used throughout the tour. That guitar represented the music they had made and breaking it on stage in front of them represented that he was breaking with the past and heading toward a different future. He broke his guitar, walked off, and didn't look back. That was the definitive moment of ending the band and moving off into a new future.

WENDY MELVOIN: After we all flew home, he rented a house in Los Angeles and he had me and Lisa come over. I guess he'd called Bobby first. Prince was really upset. He was crying, saying, "I don't want them to go!" Bobby's like, "Well, then don't fire them! Don't fire them!" We were at his house and we were having dinner and Randy, who was his cook at the time but who has since passed away, bless her heart, cooked homemade paper wrap chicken. Lisa and I call it our paper wrap chicken dinner firing because he said, "I'm going to go in a different direction." We said, "Okay." He said, "I can't ask you and Lisa to wear nippleless bras or crotchless panties, can I?" Both of us were wide-eyed. We were like, "No. I never wear that stuff." He goes, "Exactly. I would never ask you to do that. But I can ask Sheila. I can ask all these other people to do it and they will. So I think you guys should go." Lisa and I were like, "I call bullshit." We were pissed because we had agreed and things were moving forward and then he just said, "Fuck it. I'm out." We were devastated by it, completely devastated. We had to pretend as if, yeah, the band broke up, we broke up, blah, blah, blah, but no, Prince just unceremoniously said, "You're done."

SUSANNAH MELVOIN: The breakup of the Revolution was a manifestation of him wanting full control of his destiny. This is complicated, but it's clear that Prince's psychology played a huge role in how everything played out. It's all about Prince's life and his destiny and we were all there to facilitate him. The Revolution was his family but he wanted absolute loyalty, and if you asked for something, then you were thinking about your needs. He wanted everything to be about his music and his needs. If you were asking for something, you were propelling your fate and destiny as opposed to his. He felt your needs were not part of his destiny.

ERIC LEEDS: The reason he fired Wendy and Lisa was because they had made it known to him that they were considering leaving the group and, to him, just thinking about it was a crime. He couldn't allow himself to be left, to be abandoned. He couldn't go through what, for him, would be emotional trauma, particularly two people with whom he felt a certain artistic closeness. He was closer artistically with them than with anybody he's ever had in any of his bands. And the emotional trauma that he was gonna go through if they were to leave him was too much. He had to do it preemptively. It was like, 'I'll be damned if I'm gonna allow them to walk out on me! I'm gonna fire them!' And that's what he did.[20]

ME: The whole family was breaking apart.

BOBBY Z.: There was trouble in paradise. It was tense. Claustrophobic. People weren't getting along. Everyone felt a lot of stress. They weren't happy. I wasn't happy. A band breaking up is like a divorce. We knew something was coming—in Japan, Jerome let me know that Sheila was coming after my job. I was more worried about that than anyone else. I couldn't believe he was ending the Revolution.

SUSANNAH MELVOIN: Prince really wanted to be in a family. He was yearning to be connected to a tribe. But vulnerability scared him. My experience of Prince was that he was very guarded and didn't trust much. To me, that suggested that he was battling a lot of abandonment issues and loss issues. He wasn't going to let you run out on him. He would beat you to it. He would run out on you to avoid the sense of loss.

ALAN LEEDS: They didn't really "break up." None of them quit. Prince let them go. While they had their share of gripes, no one wanted to quit. Wendy and Lisa wanted more of a part in creating new music. Mark Brown thought he deserved more money, and he felt overlooked and in the shadow of Wendy and Lisa. He wanted to write and produce other artists, like his group Mazerati. The five of them were unhappy with the addition of Eric [Leeds] and [drummer] Matt Blistan. And then, the addition of [the background singers and dancers] Wally [Safford] and Greg Brooks and Jerome [Benton] became a last straw.

ME: Most of these new folks had come over from one of Prince's satellite groups called The Family—Leeds and Benton—and The Family's touring band—Weaver, Brooks, and Safford. Susannah Melvoin and Paul Peterson had been The Family's lead singers but after they released an album called *The Family*, Peterson was offered a $250,000 record deal. He left and the band fell apart.

SUSANNAH MELVOIN: Just before we started promoting the album, Paul got a solo deal and that threw a wrench in the whole thing. The band was over, but Prince didn't want to say it's over because he felt like it was a huge disappointment. He felt responsible for giving people gigs. So he said to us, "It's gonna be okay. You'll all still have a gig."

ME: The Parade Tour was starting, so Prince invited most of the remaining members to join the Revolution on stage in Europe and Japan.

BOBBY Z.: That was the volatile atomic water that spilled and killed the Revolution. When we inherited The Family on stage, things changed. That was the beginning of the end. The end of the band is a long story, but The Family joining us was when the earthquake happened. That cracked everything open and the band began to die. The Parade Tour was great, but it wasn't that tight family with all these new people around.

SUSANNAH MELVOIN: There was too much input. There was too much going on, too much noise for a guy like Prince. It started to fray. He needed more control. He needed the noise to be quieter. The existential noise, he needed to quiet down.

ALAN LEEDS: At that point, particularly, Wendy and BrownMark felt overshadowed on stage. After all, the newbies hadn't paid the dues of grueling single-bus club tours and getting attacked by angry Rolling Stones fans. The original five had shared the intoxicating ride of "trying to make it" and had become "movie stars." So, how dare someone invade their space on stage! The Revolution was a carefully assembled group of "sidemen," but one that Prince marketed as a self-contained unit, hinting that they all had shares of creative (if not financial) equity. Both *Purple Rain* fans, and to some degree the band members, bought into the hype. But the reality was that they were always salaried guns-for-hire who had no substantial input in the music, production, their individual images or wardrobe— nothing. It was Prince's house and he was just renting them rooms under one-way leases. I don't recall him ever seriously expressing his real reasons for replacing them. I assumed he didn't want to say anything that might negatively reflect on either their musicianship or loyalty. But we had all witnessed Prince's own growth as a musi- cian/composer/performer, so it was logical that he would want to surround himself with musicians who were more versatile and more experienced. Remember, none of the five Revolution players had really been members of any other bands. Despite their individual talents, their only experience and reference points were what they shared with Prince. He felt they couldn't up his game in the same way that Sheila or Eric [Leeds] could. He also reasoned that players like Miko [Weaver], Levi [Seacer], and Boni [Boyer] would enter the band fully aware of their status with no illusions about who they were and what their roles were. The newbies were coming in as accompanists to a now-established superstar, whereas the Revolution had shared Prince's rise to stardom and harbored exaggerated ideas of what they contributed, so they simply no longer fit Prince's agenda.

ME: After they got home from Japan, he blew it all up.

BROWNMARK: After the tour ended, Prince fired the girls and Bobby at the same time. The Bobby thing had nothing to do with a falling out; it was about Prince wanting to perform with Sheila E. Then Prince called me and said he'd fired them. He gave me the option of staying or going. He said, "I don't want you to leave the group, but if you feel bad about me letting your bandmates go and you choose to leave, I will understand." He thought I would be deeply pained by them being fired and I was. These people were like family to me. But to have him give me the option of staying or going was kind of odd. I said, "I have no desire to leave the group. I'm not dissatisfied with anything, except that I feel like what you're doing right now is a huge mistake." I tried to persuade him to not let the three of them go but he didn't listen to me. He said, "I've made up my mind—that's it." I stayed in the band.

ME: Prince never again had a band that felt like a family.

ALAN LEEDS: I don't get the sense that there was a relationship like that with the later bands. It's not to say he didn't like them or respect them or sometimes kibitz in the studio and have laughs, but I get the sense that with the later bands, when they were done with work, they went home and they didn't hear from him.

WENDY MELVOIN: After us, he wasn't that close to his bands. I know he was very close to Sheila and I know that there were people who represented family to him, but it was a different vibe.[21]

BOBBY Z.: The Revolution was the last band Prince was in. I don't want to hurt anyone's feelings, but the way he treated the bands after us was different. He would tell them that they were important, but he didn't treat them that way. He'd be like, "Here's a tape; learn it." With us, it was this group effort. Once, John Lennon is supposed to have tried to get Eric Clapton to join the Beatles. Years later, when Clapton was asked about it, he said, "There were times when it was like the closest-knit family you've ever seen in your life. But the cruelty and the viciousness was unparalleled." When you're in a band, in order to get perfection, you have to beat on each other. Things have to get messy. With us, with the Revolution, Prince was in the battle. He was in the trenches. We were together as a unit fighting to figure out every step. We took on the world with him. It was bloody and beautiful.

ME: After he fired Wendy and Lisa, Prince's relationship with Susannah began to wither.

SUSANNAH MELVOIN: We weren't moving toward marriage. We weren't doing anything. Well, he was doing things. We would have these moments where he just needed to get away and he would get on a flight to London or LA or wherever, and I'd be like, "You're not just working. I know what you're doing." When that started to happen more frequently, I was like, *Ugh, something's going on.* He'd leave me alone in the house, then he'd come back and everything would be fine. There were more and more of those. At some point, I ended up leaving the house and getting my own place in downtown Minneapolis. He wanted me to move out. He told me to. I've never talked about this, but he said, "I just don't think I'm ready to be living with you." He goes, "I'll do what I can to make you comfortable, but I think I need the space here." He broke my heart. I ended up in my own place and still having the same relationship with him, just not in the house all the time. I'm certain that he had other women in the house that I built. It was super painful. Finally, I said I just can't do it anymore. I packed my shit up and left in the middle of the night. He did everything he possibly could to get me to come back. I said, "No. Not doing it. Just can't do this anymore. No more of it. No more. Cannot. Can't. None of this is worth it to me, to not be around my family and my sisters and the love we have and the total ease in which we all express ourselves." It had been many years of that. It was just too much. It had to be over. I was scared shitless of him anyway at that point. I ran away. But he continued to call me. Six months after I left, he would be in Germany and say, "You want to come over and hang?" But he wasn't even that open. We'd be talking on the phone and he would say something and I knew where he was going with it. I was still slightly attached, so I'd say, "Okay." "I'll have a ticket there in the morning and somebody will come get you." I'd go and then stuff would happen and I'd come back. I didn't want to be that girl. I didn't want to be that self-conscious with my life. I just didn't. I was spending too much time alone and I couldn't handle the time alone. I went back to LA and moved in with my sister and Lisa. He spent the better part of two or three months trying to get me to come home. I said, "I can't do it. I can't come home."

ME: He went to LA to try to get her back.

SUSANNAH MELVOIN: I was at the house with Wendy and Lisa when Gilbert Davidson [Prince's bodyguard and later manager] came and said Prince was in a car outside. He said, "You've got to go out there. You've got to talk to him. You've got to talk to him." I was like, "I don't.

If I go and talk to him, I'm going to go back home with him. And I can't." Finally, I got in the car. It was heartbreaking. Prince said, "Are you coming home?" I said, "No, I'm not. I can't." He said, "Why not?" I said, "I don't want to be alone anymore. I can't do it." He said, "You won't be alone. I'll be there." I didn't know how to answer him. I was thinking, *That's the problem—that's lonely.* I think I blacked out at that point. I don't remember how it totally ended. I really don't. All I know is, I got out of the car and he was really upset, and I was a wreck. I went back in the house and I cried and cried. Of course, within a few months, he's on the road with *Sign O' The Times*, and I'm flying all over the world to hang out with him and be with him. And I'm sure he's with other women and they have no idea that like, "Oh, Susannah's in town. She's with him," and I'm like, "Ugh." This went on for years. It took another two years before I was fully, fully, fully, fully out.

ME: She was there the day Prince recorded "Wally."

SUSANNAH MELVOIN: "I remember him going downstairs with Susan [Rogers] and he was in and out from the studio, getting a cup of tea here and there, and then he'd go back down and Susan would come up and she'd say, "It's incredible, Susannah. It's about you and it's the most beautiful thing ever." Twenty-four hours later she comes upstairs crying, saying "I can't believe what he's done. It was a masterpiece. The best thing he's ever done. And now there's nothing left of it. Nothing." She said it had my name in it and it referred to me and him in the most intimate way. She was upset about him erasing it.

ME: Susan says "Wally" might be the saddest, deepest, most honest song Prince ever made and maybe Prince's best song ever. We'll never know.

SUSAN ROGERS: I'm reluctant to talk about this because I've spoken about his personal life and I've regretted it, but it's okay for me to speak about my personal life, so I'll tell you what I saw. His long relationship Susannah was finally off for good. He started wearing different clothes and I expected that there would soon be a song reflecting how he was feeling. I said, "I wonder when it's going to come." It came one day when we were in Minneapolis. It was a Sunday, it was winter time, and there was snow on the ground. He called me to his house to record. I put up a roll of fresh tape and he played every instrument. He had me mic the piano and give him the long reverb, which is what we would do for ballads. As usual, he played the drums, then the piano, and the bass and strings. When it came time to do the vocal, I left the room so he could do the vocal by himself. When I came back in, I heard the vocal. It was called "Wally," and he started by speaking through Wally Safford, his dancer and bodyguard. Prince is talking. It's a monologue and he's saying, "Wally, those glasses are really cool, can I try them on? Cause I'm going to a party and I want to look clean." He tries on the glasses and he says "This is great" and then he says, "I want to look good 'cause I hope I meet someone because my woman left me." Then it goes into the chorus and the melody was just beautiful, he's a genius with melody and this one was gorgeous. The words of the chorus are "Oh my la de da, oh my la de da...my la de da, oh my melody, oh my malady, my sickness, oh my la de la..." It was beautiful. All based on piano but with a lot of strings. At the end, the music breaks down and he hands the glasses back to Wally. He says "Keep these glasses. I don't need them now. I'm going home." The song was confessional, it was close to the bone. He was saying, "This is what I'm feeling. I feel terrible." The song was a message of sadness and regret and it was a window into his pain and into who he really was. It was beautiful. He was layering the piano and layering the backing vocal into a big choir that was Phil Spector-ish, really big and beautiful. We spent the whole day tracking everything and mixing it, and I made him a cassette. Then he looked at me, pointed to the multi-track, and said, "Now erase it." I said, "What? Excuse me?" He said, "Put all twenty-four tracks in record and erase it." It was one of the best things I'd ever heard him do, so I said, "You've got to be kidding me." He said "If you don't, I will." He'd never said anything like that before. I said, "Please, will you just think about it? Can we just put the tape away and just think about it overnight? Tomorrow, if you still want it done, I'll do it." I felt, as a fan, that that was wrong. *Don't do this. You're depriving us of this great song and you're depriving us of a window into who you are.* It's so hard to put that much care into something and then destroy it. I did not know that this was being created to be destroyed, but it was too close to the bone for him. He didn't want it heard. He stepped toward the machine and he put all twenty-four tracks in ready record, hit record, and wiped the whole thing.

ME: In the years after their relationship finally ended, Prince continued to need Susannah and, every once in a while, he called her.

SUSANNAH MELVOIN: He loved being hugged by me. I always knew when I was with him that he had this intense, kind of, visceral thing around my hugs. One time, years after we'd broken up, he called me in the middle of the night and said, "Can I come over?" I told him how to get to my place and he comes in and he said, "I just came here because I needed to get a hug from you." I wrapped him in my arms and I gave him this big, giant hug. He just melted into my arms and was smelling the back of my neck. He was like, "I needed to be hugged and nobody hugs me the way you do." It was heartbreaking. I was like, "What's going on?" I couldn't figure out what was going on with him but he was struggling with something. He stayed for about an hour and when he was leaving, he stopped at the door. He looked at me, and he was like, "I'm coming back for you. I'm coming back for you." I said, "Okay, I'll be here. You know where I am."

ME: Her love is eternal.

SUSANNAH MELVOIN: My relationship with him was layered, complicated, beautiful, heartbreaking, and never to be. But it was a beautiful ride. He was the coolest alien that's ever landed and I got the abduction. I'm totally happy about it.

ME: Prince was approaching middle age and he wanted a family. He wanted love and connection, but he also needed something to protect him from himself. He was still taking pills and people around him were realizing that something was wrong.

14

Moonbeam Levels

Addiction (1985–1988)

SUSANNAH MELVOIN: The 1985 to '87 period was probably the most prolific songwriting period of his life. He made five albums' worth of songs. He made *The Black Album, Camille, Crystal Ball*[22], *Dream Factory,* and *Sign O' The Times*.

ME: *Camille* and *Crystal Ball* were going to be released in the voice of Prince's feminine alter ego, Camille. He lost interest in Camille, but...

SUSANNAH MELVOIN: He presented *Crystal Ball* to the label as a triple album. They said, "No way. No triple album." He went back and plucked songs from each of those projects to make up *Sign O' The Times*, a double album.

ME: The Revolution played on *Sign O' The Times* but in several ways, it was a return to form.

BOBBY Z: When he made *Sign O' The Times*, he had broken free of having the Revolution as a weight and I mean no disrespect in saying that, but now he was back to being Prince the soloist. I was there long before there was a band, when he was in LA making albums by himself, and I was surprised when he wanted to cement himself to a band. When I saw the cover of *Purple Rain* with the band, I couldn't believe he would go so far as to have the band branded along with him because at his core, he was a solo guy. *Sign O' The Times* goes back to that. And there's amazing grooves and the instrumentation is lush.

SUSAN ROGERS: *Sign O' The Times* was an opportunity for Prince to try to return to his original audience. An attempt to be more soulful and speak to people who he may have been accused of neglecting. People who listened to R&B radio and bought soul records. "Adore" was important in that quest. It was a conscious attempt to win back those fans he had been steadily losing.

ME: The colors he chose to present *Sign O' The Times* say something about where his mindset was.

SUSAN ROGERS: He went into peach on *Sign O' The Times* because Susannah wore it a lot.

SUSANNAH MELVOIN: It was the '80s. All that horrible pastel was a thing. I wore peach. He wore peach. I had dresses in peach; we had peach pillows in our house. We had a lot of it in the house. Pastel was everywhere in the '80s.

ME: Prince always chose colors for his albums' artwork that spoke to what he was thinking about musically.

SUSAN ROGERS: He'd gone black and white for *Dirty Mind* because it's artsy and minimalist and that was a minimalist record. *On Purple Rain,* he was making a grand statement, so he used purple because it's royal. It makes a splash. *Around the World In A Day* is rainbow because the album is utopian. He was in a moment of rebirth. *Parade* goes back to black and white because he's making an introspective art record—the movie was in black and white. It's artful, it's a deeper musical expression. And on the cover of *Lovesexy,* he's naked because he's baring his soul and talking about his spirituality, which means so much to him.

ERIC LEEDS: When we were recording *Lovesexy,* we did two versions of the song "Lovesexy." The original version was musically quite different from the released version. We recorded it and then a few days later, he called me and said we were going to do a remake of the song. Same lyrics, completely different music. After the session, I asked him why the remake and he said he had taken the original version out to California to play for people at Warner Bros. and no one understood it. No one could figure out what the song was about or what he was trying to get across. He said he needed to redo the music to get people to understand it more. He looked at me and said, "You understand it, don't ya?" I didn't really understand it, but I said, "Maybe I do, but why don't you explain it so there's no misunderstanding?" He looked at me and said, "It means God is love. God loves you."

Alan Leeds: His whole *Lovesexy* thing was about the merging of the words love and sexy, which underlined his whole ethos that those two things are one in the same. The love of God and the sexual urges we feel are somehow one in the same. That's what he was trying to say. They both come from the same root inside a human being. God planted these urges and it's never wrong to feel either. Lust is a holy urge just as love is a spiritual imperative. That was at the core of his personal philosophy, so in revealing that, he was sharing who he really was. It was a really vulnerable thing for him.

Me: *Lovesexy* is one of Prince's great albums but for several reasons, it was a commercial flop and that was deeply hurtful to him. He did not normally fixate on such things—when I interviewed him, he said, "To me, the album is a success when I release it. I don't care what fans and critics think." But this album was different because he was revealing himself and his spiritual philosophy. To him, sex and God or sex and spirituality were not separate; they were one. He pulls this together in "Adore," where an intertwined couple is being watched by angels in Heaven who are moved to tears by their love, linking sex and Heaven in a way seldom seen in pop music or even poetry. Most religions tend to make sex feel forbidden, but Prince's vision of the spiritual world fully embraces sexuality. He fully merges Saturday night and Sunday morning. That communion has long been at the center of R&B music—the bastard child of gospel—but Prince took both sides further than any other songwriter. He made lewd songs like "Darling Nikki" and "Sister" as well as songs like "God" and "Controversy," in which he recites the Lord's Prayer unironically. How did he reconcile these two sides? In *Lovesexy*, he explains himself. But there were several issues with *Lovesexy*. Prince sequenced the CD so that it played as one single song because he wanted people to listen to everything he was saying about God and evil. He did not want people skipping around. It made the listening experience cumbersome—people didn't want to always start with the first song, and they didn't want to fast-forward to get to later songs when they were used to just pushing a button to skip to the next. Fans and radio programmers alike were annoyed, which reduced both the amount of airplay the album received and the word of mouth around it. Also, shortly before the album dropped, Prince decided to launch the Lovesexy Tour, but both Madonna and Michael Jackson were already slated to tour America that summer, so Prince had to tour Europe all summer and do America in the fall, taking him far away from American consumers and media when he should have been home promoting the album. On the cover, Prince put a tasteful and artful photograph of himself naked to symbolize that he was baring it all—he was baring his soul—but Walmart, the country's biggest retailer, objected to the nudity and refused to sell the album. None of that had anything to do with the quality of the music or the nature of Prince's message. But the album was a commercial disappointment and that hurt Prince deeply. For someone who had spent so long hiding his true self, to reveal that and have the public dismiss it was painful.

Eric Leeds: When that album flopped, he took it very personally. He really did consider that to be one of his most personal albums. He went through a crisis of conscience and a crisis about his place in popular music. He took it hard.

Me: Part of why the rollout for *Lovesexy* was a bit rushed is because it was a replacement—a few months earlier, he was set to release the *Black Album*, a much more lewd and aggressive record, but then he had a bad feeling about the album while doing ecstasy with his then girlfriend Ingrid Chavez and decided to shelve it at the last minute.

SUSANNAH MELVOIN: I went to visit him at the house. He told me that he'd had a divine intervention the night before and that he wasn't going to release the *Black Album*. He said it was too dark. He said he was told to stay away from that negative place. The record had already been manufactured, but he stopped the release. Later, I heard that he had had an ecstasy trip.

SUSAN ROGERS: Apparently, Prince stayed up late one night and got some drugs from somebody. He had a bad experience and it made him really unhappy. He had wanted to try it because Hendrix and some of his idols took drugs. He said, "Well maybe I should try," but he didn't like it. The song, "Moonbeam Levels" was about the feeling of coming down from being high. I think he scared himself.

JILL JONES: He started doing hallucinogens with Ingrid Chavez and all these different people and looking back, now, for me, that's a red flag.

ME: The man who had always rejected drugs and did not want anyone around him doing drugs or even getting drunk, was suddenly open to doing drugs recreationally. His attitude toward taking substances had changed. At the same time, he was struggling to manage the chronic pain that dogged him through the last few decades of his life.

MORRIS HAYES: I did notice that after some of the shows [in the '90s] he would have on these spongy little flip-flops, and I'm thinking the only reason why you would put something like that on is to try and absorb some of the impact. At one tour, we used lots of smoke machines and had these ramps on the sides of the stage. The fog from the machines would make the ramps very slippery and once, coming down on one of the ramps, Prince slipped and fell hard. He told me he broke his toe. He said, "My toe went like under my boot." I was like, *Ew, that's tough*, and after that, I started noticing that he had these really dope canes he would walk around with but I could see that he was wincing as he walked and favoring one leg over the other.

ME: Did he go to the doctor?

MORRIS HAYES: Prince never liked doctors and he never liked the hospital, so any way that he could avoid dealing with any doctors, he'd be like, "Yes. I don't have to deal with them."

ME: He may have been self-medicating as early as the early '90s. That's when Morris Hayes believes Prince went to rehab.

MORRIS HAYES: This one time in '94, Prince had been real hard on us, just killing us. For a whole week, every day he was rough. One day after rehearsal, the guys get to talking and they're like, "Dude, what's the matter with Prince? He's on a trip right now. What's his problem?" We're all just sitting around chewing at that and one of the guys is like, "Word on the street is he's messing with drugs." I'm like, "What? Do you believe that?" The guy said, "Yeah. Probably. Maybe." I said, "Well, then, you should say something." I said, "I'm gonna." But first I went home and thought about it. I was feeling like, okay, I can be here a while, I like my job, I'm getting paid to do great music, it's like my dream has come true and I don't want to rock the boat but then I'm thinking, *If he is doing drugs, if something happens to him, I'm not gonna have a job anyway. If I know that there's a problem and I don't try to help then that's horrible.* So I called and asked if I could have a meeting with Prince. When I go in his office, I'm nervous. He had a suite up in Paisley Park that was an office-slash-bedroom. I go in and he's marching around doing his thing. He's always busy. I'm nervous because I don't know what this dude is gonna do when I say what I gotta say. I could be walking into a big, bad situation. But I sit down and I say, "Hey man, look. I don't mean to come in here casting aspersions or anything. I don't mean to cause no problems and I wouldn't even say nothing, man, it's just that you've really been weird and acting really out of character, lately, and I'm sorry, bro, but word on the street is you're messing with drugs and if you are, bro, your slip is showing. If not, then, I'm sorry. I don't mean no harm." He said, "Aw, man. I'm not doing anything like that." He says, "I'm a taskmaster and, you know me, I'm working. I'm doing stuff. We've got a lot of stuff to do. It's nothing like that." I'm like, "Okay, man." He said, "It's nothing like that and it's cool and you can head on back down. It's cool." So, I go back down. But Prince doesn't show up to rehearsal. We're just waiting on him to come down but he never shows. We come in the next day, no Prince. We come back each day, no Prince. This goes on for a week. Now usually, if Prince goes out of town, or if he's got meetings, he would give us instructions saying, "Alright, do this and this, and then, send him a tape so he can watch rehearsal." There was none of that. It was like he just vanished. About a week later, he's back. As soon as I walk into Paisley, he comes over the intercom like God. "Morris, please come to the office." I'm like, *Oh snap. I got summoned by the man.* I knew for sure I'm getting fired. I get up to his office and I'm shaking in my boots like, *This is over.* He said, "Hey, man. I want you to understand that in the time since I've been a professional, I've never taken a week and not picked up my guitar and not written a song. I want you to know that I appreciate you coming in here. I took some time to lie about and kind of cool out and I appreciate you coming in here and saying something." That's not what I was expecting him to say. Now, it's weird that at no other time that I worked with him did he leave without leaving instructions. And that he didn't play or write for a whole week was really a big deal. I've never seen Prince go a day without doing something musical, much less a week. Prince would write a song every day, so for him to tell me that he hadn't picked up his guitar or written a song in a whole week, I was like, *Well, what did he do?* We didn't hear from him; no one in the band did. I don't know what else he could've did other than go somewhere where he was sequestered. I think he went to rehab. I hope he went to rehab. I think he was dealing with an issue and I hope that's what he did.

ME: Prince's battle with chronic pain had him debating for years whether or not he should have surgery.

MORRIS HAYES: I was at his house in LA and he was talking to Tyler Perry and me. Prince said, "I talked to Tiger Woods's doctor and I'm gonna get him to do my knee operation." I always kind of thought

Prince needed hip surgery done because he used to jump off of speakers and do splits and do all of these things. I don't know how anybody could physically do what he did on a year-by-year basis and not be completely racked in pain. I just know that there were many times where he was filled with pain and just powered through it. I don't know how he could do it. It would make me hurt just looking at him do it. So when he mentioned surgery I said, "Prince, please, do it. You'll only be pissed off that you didn't do it sooner."

ME: It's unclear whether or not he ever got surgery. But his chronic pain and his drug use continued, as did some strange behavior.

MORRIS HAYES: One time in 2010, Prince went to San Francisco and for whatever reason, he wanted me to book the hotels and planes and stuff. Then I got a call from one of the people from the Ritz Carlton saying they were a bit concerned because Prince got spooked out about the room and decided to go to some other place. The guy at the hotel says, "You're the only guy we know to call and we're concerned about him." I'm like, "What?" I was in Minneapolis, so I called the head of his security detail and said, "Hey man, what's going on? He says Prince had gotten away from them. He went out on his own. "He lost us. He ditched us." I was like, "What? Well, you've got to find him!" Eventually they did, and when I talked to Prince afterwards, I said to him, "What did you do?" He said, "I went with these nice people. They bought me breakfast and some other stuff." I'm like, "Are you kidding? You can't do that! What in the hell are you thinking?" That's when I started thinking it must be something heavy because that is not what you do in a normal situation, ditch your security detail and go have breakfast with some strangers. When he got back to Minneapolis, I said, "Prince, you have to stop whatever you're doing, bro. This is not clear thinking. You've got to stop." I just hugged him up, man. I grabbed him, and I hugged him, and I started crying, and squeezing him. I actually caught myself because I was squeezing him in like a mad squeeze. I'm hugging him and he's like a ragdoll, not trying to like break loose, just taking it. I said, "Prince, you have to stop. Whatever you're doing, you have to stop."

15

Let's Have a Baby

The Birth and Death of Prince's Son and the End of His Marriages (1996–2006)

ME: The year is 1998 and I'm inside Paisley Park playing one-on-one basketball with Prince. There's a single movable hoop set up just a few feet away from a rehearsal stage. He's in a tight, almost sheer, long-sleeved black top, tight black pants, and black boots, until he digs into a box of used sneakers and pulls out some Nike Air Force high tops that are red with a white swoosh. Then he takes my ball and makes a face that anyone would recognize as *I'ma kick yo ass* and starts knifing around the court. As he dribbles and moves and defends and shoots, he looks like a ballplayer. His form is perfect, his movement is smooth and athletic, he's clearly at home on the basketball court. He moves quickly but under control, dribbling fast, sliding under my arm to snatch rebounds I thought for sure I had, making jukes to create space and rapidly rising up to shoot. He plays like one of those fast, darting little guys you've got to keep your eye on every second—blink and he's somewhere you'd never expect. Lose control of your dribble for a millisecond and he's snatched the ball. He's energetic and plays with a fast tempo and always thinks he can make the shot no matter where he is, so it's a rapid game. He shoots a lot, but he's never manic or out of control. We're both rusty so a lot of shots miss, clanking off the rim, and after ten minutes, there's not much of a score: it's 4-4. Finally, I get past him and lay it in, scoring on a drive that feels too easy. As I grab the ball I just put in, I look back at him like what happened? He said, "I don't foul guests." Oh really? On the next play, I fake left and again drive right and just when I think I've got a step on him he bumps my arm hard, knocking me off course, fouling me. He makes a look like, *What? I didn't see anything.*

This all started days ago when I interviewed him in a small conference room upstairs and walked away unhappy. To write a good cover story, I need a lot of comments, I need some introspection, I need some stories, I need a deep talk about who you are, and I need a few hours of talk time plus some hang-out time. Prince had given me about thirty minutes in a conference room and a lot of what he said were talking points. He wore a maroon velour Prince suit—it had a slim cut vest as a top and a matching pant. He gripped a gold cane and maintained a sly, Cheshire Cat smile. There was base makeup covering his face and his frame seemed so small and wispy that it looked like a strong man could snap him like firewood, but I never once thought that he seemed short. It just never occurred to me. Later, realizing that, I remembered the iconic dancer Rudolf Nureyev saying, "On stage, I can be as tall as I want."

Before I could ask a question, he took over the conversation, speaking in a deep, warm, masculine voice, launching into his core issue like a politician on script. "We've been talking about how freedom has affected our people," he said. "It's so liberating to work on music with no dogma at all. It's so freeing to record without a clock ticking, without knowing you owe someone royalty money." I would have preferred to talk about music rather than the business of music, but this was important—he had recently split from Warner Bros., his record label of eighteen years, after a bitter battle. He had named himself an unpronounceable symbol as a way of distancing himself from the label—he was trying to renounce his old self by giving himself a new name, thus declaring he no longer owed the label anything because he was no longer Prince. The label said, "No, you're still Prince." (Before we met, a publicist told me to not refer to him as Prince but later, I made a mistake and did call him Prince and it was...a thing. But we'll get to that.) He had written "slave" on his cheek to say that he was a slave to his record label as if they owned him because he couldn't do anything he wanted like, say, release a triple album or leave the label. He wanted to know, does the label own my music or my body? Am I stuck working for them even if I want to leave? A lot of people thought he was either crazy or disrespectful to bring that loaded word into his dispute. Could a multimillionaire musician really be a slave when he was his ancestors' wildest dream? He was determined to focus our interview on that.

"For me to create an album, tour all over night after night and get less than the $140 million it grosses is ridiculous."

"How much would you get?"

"I'd get at most $7 million."

"Still, how could you call yourself slave in light of the history of that word among our people?"

"Imagine yourself sitting in a room with the biggest of the big in the recording industry and you have slave written on your face. That changes the entire conversation. You know what they think of us. They say 'It makes it real hard to talk to you with that on your face.' Why? And it got real quiet. They don't wanna get into all that. Adding that language into the conversation worked perfectly. It changed the dynamic of the conversation."

"Is there a difference between Prince and the Artist?" He was then called The Artist Formerly Known as Prince" or "The Artist."

"Only that Prince owns nothing. None of those songs."

"So you're happier now? Did the old music come from a place of pain?"

"I won't speculate on where the music came from. I look back in awe and reverence. It's made me become courageous."

"Courageous around music?"

"Regarding everything."

"Do you realize you've changed a generation with your music?

He got defensive. "I don't think about that. Why would I? There's no gain in that. Being in control of someone's thoughts? You'll second guess your writing."

I felt stifled. I was unable to get to the real Prince. He was closed off. He wasn't really answering my questions and allowing us to have an organic conversation: he was just steering our talk back to one issue—his dispute with his label and the importance of recording artists owning their own masters. I understand him making that point and moving on, but I didn't feel like I was getting to see the real person, it was more like a robot diverting everything back to a single command. It was more of a performance, not him letting me get to know him. This was what people had talked about, the way he prevented people from ever seeing the real him. I had to do something. I had to break through somehow. I kept thinking, *How can I get him to loosen up and really talk to me?* I was also thinking *Oh my God, I'm talking to Prince.* Also: *How in the hell am I going to get these quotes down?* He had banned media from recording him so I had to furiously scribble his words as we went along. I had to recall what he'd said while listening to what he was saying while thinking about what to him ask him next, do I need to follow up the question I'd asked or move on to another...?

I asked him about basketball and I could see his body relax.

"What's your team?"

"Bulls," he said, like, *Of course.*

This was when they had Michael Jordan, Scottie Pippen, and Dennis Rodman and they were the best and most beloved team in American pro sports.

"It's gonna be rock 'n' roll time next year," Prince said. "The Bulls are gonna be like the Beatles. He's Superman," he said, meaning MJ, obviously. "He don't have to do that much to whup them people."

We laughed together. I loved Jordan, too. His success, his excellence, his athletic beauty were somehow uplifting. Then, a moment later, somehow, we were back on recording artists and money. Prince said he admired the music of Erykah Badu, De La Soul, A Tribe Called Quest, and D'Angelo, then said, "D'Angelo's really gotta search his heart deeply on being part of the problem or the solution. What's his whole consciousness? He's got to own his masters," he said, referring to the tapes that confer true ownership of a song. "Black Americans are walking away and getting nothin'! How can you not own your masters and try to uplift the community? Let's all of us be part of the solution or we gonna get our problems solved for us. The situation in Africa is testament to that. Twenty-one million with AIDS! Don't that spook you? We got to solve our problems or they'll be solved for us. And a man can't solve your problems for you. You and your faith will solve 'em for you."

What? How did we get from D'Angelo to owning your masters to AIDS in Africa to faith solving your problems? It was fascinating and frustrating to talk to him. It seemed like an act, and surely an act he believed in but not an honest human connection. He told me another journalist had asked him, "Do you ever get tired of being so flamboyant all the time? Don't you ever wanna wear a T-shirt and jeans?" He reared his head back, eyes wide, in mock indignation, as if to clutch symbolic pearls and say, *How ridiculous! Don't you know who I am?* He thrust the cuff of his maroon Prince suit out toward me in a very macho gesture and said, "Feel that! If you could wear that every day, wouldn't you?!"

I felt the cuff. It wasn't a rare and special feeling. "What is it?" I asked.

Immediately, his entire demeanor switched. It was an emotional stop on a dime. He went, in a heartbeat, from larger than life to hushed and humble.

"Oh, I don't know," he said quietly, dismissively, feigning ignorance of the fabric of his fabulous garment. "If you have money, you should act the same. It's currency. It's supposed to move like a current. You ain't supposed to hoard it. You get sick otherwise." So now money isn't important? I'm confused.

After we finished, I walked out feeling as though I'd gotten far too little for a cover story. He'd never truly shared himself. I'd been given the day's propaganda. And today's propaganda had made me feel like I'd spoken to Curt Flood, a 1960s baseball player known mainly for sacrificing his career to force the introduction of free agency, when I'd hoped to better understand Willie Mays, the greatest. Or maybe: I'd met Lebron, but instead of basketball, he would only discuss the collective bargaining agreement.

I didn't have nearly enough for a cover story. I asked the publicist if I could email him some questions. She said okay. So I wrote twelve questions, mostly about music, and at the last second I tacked on one more: will you play one-on-one basketball with me? Then I emailed the queries into cyberspace—this was back when we called it the information superhighway or the world wide web.

Two days later, he emailed me his answers. I wish I had kept that page. Why didn't I print it out and frame it? I don't know. The impermanence of the Internet seemed clear even then. If he'd written me a letter, I would've put it in a safe deposit box, but his email to me is lost to time. I no longer know what my questions were, but I have his answers. He used the letter u for the word you and the letter r for the word are and the number 4 for the word for and 2 for the word to or two. That's where he wrote "Ultimately, spiritual evolution is the axis on which inspiration and creativity spin...there r so many songs that I've written and recorded, sometimes it is hard 4 ME 2 believe it comes from one source!" And, intriguingly, he wrote, "All of my musicality comes from GOD...the blessing/curse ensued when I kept sneaking back in2 the talent line dressed as another person...I got away with it several times be4 they caught me!!"

As for my last question, will you play basketball with me, he wrote "Anytime, brother." Anytime? Basketball with Prince sounded amazing. Nah, he didn't mean it. Did he? I'd get to Paisley and there'd be some excuse. Right? But how could I risk not trying? When it was time for the photo shoot that would accompany my story, I went back to Paisley and just to minimize the potential for excuses, I brought my own ball.

After a while, our one-on-one morphed into two-on-two—Prince and I against six-foot-five Morris Hayes and my photographer, a normal-sized human. Prince told him not to take pictures of the game, so there's no visual record. With two-on-two, the game became more exciting. Prince was setting picks and making smart passes and moving with purpose like someone who knows the fundamentals of strategy. Whenever he saw a slight opening, he drove to the hole boldly, sometimes flying through the air in between both opponents, being too aggressive, yet showing the confidence of a man who's taken on the world and won. He scored on a lot of those too-bold drives to the hoop and on some jumpers, too.

At one point, I was dribbling at the top of the key when I saw that he was in good position under the basket. I quickly flicked the ball at him. I grew up idolizing Magic Johnson so, to me, the best pass was always a no-look pass. This was one of those except while I was not looking at Prince, Prince wasn't looking at me. And the ball was flying right toward him. A millisecond later, I realized he didn't know the ball was coming. I had to do something. I yelled out. This man had been a part of my life for about twenty years, so I yelled out the only name I ever knew. I yelled out, "Prince!"

But he was not Prince. And in the milliseconds between the word escaping my mouth and me realizing my faux pas I had a vision of him storming out of the room and banishing me from his Paisley Palace. I put my hand over my mouth as if to catch the word out of the air and put it back before it reached his ears. But the word was out there and the ball was still flying toward him when he turned to see it. It missed hitting him by a lucky inch—by the grace of God I didn't bust Prince's nose. The ball flew past him, out of bounds and he jogged off to grab it. As he walked back holding the ball, he smirked. I said, "What's so funny?" He pointed at me and said, "He didn't know what to call me." He was laughing at my quandary, enjoying seeing me off balance, forgiving my mistake, and just being cool. Finally, I was seeing the real man.

After that, the game teetered back and forth with one team gaining point-game then the other—Prince made most of the shots—until it was 13-12, our lead. It was a bit tense. We definitely wanted to win. I took the ball out at the top of the key, dribbled while he made some moves, passed it to him when he was on the baseline and looking. My pass hit him in the hands, and then, full of poise, he coolly rose up, shot, and it swished in. We won.

MORRIS HAYES: Prince had gone through this time where he was really fed up with interviews. We had had a couple bad interviews and he had just gotten sick of it. Then we had a lot of records we had coming out so he says, "You know what, man? I'm not gonna have any more of these interviews with people who are not cool, who either can't play music or can't do something that we love. I don't want to have these boring interviews." So when people would show up, he'd say, "Okay. What can you do? You play something?" If you said, "I play a little guitar," it was "Okay, Levi, give him your guitar." The guy would be on the spot, but if they just could play even a little, he said, "Okay. I'll talk to you." When you came, it was cool because he said, "Alright. We're gonna play some ball. This dude looks like he could be a lot of fun. We gonna get it on here." When you came, he was like, "Alright. We gonna put him to the test. We gonna see what he can do." Man, we laughed about that for days on end because it was a lot of fun. It became a great story for us.

ME: Prince was excited to play basketball with me? Prince had fun playing basketball with me? I can die now.

MORRIS HAYES: That was one of his favorite sports. He loved, loved, loved basketball and any chance he got to play, man, he took it. Like we'd rehearse all day and then, go play. I played with him a lot and he killed me so many times. He knew how to get me to commit to moving or jumping, and once he's got you off your feet, you're a done deal. He was already past you, through you, put the basketball through your legs, whatever, and then, you're beat. He could fake me out and go by me every time, man. He loved, loved basketball, and he probably could've been like Spud Webb or something like that. Could've been but he didn't have the height, but he had handles, man. Damn, he could shoot. One time, he beat the tar out of me, he was beating me so severely. Remember that movie, *Pleasantville*? There was a scene where nobody missed a shot? Everything went in? That was Prince. Like, he'd shoot the ball, just throw it over his head, and it'd go in. I'm like, "Dude, come on? Really?" He said, "You know, Morris, I see the goal, I see the ball in the goal, and it's just execution. I see the shot finished in my head."

BROWNMARK: He was a ballplayer who knew how to play guitar. If he had any height to him, he would have definitely done something with basketball. If you could put another foot on him, man, it would have been a mess. Yeah, I just stopped playing with him because he used to kick my butt in heels. Whoever seen somebody play ball in four-inch heels? The dude wouldn't miss a beat. When I first started playing with him, I was like, I don't want to hurt him because he's way shorter than me, but if you gave him any kind of leniency, he would get mad and he would get better. That dude could ball, man. He was rough. He'll school you. He'll leave you sitting there looking stupid, sucking your thumb. He's bad. I didn't even want to play with him no more.

DEZ DICKERSON: He had a good outside stroke. Not Steph Curry, but that ilk. He'd set up outside and hit those threes all day. And he can handle the ball. He was a good player. Obviously, height is a factor, but he was legit. It's not like the showbiz version of, "Yeah, he's an athlete too." In this case, he really was. Playing basketball was part of the culture of the band. A few of us had been jocks before the music, so it wasn't like, "Oh, let's try to shoot a basket here." It was an authentic thing we really enjoyed and we all played hard. At Sunset Sound in LA, in the courtyard; they had a hoop and on breaks, we were out there shooting hoops many, many times. When we shot the "Little Red Corvette" and "1999" videos in Lakewood, Florida, when there was a break, we played basketball, like five-on-five, full-on, got the heels on and still killing it. He knew how to be normal at that point in time.

ME: Did I mention that Prince enjoyed playing basketball with me? And that he had fun? It was definitely one of the highlights of my life. But I did not know Prince was then slogging through one of the worst periods of his life. While I was at Paisley, Mayte pulled up in a hot pink BMW. They had met at a concert of his when she was a teenager—her mother gave Prince a videotape of her belly dancing, which led to them talking on the phone until she was legal. The day she turned eighteen, he flew her to Minneapolis. When I interviewed Prince, I asked him how he knew she was the one. He said, "God tells you who's the one. If you don't have a relationship with God, you're in trouble. That gives you something to put everything in line."

THEY MARRIED in 1996 in front of a dozen people and thousands of flowers that had been flown in from Japan. The couple honeymooned in Hawaii. I asked Prince if he enjoyed being married.

PRINCE (from our interview): I'm not afraid of the rain anymore because my wife built me a garden. Now the lightning and thunder put energy in the vegetables and give me energy to talk to you.

ME: She definitely made a difference in his life.

MORRIS HAYES: His whole lifestyle changed, bro. I hung out with Prince before her. We were rock stars, bro. We were seeing girls. When Mayte came in, it kind of grounded him. It kind of took all that rock 'n' roll life and shrunk it into family life. He had the dogs and everything. It just went to a family situation. It was a whole different kind of thing.

ME: Shortly after their wedding, Maye got pregnant. Prince sampled the baby's heartbeat for a song on his album *Emancipation*. During the pregnancy Prince transformed Paisley into an eye-popping wonderland. I noticed all sorts of colorful, whimsical paintings on the walls—a flock of golden doves seeming to tumble from the sky and rainbows and soft pastels. All over the place, there were oversized comfy chairs of all colors on pillars topped with gold disks. Underneath was thick blue carpeting dotted with zodiac symbols.

PRINCE (from our interview): There was no color in this building before I got married. It was all white with gray carpet. For fifteen years, I was just in the studio every day, on a grind, not even thinking about it.

ME: At Paisley, in the back, in a yard, there was a wooden jungle gym. It had never been used.

MORRIS HAYES: Before the baby came, he said to me, "I built a play yard out at Paisley." He put the swing and the full nine out in the back. I was like, "Prince, you know they can't use that when they're infants. You do realize that if you put that baby on that slide, it's just gonna not go well, so why do you have a slide?" He was like, "Morris, things are gonna change around here. You're gonna have to do a lot of things by yourself now because I got a kid, you know, and I'm gonna be busy doing stuff, so you got to handle it." He talked about when the kid's grown up, how that's gonna be, how they're gonna take over all of his estate and all of these things.

ME: But it was a difficult pregnancy. From early on, doctors knew something was wrong but Prince refused to allow them to intervene or even do routine checks. He said, "God will take care of us." Friends say Mayte considered having an abortion, but Prince refused to let her. He just knew that God would deliver them. The baby, Amiir, was born severely deformed. In her memoir, Mayte wrote about the moment of birth. "I don't know how to describe the look on my husband's face. Pure joy. Pure love. Pure gratitude. I'd seen this face when he stood in a stadium filled with forty-eight thousand screaming fans. I'd seen him experience the ecstasy of creative genius. None of that compared to the look I saw on his face in this moment when he became a father. And then they held the baby up in the glare of those harsh lights. The pure elation on my husband's face turned to pure terror. It was as if we were at the center of a whirlpool and the room was turning in on itself, contorting, twisting everything." The baby was born with Pfeiffer's Syndrome, a rare genetic disorder. Doctors rushed the child to intensive care. Prince called in the best specialists he could get. In her book, Mayte described the many issues the baby had. The child's severe birth defects are hard to read about. His eyes were outside his sockets. His hands and feet were weblike. He had no anus. They named him Amiir which means "Prince" in Arabic and relates to Mayte's mother's stage name from when she was a belly dancer—Amira, which is "princess" in Arabic. Mayte wrote, "He was Amiir's father, a protective papa bear thinking only of our son. From the first moment of our son's life to the last, my husband thought nothing of himself, his vanity, his ego, his needs—all that had been stripped away. All that remained was a solid core of unconditional love. There was a lot of surgery and a lot of fighting for his life but after nine days, both Mayte and Prince decided they had to let him go. They took him off of life support. Prince brought his ashes home in an urn. There was no funeral because Prince did not want one.

MORRIS HAYES: I saw what happens to a person, a human, when you have a loss like that. Prince was heartbroken.

GREG BOYER: He didn't really want to talk about it, but you could tell it was hard. He had a baby gym at Paisley Park and on the back wall of that gym was a lot of baby toys and baby items and they just sat there untouched. I just remember seeing it and thinking those toys never found a kid. I just couldn't imagine. I don't think those were easy days for him, but he tried his best to make it look like, "Okay, let me just keep going forward." I wondered what he was thinking 'cause that gym, you kind of had to walk through there to get from one of the studios to the main entrance. Did he go another way or did he walk through the gym and not look over there? Did he look over there and just feel this pain in the pit of his stomach? I don't know. He tried his best to mask it and he was successful at times, but I could see it. That might've been one of those instances where if he blows up on you for no reason, it's not you. That might've been one of those reasons why he fell off the horse.

MORRIS HAYES: It was an incredibly tough time. That's really when I saw the humanized Prince. I'd always seen his rock star side and I said that guy's as tough as nails. But I believe at that point I saw the humanized Prince. I think he realized that "I'm not God and I can't do anything more than I can do," and he felt what other people feel, that heartache of "I've done everything I can, I've spent all the money I have, and I'm just like anybody else and I'm hurt and I'm sad." I didn't really know what to do, other than to just try to comfort him. I'd never before seen him in the condition that he was in when all that happened. It was very heartbreaking. It was really tough. And he had to continue after that. That was so difficult because he was trying to do all of these things to get himself back into the headspace where he knows I've got to go do these tours, I've got to do this record, I've got to go do this stuff, and that's when you see the mental fortitude of somebody who is able to absorb all of that grief and find some way to keep going.

SUSAN ROGERS: From what I understand, this was really a turning point in his life.

A FRIEND: The experience left Prince broken. Losing the baby hurt him deeply. Losing a child is something some people never recover from.

ME: Mayte once said, "Losing a baby is a terrible thing. Some couples are brought closer together after the loss of a child; others are driven apart. In our case, the latter happened." After he lost the baby and the marriage, Prince was in his late thirties and without any family. He tried again with Manuela Testolini, his second wife, but their relationship ended after just a few years.

SUSANNAH MELVOIN: He saw her as a safe place. She was the salt of the earth. Smart, beautiful, grounded, strong family ties. He loved her.

ME: He bought a house in her hometown of Toronto so they could be closer to her family, but Prince was not up to the job of making the relationship last. After a few years, they separated. He was at an age when most of his peers are building families. He had nothing and that can be quite lonely. After losing the baby, he became a Jehovah's Witness—in my interview, Prince told me that it all began with him becoming close with a Witness named Larry Graham[23] who was the legendary bassist for Sly and the Family Stone and Graham Central Station. Prince also told he and Graham had had a multiyear argument about religion, which Prince said, "He won."

A FRIEND: Prince felt lost in the world after losing his baby and he became a Witness as a way of trying to find himself again.

ME: He went all in, attending service and knocking on strangers' doors to proselytize. People in Minneapolis told me it wasn't uncommon for him to knock on your door during a Minnesota Vikings game. He also proselytized within his own world.

WENDY MELVOIN: He asked me and Lisa to come back, but he asked me and Lisa to renounce our homosexuality with a press conference. We said, "That's just not going to happen." He also asked Bobby and Matt to sort of renounce their Judaism.

ERIC LEEDS: One afternoon in LA, he picked Wendy up under the guise of going to a recording session with him and he took her to a Kingdom Hall and made her sit through a service.

ME: As he moved into his forties, he was, more than ever, The Lonely Guy.

A FRIEND: He had become a sad and lonely person. He was not the fun guy he had been twenty years earlier. He used to be fun, a prankster. But after Mayte and the baby and all that, he was very sad.

ME: The only place he found community and love and acceptance and any sort of family was in his music and his fans.

JILL JONES: He definitely tried to make the fans into a family.

ME: They were his only real family. But that meant that he had to keep that relationship going no matter what his body felt like because without that, he would truly be alone in the world. He was still creative enough to keep it going and he still had fans around the world who loved him, but he also had chronic pain. In order to keep touring and getting on stage and doing the sort of show that would keep earning him love, he needed to dull the pain. He wasn't doing drugs like a hedonistic rock star; he was doing drugs like so many working-class Americans who need pills to get breaking-down bodies through the workday so they can show up for the people who rely on them. America has an opioid epidemic because many working people are using painkillers so they can work. Prince was one of them, but he was taking fentanyl so he could keep creating and touring. It wasn't because he needed the money; it was much deeper than that. Creating and touring were essential to his identity. This is someone about whom people said music is not what he does—it's who he is. They said you cannot divide Prince from the music. They said the guitar was an extension of him. When you are that deeply intertwined with music, then how could you stop? If you have no one to go home to, no wife, no serious girlfriend, no kids, and your family is your fans, you would do whatever you had to do to keep the connection going.

Morris Day: I think he used the drug so he could work and I think the feel-good part took over. He didn't realize what he was up against. He didn't realize how powerful it was. He must not have realized it because he ended up abusing it.

16

Sometimes It Snows in April

The Death of Prince (2016)

JILL JONES: After we fell out, I didn't speak to Prince for ages and the last time we really spoke was after Vanity died.²⁴ I was there talking with Apollonia and Susan [Moonsie] and her sister Loreen. It was all of us girls in a huddle and I just looked across the room at him and said, "He's on something." The girls were like, "What?" I said, "He's on something." I'm super, super tall, I'm like 5'8", 5'9" and these girls are all like 5'2" little chipmunks, and I'm in high heels. We're in the corner, and I'm leaned over, bent down talking to them. It looks like I'm gossiping and maybe I was, but, of course, he shows up. He goes, "What are you guys talking about?" And Susan, I totally love Susan, she's like, "You. We're talking about you. Why are you so thin? What's going on?" He didn't say anything but he looked at me. We still have a connection after thirty years: I could still feel his spirit, like a reading of the minds, and I knew what was up with him. I knew something was wrong, and I know he knew what I was thinking. Then the conversation turned into, "You're so thin," and each girl was saying, "We'll come up and take care of you and make some food for you and put some meat on those bones." Apollonia said she was going to go and look after him and I said, "You know what, let's all get together

228

like once a year. We're getting a little long in the tooth to not see each other more frequently, so let's just check on each other once a year. Let's just make that agreement." I was like, "Let's go do something we've never done before!" He goes, "Well, what do you want to do?" I said, "Let's all go skydiving together!" He was like, "I'm not going skydiving. You ain't gonna get me up there skydiving." I still think about how this is the guy who told me he wouldn't skydive, but he was taking fentanyl. That messes with me still.

BrownMark: I feel that the whole fentanyl thing was just him escaping pain from the hip and it got out of hand. I really believe that. I don't believe that it was anything recreational because Prince wasn't like that. I never knew him to recreationally take drugs and get high just to escape. That wasn't him. I think the opioid addiction is so strong that if you don't get an intervention, you can't come off of it. It's too addicting. My opinion is that it had everything to do with the pain from his hip and needing something to take that pain away but then it got to a point where the addiction settles in, but he's keeping it hidden because nobody's going to see me sweat. That was the thing he lived by. "Never let anybody see you sweat."

Me: But people knew he was off.

BrownMark: He invited me out to Paisley when he was thinking about doing a new group. He flew me in but he forgot, so I was sitting in the hotel for three days. You can't just call him, you can't get a hold of him, but how do you fly somebody and forget? I thought that was strange. Finally, I got in touch and when I got to Paisley, he was in the parking lot riding his bike in circles. I got out of the car and he looked at me, gave me a hug and said, "You look really good. I can tell you're taking care of yourself." I said, "I'm trying, I'm trying." He said, "Did you bring your guitar?" Weird. I said, "Bring my guitar? Prince, I play bass." He goes, "Oh. Well, okay. Well, somebody got to play guitar." I thought it was all really strange. I didn't know what it was, but I knew something was different.

SUSANNAH MELVOIN: I saw him on the American Music Awards and I had never seen his face so thin. He'd lost a ton of weight.

WENDY MELVOIN: By the time he died he was like 107 pounds. On the Parade Tour, he was 145 and all muscle. By the time he passed, he was like a baby bird.

SUSANNAH MELVOIN: He was super sallow. I was like, "Something's not right."

ALAN LEEDS: Chris Rock told me about seeing Prince near the end. He knew him rather well. Chris was in Saint Barts with Seinfeld and a whole bunch of other elite-level personnel and bold-faced personalities. Zuckerberg's there. It's that crowd and it's New Year's Eve 2015. Somebody had hired Prince as the entertainment. Rock said that he had never seen Prince with such a look of despair in his eyes. He looked so lonely. He's at New Year's Eve with just a bodyguard, no date, no girlfriend, performing for all of these people who are his peers, people he should be sitting and having a mint julep with. Now he was terrific on stage. He sat at the piano, played some guitar, was mesmerizing on a musical level, but he had no interest in socializing with the rest of the gang. Rock said he looked so sad it was striking. He said, "You know, I should have known something was up. He just wasn't himself."

ME: Being a rock star was no longer enough to sustain him.

ALAN LEEDS: Thirty-year-old Prince didn't care about anything in life beside music, but Prince in his fifties obviously wanted something else. Here's a guy who had two failed marriages, no surviving children, was estranged from most of his blood family, had very distant relationships if any at all with his sister, his half-brothers, and his half-sisters. At the end, he was living in an apartment in the huge complex, a space that was really an office. It wasn't really meant for sleeping. He was having a chef bring meals in, having an assistant bring him mail and run errands. It's this very lonely existence.

ME: On April 15, 2016, Prince was flying home in a private plane after a show in Atlanta when his plane made an emergency stop in Molene,

Illinois. He was just an hour away from Minneapolis. An emergency stop so close to home sent alarms through Princeworld.

MORRIS HAYES: Knowing Prince, there's no way they would've landed that close to Minneapolis unless he was in dire straits. I don't care what he felt like; he wouldn't have wanted to stop. The fact that it landed there meant it was big trouble.

ME: It was announced that Prince had the flu. Insiders didn't buy it.

SUSANNAH MELVOIN: I said, "That doesn't sound like the flu." I called and I spoke with Apollonia and she said, "I think he's okay."

JILL JONES: Apollonia told all of us that it was the flu and I kept saying, "Why would you come down in a plane that fast with the flu?"

MORRIS HAYES: I called one of Prince's folks and I said, "Hey, man, is, like, stuff cool, man? Because what I'm seeing on TV, this don't look good. If you don't get a handle on it, this dude's gonna be out of here so whatever you all doing, it needs to get tightened up, 'cause he don't look good. The situation doesn't look good. I know it's trouble. He looks out of control. Are you guys okay?" I got one of those responses like, "Yeah. Well, we good. It's all good."

ALAN LEEDS: I talked to Questlove, who had talked to Prince and been assured that he was okay. But what got me was Prince was so private about anything personal. He could keep anything secret because he would orchestrate a private entrance to a private hospital and have a private doctor sign an NDA, so the fact that this was something that couldn't be managed discreetly, the fact that it was public, that really spoke to the urgency of it. And then, I don't know where I got it, I can't think of the sequence of calls or who said it, but it was common knowledge among people who knew him that he had had some kind of reaction to drugs.

ME: When Prince's plane landed, he was carried to an ambulance that was waiting on the tarmac where he was revived with a shot of Narcan, a drug that combats opioid overdoses.

MORRIS HAYES: I remember calling Kiran, who had been Prince's manager, and telling her, "I just don't feel good about this. Something's really off. But I don't know what to do. But I think we gotta do something." One of my big regrets is that I didn't go there and just show up and take my chances and get kicked out if necessary.

BROWNMARK: I would've been like, "Dude, you just flatlined. You need to sit your butt down." He needed help. I knew he was in danger. If you're addicted to something and you zero out and you got nobody monitoring you, that's a concoction for trouble right there. And I heard he went right back to using. I heard it was even some street stuff.

SUSANNAH MELVOIN: I know addicts and I know what it's like to ask somebody to go into recovery. It's not easy. You can't just make somebody go do that. They have to call themselves an addict, they have to know that they are. He did not think he was an addict.

ALAN LEEDS: Nobody could have stopped him from taking whatever he was determined to take. Prince is someone who absolutely cannot be forced into doing something against his will, no matter how good your intentions are. I also know that one of the side effects of those kinds of drugs is depression. If you've got a guy who's already lonely and he's in chronic pain, and you add depression to that, it's not a good recipe. I'm not so sure his death was preventable. That said, the autopsy proved that the drugs he was taking were tainted. They were masquerading as one thing, but they were much, much, much more lethal than he could've known.

ANNA FANTASTIC: I heard he took enough to like kill a thousand-pound whale. I don't think he just went out in the streets and got these counterfeit pills himself off of just anybody, so something's not right. I don't think people had his best interest at heart. I just don't.

ALAN LEEDS: He was full-blown addicted. Based on what was in his system according to the coroner's report certainly suggests that he was addicted. It seems to me that someone around him should have had a responsibility to encourage him to get off, which apparently was happening. They were already in touch with this counselor doctor in California, who sent his son, who was supposed to ween him off pills.

ME: The day before Prince died, someone in his camp called an addiction specialist in Los Angeles and said they needed him to come right away. He said he could not come that day but he could be there in two days. Prince's camp said, "That's too long." Can you imagine knowing that one more day is too long? The specialist dispatched his son, who was also an addiction specialist.

JILL JONES: I grew up with people who had addiction problems and I know what it's like. I wouldn't have left him alone. Plus, the building was so big, you didn't have to leave. You could pretend that you left and be in a whole other side of the building. For me, it just seems like once you do an intervention or something like that, you send the person to rehab immediately. I've never seen an intervention where they tell somebody, "We're going to do it now, but do you have a whole day to wait." It usually happens right then and there. Not saying that the people around him were bad people but they didn't inspire any alchemy. They inspired nothing. There was no nurturing going on at that difficult moment, and I'm not saying they weren't all up in arms about what to do for him or how to help him, but they brought in people who could help a couple of years too late.

ME: On April 21, 2016, Jill Jones woke up abruptly, engulfed in immense sadness.

JILL JONES: I woke up gasping for air in the middle of the night. It was around three or four in the morning. I got up, went to the kitchen, and got some water. One of Prince's old assistants had a similar experience. She woke up in the middle of the night and couldn't catch her breath. She had a feeling someone was gone. A few people had very weird things happen to them early on the morning of the day when he transitioned like, right at the time when it probably happened. It's very odd. A few hours later, I was on the phone with my daughter when the image of Paisley Park popped up on CNN and they said that a body had been found. I immediately knew it was him. My daughter was like, "It could be anybody. Calm down. Calm down." But my gut was like, "It's him. It's him. It's him." I became physically ill because I knew it was him. I became very, very ill, and sick to my stomach. I started throwing up. It was terrible, just awful. Then I went and got a bottle of scotch. I was really sad. I kept feeling like, *God, why didn't we go there quicker?* We knew from the plane thing that it was bad. And then you want to blame everybody, and I still kind of do blame them. The people who were around him at the end have to live with whatever it is they did or didn't do. Addiction doesn't just happen overnight. I don't think he had anybody around him who stood up to him. I know it's hard to say no to an addict but if your friend is going through withdrawal, do you like say, "Okay, see you later. You know, your guy's coming tomorrow, so just binge like crazy tonight."

ME: The addiction specialist's son was among the group that found Prince's dead body.

JILL JONES: They said there were like thousands of pills all over the building.

ME: Investigators moved through Paisley, finding painkillers in vitamin bottles and aspirin bottles, as the horrible news began to spread.

BROWNMARK: I was at home; I'd just woken up and my boy Hucky Austin called me up. He used to be a bodyguard, so he's got close ties with the police department and they'd always call him and tell him what's up at Paisley. He called me and said, "Mark, an emergency call came in this morning and something bad happened at Paisley. I'll call you back in fifteen minutes." I'm like, "You couldn't wait until you got the whole story to call me? You call me and say something's bad; I'll call you back?" Now I'm sitting at the edge of the bed like, *What is going on?* Finally, he calls me back and he said, "You ain't going to believe this, man. He's gone. He's gone." I'm like, "What do you mean, he's gone? What are you talking about? Who's gone?" He says, "Mark, Prince is gone." It's still hard for me to talk about because that's like losing a family member. I hung that phone up and I cried for like two days. Couldn't stop because I kept reminiscing about all the fun, you know? That was the most mind-blowing thing ever. There was so many things I wanted to finish with him and never got that closure.

JEROME BENTON: My niece comes to me and says, "Your phone's blowing up." I said, "Okay, I'll be there in a minute." Two minutes later, she's like, "Your phone is blowing up." "Okay. Leave me alone. Let me finish doing what I'm doing." "No, your phone is really blowing up." So I come in and my wife is watching CNN.

ME: Manuela Testolini, Prince's second wife, called Mayte, his first wife. She was driving. Testolini told her to pull over and park. She did. Testolini told her Prince had died. They cried together.

ANNA FANTASTIC: My daughter walked into my room. I was half asleep. She's like, "Prince died." I was like, "Oh God, stupid tabloids." But then I was like, "Are you sure?" She was like, "Yeah." I just pulled the covers over my head and cried.

MORRIS HAYES: I hear the phone going off constantly. I'm like, *What is going on?* I go in the room and it's just moving on the table like it's gonna vibrate off the table. I turned it over and I had like four hundred texts. I had never seen a number like that on my text messages before. I turn on the TV and it's helicopters flying over Paisley and they're like, "Yeah, you know, we got reports that Prince is..." My stomach just goes into my shoes. I just broke down, bro. I was crying like a baby. I had said, "If they don't do something, he's outta here." I said, "They have to do it. They're the inner circle now. They have to fix it." When I saw that that happened, that he was gone, I realized they didn't do it. And I just fell to my knees. It was like somebody stabbed me. I said, "I screwed up. I shoulda went. I shoulda went. I shoulda went." Prince told me he wanted to do a Broadway musical. He wanted to do an opera. He wanted to do all of these things and I couldn't imagine how this could happen when there was so much more that he wanted to do.

SUSANNAH MELVOIN: I was in college, in class, and I heard a woman behind me say, "Prince is dead!" I turned around and I was like, "Where did you hear that? What are you talking about?" She was like, "It's right here on the news!" Nobody in that class knows who I am. It's just a bunch of eighteen- and nineteen-year-olds. I said, "Well, you can't always believe what you hear," but then I pick up my phone and it's on fire. I grab my books and I go up to my professor to say, "I've got to go." I called Wendy. She was at home and we cried together.

WENDY MELVOIN: It's deeply painful to not have him on the planet. I kind of measured my personal abilities based on what his reaction would be or what he would think of something. He was my thermometer. And to not have that compass anymore is devastating.

MORRIS DAY: I was flying from Las Vegas to Florida. We had a layover in Chicago and my wife and I sitting were there at the bar, having a drink. I saw Paisley Park on the news and, these cop cars and all that and a buddy of mine calls me and he's like, "You hear about what's going on at Paisley?" I said, "They found an employee dead there." He's like, "No, man. It was Prince." I said, "You're lying." I really didn't believe it.[25]

ALAN LEEDS: I was on a train in Canada. My brother Eric and I, on our bucket list was to take The Canadian, which is a refurbished 1950s-era streamline train that runs like three times a week. It runs from Vancouver all across Canada to Montreal. We're both train buffs and the novelty of the train ride plus the scenery, which is mostly breathtaking all through the Rockies, is like a time machine. We had flown to Vancouver to get on and we'd been on it for a day and a half just chillin', when my phone started buzzing. Service was spotty where we were. This is right where you'd look out the window and there'd be moose. But I got a text saying that somebody had heard there was something going on at Paisley. The police were on the way. Did I know anything? No. Then I got a phone call from Questlove and he was in tears. He patched in D'Angelo and the three of us sat on the phone crying. Shocking is not a strong enough word for how I felt. It was kind of paralyzing because he was one of those people that you never really thought of dying. Then Eric said, "You know what, people like Prince aren't meant to get old," and he didn't mean that in a mean-spirited way at all, just that some people are not built for old age.

Morris Day: It hit me like a ton of bricks, all the stuff we'd been through and what an important part of my life this dude was.

Morris Hayes: I immediately called the other members of the Revolution and we all were boohooing. They're like, "What do we do?" I said, "I don't know. I'm getting on a plane and I'm heading to Minneapolis. I'll figure it out when I get there." So we all went there. We all stayed in the same hotel.

BrownMark: I immediately booked the airline tickets and flew to Minneapolis and so did the rest of the Revolution. We didn't get invited to the funeral, which I thought was absolutely weird, but we made our own.

Susannah Melvoin: I ran home, got my kids, got a bag, and flew to Minneapolis. Where was I going? I don't know. I thought I was going out there because we have a very deep connection. My family, Wendy, and Lisa, we were all like, "If he's not here, we need to be there. We need to hold him, and his spirit. We need to do that." I was the first to get there and it was awful. We were shut out of the funeral. Like, "You can't be here. You're not part of this." Like, "You don't know him, you're not part of him, you don't know." I sort of sat in this mire with my kids, and my friends and we're all sitting around, and I was like, "God, I feel like such an asshole. Why am I here? Where are my tears coming from? Why am I so sad?" It felt really awful, and then I was like, "Nope, just get it together. You're here." I drove around and went to our old house. I literally snuck under the gate, got underneath there, and I walked the entire property, just sort of doing my goodbyes. Then Wendy and Lisa got out there, and Bobby and Mark and Matt and everybody who's worked with him. Everybody, just everybody. All the techs, all the sound guys, Mayte. And we had our memorial.

ME: Prince was cremated within hours of his death.

BROWNMARK: The family had a funeral, but it was invite only. We were not invited and I was pissed. I was so mad because I was like, *What kind of crap is this? We didn't get invited?* I don't understand that. I really don't. Here we were, the beginning of his family, his musical family, the ones who were with him at the pinnacle of his music career. We were at the top with him. He never outdid that time period. And to think that we weren't invited to that funeral? I was so insulted. We all were. We didn't even know who was in charge, why it happened, how it happened, but we were grieving so badly and to not be able to go into Paisley, to not be able to connect with that, it was the hardest thing. I was angry. I'm still angry. I'm angry to this day, I'm just not going to speak on it, but that's what made the hotel feel so bad for us that they just gave us the floor. They just said, "You guys can use this," and we all just kind of gathered together up there and that was our own fare-well to him. A lot of people showed up. I got to meet Mayte for the first time. That was a wonderful thing. Me and her connected very quickly.

MORRIS HAYES: We all kind of congregated together. We just didn't know what to do. Who knows what to do with something like that? So, we had our own little memorial, all the PRN people, all the people from *Purple Rain*. There was about a hundred of us in the lounge on the third floor, all gathered in there. It was just so surreal. We just talked and talked and talked all night.

BROWNMARK: We had our little grief moment and we just told stories, fun stuff. It was fun to reminisce and talk about all the fun times we had on the road together. We spent years together on the road with these people. We were a family, probably twenty-two trucks and buses. It was a huge production, so it was fun to be able to see every-body that we hadn't seen in decades and just grieve together and talk about him. I mean, if I hadn't met him, I probably would have been an architectural draftsman. That's what I was in school for. But he gave me the dream that I always wanted. He changed my life.

ME: In his last years, when the downward trajectory was clear and he needed someone to change his life, no one came for him until it was too late. Yes, you cannot force a drug addict to get clean if they don't want it for themselves, but Prince needed something, he needed help, he needed family, i.e., people who loved him, and it seems like there was no family around him. When he was a boy with no place to live, one family had saved him. When he was in the early years of his addiction, a member of his extended family had said, "What's going on?" But friends say that most of the people who were around him at the end were too enabling.

A FRIEND: The people who worked with him in his last years treated him like porcelain—gingerly. He hired people who were in awe of him or were so afraid of losing their jobs that they seemed scared to say stuff, scared to be themselves, afraid of being fired. He was looking for yes people. Which makes sense if you're on drugs. You don't want anybody questioning you.

MORRIS HAYES: Prince died because there wasn't that woman figure in his life when he really needed it. If he had somebody like that in place, the whole outcome could've been different.

JILL JONES: Prince died from neglect. People who claimed to care about him abandoned him. Just like he was abandoned at twelve. The whole thing went full circle in my mind. But this time, there was no Bernadette to pull him up and make him strong.

ME: He needed family, by which I mean people who truly loved him. But no one was there.

Endnotes

1 Allow me this one reference to one of my favorite lines in one of my favorite novels, Lolita. Also, the "crazy man" is not Vladimir Nabokov, it's Humbert Humbert.

2 Prince was an elite songwriter and he knew everything there was to know about music except for how to read sheet music.

Morris Day: I can understand why he didn't really want to read. I'm sure he could have learned that if he wanted, but I think he had so much music in his head and had picked up these instruments so easily that it probably would've hurt him creatively to try to be a more formally trained musician. He was all ear training. Of course, he could call out chords and keys and all of that stuff, but as far as being able to write a chart, he wasn't trained like that. But to write a song, arrange it, and put the backgrounds and all the instruments together, he didn't need any charts.

Me: But when he came up with new songs, how did he communicate them?

Morris Hayes: That was easy. He played everything.

Greg Boyer: He would just sing it like, "Okay, right here I want this thing, dah, dah, dah, dah, dah, dah." I used to laugh because it was very brittle sounding and, as a matter of fact, he sounded a lot like the little Sweet One Dr. Pepper commercials when he was singing the horn lines or whatever. I didn't want to laugh 'cause I had to get it down, but it always sounded funny to me.

Me: Greg was the Prince translator in the band.

Greg Boyer: I would write out what he was saying and give it to everybody in the horn section. Then we'd play it and he'd be like, "Yup, that's it." I made a career of what was taking his ideas and putting them down on paper, and handing it out to the rest of the band.

3 **Me:** He was much more than just a poet—his entire songwriting ability was extraordinary.

Susan Rogers: He was a strong enough songwriter that you could strip away the whole record, strip it down to just the skeleton, and you'd still have something valid. You'd have good lyric writing, you'd have strong melodies, you'd have what you need. And he was able to add harmonic progressions that were innovative and smart. He was able to add rhythmic foundations that were great. He taught me so many things. One thing I learned from him is that you should be able to strip out everything except the bass and drums and maybe one rhythm instrument and it should sound like a record. He was a master craftsman who understood how records function. I'm a psychologist. I know that there are three main avenues through which listeners can bond with a piece of music. There's our motor system—music can make us move. There's our emotional system—even something without drums in it, like classical music, can move us. Chord changes alone can move us emotionally. And there is our cognitive system—lyrics make us think. If you're a genius at any one of those, you don't need to be that good at anything else. James Brown makes us move, even if you don't understand English. That rhythm is going to engage your motor system and feel good no matter what. People who are geniuses with melody can write a great chord change that will make us feel something. People who are geniuses at lyrics, whether it's Bob Dylan or Bob Marley, will make us think. Prince understood all three avenues and, unlike most artists, he was a master of all three.

4 **Me:** Prince was also incredible at ping-pong.

Randee St Nicholas: Did you ever see the ping-pong sequence in Forrest Gump? Prince was like that. He would just effortlessly hit the ball while everyone else is struggling and running back and forth. He would just flick his wrist and make it look all so easy. He beat everyone. He was brilliant at it.

Alan Leeds: Prince was a master table-tennis player. You do not try to play table tennis with Prince. He will humiliate you. I imagine he could hang with a professional table-tennis player because he was serious.

Me: He was also a pool shark.

Alan Leeds: Don't play 8-ball with him. He will embarrass you. You will never get a shot. If he shoots first, you will not play. You'll just hold your cue all night. He was that guy.

Afshin Shahidi (photographer): I joke about having paid for college by shooting pool, so I'm not bad. The first time I played him, I thought, Okay, let me go easy. I don't want to beat the boss too bad. That's not a good look. Then he cleared the table. I didn't even have a chance. He walked around and did a little bit of the Color of Money, Tom Cruise thing with his pool stick, using it like a nunchuck as he's going up to the ball. He was pretty cocky. But he was cocky when he did anything.

5 **BrownMark:** He used to eat Doritos like they were going out of style, like he had stock in the company.

6 They say Prince got a lot of crap for having a half-brother, Duane, in the same grade, especially because he was handsome, tall, and one of the stars of the basketball team. Duane ended up working for Prince as a bodyguard.

7 **Jill Jones:** These were two parents who were okay with their son not living at home. What could a child possibly do that would make you not want them there? I hope that brings some kind of perspective on what he had to deal with.

8 Robert Johnson died at the age of twenty-seven. The cause of death is unknown and his death went unreported. He just vanished from the historical record. The exact location of his grave is unknown. The final destination of his soul after his death is also unknown.

9 **Me:** Prince loved his costumes.

Jerome Benton: He got really excited about his attire. He really did. He would take you to whatever warehouse he had and he would say, "Come see this." He would lay his stuff out and start dancing around all excited. The way he dressed was a form of performing. He loved the presence of being a star

10 **Me:** Morris doubts that Prince was ever R&B.

Morris Day: On his first record, "For You," he was in the mindset of an R&B album, if you will, but if you really pay attention, his music was never R&B. I don't think "I Want To Be Your Lover" was an R&B song. That had pop overtones all day long.

11 **Me:** The influence of "Miss Me" pervaded "Controversy" as well.

Morris Day: Prince was feeling "Miss You" so much that he wanted something like that for himself. That's how "Controversy" came about. He and I started out jamming on drums and bass, then I took off and Prince stayed and when I came back the next morning the whole song is done. Vocals, everything. All the other instrumentation on the record, everything, done. And that's how he did "Controversy."

12 **Alan Leeds:** Susan Moonsie was a student at U of Minnesota who dated Prince in his early days. She was a spirited young woman with too much self-esteem to fully submit to his dominance. She never had showbiz ambitions. When Prince presented her with the concept of a girl group, she just thought it would be a fun adventure and she joined Vanity 6, but even with a hit record, "Nasty Girl," she never took it too seriously.

13 **Alan Leeds:** When he hired people, there was some point in the first month or so of your employ that he'd catch you in the cafeteria or in the tour bus or somewhere where it just happened to be the two of you. Out of nowhere, he would look at you and say, "Do you believe in God?" That's your litmus test because depending on your answer, you may or may not have a job tomorrow.

14 **Me:** Prince was so at home in the studio that he put others at ease. You might think it would be intimidating to be in the studio with this impetuous genius, but no.

Anna Fantastic: You would imagine that you'd be quite nervous in the studio with Prince because he's obviously so talented, but I wasn't. He made me feel really comfortable. I never felt like I was not getting it right. He made me feel like I could do no wrong. Everything I did, he's like, "Yes, yes, yes." He was very positive. He wasn't like, "Ah, that's not right." He was able to really go deep and pull out your feelings so you're not just singing like some robot, but you're putting your feelings into it and you're really feeling what you're singing about.

Chuck Zwicky: I've never saw him come off as grandiose or pompous or particularly maniacal in the studio. Obviously, he's introverted and quiet, but he's also an incredibly intuitive person. He can be extremely gentle with people when he's in his persona.

15 **Jerome Benton:** We were in Rio De Janeiro and some fan gave Prince a note talking about how much she loved him. It was broken English and it said "I wonder you, I dream of you, for all time, though you are far." He took that and turned it into "I Wonder U." The lyrics in the song are exactly what the letter said.

16 **Susan Rogers:** Around *Parade*, he was listening to Kate Bush and Joni Mitchell and Ray Charles a lot and he was focusing on his arranging skills and his musicality.

17 In one of those rehearsals, a spontaneous moment became something unforgettable. In The Time's shows, Jerome would play Morris Day's valet and mid-show, he'd come out in a badass suit and sunglasses and hold up a full-length mirror so Morris could make sure he looked perfect. Jerome would dance as Morris primped himself to the beat. That emerged from rehearsal.

Morris Day: Jerome wasn't in the band; he was a valet for real. He used to get the band's bags and set them out and make sure the dry cleaning was done and all of that; that was his gig. One day, we're at rehearsal at this little raggedy studio in south side Minneapolis.

Jerome Benton: We were rehearsing at this place where the owner was fond of making homemade mirrors and hanging them on a wall and then selling them. So all around the room, there were these plaster mirrors that were painted gold lamé. We were there going through that exercise of rehearsing one song for hours on end.

Morris Day: I get to the part in the song where I say, "Somebody bring me a mirror!" And Jerome jumps up.

Jerome Benton: I grabbed one of the weird mirrors off the wall and I ran up to Morris and put it in front of him and he just looked in it and smoothed his hair back and fixed his clothes up.

Morris Day: He brings it up and holds it up in front of me and it was just one of them moments. We all kinda stopped and started looking at each other.

Jerome Benton: Prince broke up! He was on the floor, laughing 'til he was tired out. Then he hugged me and said, "I want you to do that every time!"

Morris Day: We were like, "This has gotta be part of the show!"

Jerome Benton: So, here we go. They're rehearsing the song over and over and I'm jumping up, putting the mirror in front of him and he's standing there looking at it and primping himself and smoothing his hair back and from that point on it just became second nature.

18 **Me:** Prince was extremely generous and loved to use money to help people he loved.

Alan Leeds (manager): Clyde Stubblefield, the drummer on James Brown's "The Funky Drummer," fought cancer for the last years of his life. Like many musicians of that particular era, he had no insurance. Prince found out about it and sent him, like, $100,000 to pay medical bills. Nobody knew that, but him and Clyde and whoever sent the check.

Morris Hayes: Prince was a really big philanthropist and a lot of people didn't know it, including us sometimes. He gave Spike Lee a few million dollars to finish Malcolm X.

19   It's terrible to have everyone on stage going in different directions musically, but, in general, Prince didn't view mistakes as the end of the world. He knew real performers could make mistakes and keep the show flowing.

Morris Hayes: He was great at making a mistake and making it seem like it was cool. He could repeat the mistake if he wanted to, and make it sound like that's what he intended to do. That's how good he was.

Wendy Melvoin: One of the greatest things he ever said was, "If you make a mistake on stage, make it twice—then it's not a mistake."

Me: Prince told his people whatever happens on stage, just roll with it.

Morris Hayes: If you stop, then everybody knows there's trouble.

Me: Once, Morris had a keyboard melt down while he was on stage.

Morris Hayes: It just died in the middle of the show. It was an Oberheim, an OB8, a dope keyboard, but it's an analog, older keyboard and it has some stability issues. It had been down the road and shaken up, and we'd had to repair it a few times and this night, it decided to die right there on stage. The oscillators went off and it just died outta nowhere. It made a death noise while I was playing. I got all of this stuff going and all of a sudden, this thing just goes dead and it makes the craziest squeal I'd ever heard. I'm like, What in the hell? I'm just looking at it like, I'm not touching it, I don't know what happened because I'd never heard or seen that happen before, and Prince is at the front of the stage twirling his towel and he turns around because he know it's me and he takes the towel and he throws it and hits me and he looks at me like, "Ugh." He was so mad. After the show, a bodyguard comes over and says, "Boss wants to see you." I'm like, "Here we go." I go in there and he says, "Morris, what happened?" I said, "The keyboard just died." He says, "But Morris, why didn't you at least make a show out of it? Don't stand there like a deer in the headlights. You could pick it up and throw it on the ground and smash it into a million pieces. At least the other way, it's a show. I'll buy you a new one. Be rock 'n' roll. Don't just stand there looking at it and telling everybody, 'Oh, look, he's got a problem.'" I said, "That thing cost like $8,000! I'm not gonna break it." He said, "Above all else, don't mess up my show. Everybody was looking at you like, 'That guy's got a problem, and he's on fire,' so I wasn't the center of the show anymore. You and your problem were. And I got a problem with that. Just break it and keep the show going and I'll get you a new one." He said, "It ain't a mistake until you stop." That's one of his favorite quotes. I remember Levi Seacer, our guitar player, did something brilliant that I learned from. One show, his battery pack went out right when it was his turn to his solo. You've got ten to fifteen thousand people in this place and he goes to hit his note, and... nothing. But he never quit playing. He knew the pack was out and something was wrong but he continued to play the solo as though it was on so everybody's looking at the sound man like, "Hey, turn him up. The guitar player's playing and we can't hear him!" You never thought Levi knew something was wrong. You thought the sound people had made a mistake. It was amazing because he went through the motions and he looked like he was just killing it. That's what Prince means when he says it's not a mistake until you stop.

Me: And Prince was not above wrecking some instruments from time to time.

Morris Hayes: One night at an aftershow, we didn't like the equipment we got. Everything was just lame, so we took a break after playing a few songs and Prince said, "Okay, this what we're gonna do. We're gonna go back there and tear all this crap up. We're gonna tear all of it to pieces. I'm gonna give you the cue and then lay waste to everything on that stage." Now, I always had to work hard and hustle for my little equipment so the last thing I would ever do is break a piece of my gear. Just the thought of stomping and smashing a keyboard was breaking my heart, because it costs money. But then Prince cued us. He smashed his guitar, Sonny karate kicked his amp, Michael Bland pushed his drums out all over the place. We demolished the stage. The people thought we had lost our minds. But we were so happy. We went in the back and we were just laughing like crazy men. And we had that mob thing come over us like, yeah, let's tear up some more crap! Let's go out and trash the streets and turn over cars! Prince wrote them a check for $50,000 to cover all of their equipment and next thing you know we're on the bus all wired up. It was crazy.

20 Jerome got fired, too, but the rationale was far different.

Jerome Benton: Shit. I got fired because I was hanging out with Janet Jackson and working on her videos and stuff. They hired me for what I learned around Prince. He had one of his people call me and say, "He wants me to let you go, but man, he's gonna miss you." That's when I talked my way into a conversation with Prince. But I knew he was hurt. He birthed me into this business. He said I was playing both sides of the fence and he had a creative formula and if I was learning his secret sauce and then taking his lessons over to another camp then that would make him less unique. He said if he gave out his secrets, and his secrets got used, then eventually he would not be needed anymore. And he couldn't have that.

21 **Me:** She says the sound wasn't quite on point.

Wendy: By the time of the Diamonds and Pearls record, everything started going a little bit odd, musically. There was a certain sonic laziness to some of it that hadn't been there in earlier records. He didn't spend as much time getting the sounds down. It became almost too fast and you could hear it. I would listen to the later records and say, "There's something missing about this. Is it a certain attention? What's happening here? Is he becoming more of a businessman?" I'm not sure, but I clocked it, and it felt slightly alienating to me and to Lisa.

22 This Crystal Ball album is totally different than the Crystal Ball album he would release years later.

23 Prince had played covers of Graham's music as a kid in Grand Central.

24 Vanity died of kidney failure after years of being addicted to crack.

25 **Morris Day:** The last time I saw him, me and the band had ripped this show at Paisley Park. We finish, we come off stage, we're going down this dark hallway and I see a shadow coming out of the corner. He was clapping his hands, like, "Bravo. Bravo. You guys killed it." He and I went into the little commissary there and sat and talked for like an hour. He was telling me all these things that he wanted to do like, "I wanna send you guys to Europe and I'll manage your tour." He had big plans. When I got up to go, the dude gives me a hug and he's like, "I love you." That caught me off guard because he had never talked like that to me. I was like, "Cool. I love you, too." That was it, man.

Acknowledgments

Thank you to my wife, Rita, and my kids, Hendrix and Fairuz, for putting up with me through the writing of this. Thank you to Chris for your help on this road. Thank you to Ryan for your loyalty and friendship. Thank you to Jacob for taking this on and slashing it into shape in record time. Thank you to Susannah, Alan, Bobby, Susan, Morris, Morris, Jill, and Questlove for being so generous and being true friends. And thank you to Prince for everything. None of this would matter if your life had not been so incredibly meaningful.

About the Author

Touré is the author of six books including the Prince biography *I Would Die 4 U: Why Prince Became an Icon*. He is the host of the podcast docuseries *Who Was Prince* and the twice-weekly podcast *Touré Show*, which has had over three million downloads. He was the cohost of MSNBC's *The Cycle* and a host at MTV and BET as well as a correspondent at CNN. He lives in Brooklyn with his wife Rita, and their kids, Hendrix and Fairuz. He grew up a devout Prince fan and among his greatest life moments are interviewing Prince, attending the private aftershow where Prince played with D'Angelo and Questlove, and, of course, playing one-on-one basketball with Prince at Paisley Park.